Sudden Loss, Slow Grieving

Sudden Loss, Slow Grieving

A Clinical Pyschologist's Personal
Journey through Grief

VANESSA MOORE

KYLE BOOKS

An Hachette UK Company
www.hachette.co.uk

First published as *One Thousand Days and One Cup of Tea* in Great Britain in 2021 by Kyle
Books, an imprint of Octopus Publishing Group Limited, Carmelite House,
50 Victoria Embankment, London EC4Y 0DZ
www.octopusbooks.co.uk

This paperback edition published in 2023

Distributed in the US by Hachette Book Group
1290 Avenue of the Americas, 4th and 5th Floors, New York, NY 10104

Distributed in Canada by Canadian Manda Group,
Toronto, Ontario, Canada M6S 2C8

Publisher: Joanna Copestick
Copy Editor: Tara O'Sullivan
Editor: Jenny Dye
Cover design: Mel Four
Production: Lisa Pinnell

ISBN 978-0-85783-942-8

A Cataloguing in Publication catalogue record for this book
is available from the British Library.

Printed and bound in the UK

10 9 8 7 6 5 4 3 2 1

The FSC® label means that materals used for the product
have been responsibly sourced.

'There is this question in psychotherapy that I frequently think about: whether it is a process that's supposed to make us feel better about who we are or to change who we are.'

'And what do you think?'

'I think, ultimately, it's about acceptance.'

VALERY HAZANOV, *The Fear of Doing Nothing*

For Emily, William and Simon
with love

Contents

Preface

I read a story recently about a magic gate. Pass through it to the left, and you would see yourself as you were twenty years ago. Pass through to the right, and you would see yourself as you would be twenty years in the future.

If I were to take a left turn now, I would find myself as a busy, working mother at the centre of a large family: three children at school, a husband whom I adored, three cats, a crazy dog, a big house, a challenging but rewarding job, plenty of friends, both parents alive and living in an idyllic place by the sea.

If that busy working mother had been able to take a right turn through the gate, she would have found me as I am now: retired, living alone in a much smaller house, husband, parents, cats and dog long since dead, children grown up and moved away. So much loss, and a life dramatically changed in a relatively short space of time.

This book is the story of that period of great loss in my life, a time when the tables were completely turned on me. I was a qualified therapist who suddenly found myself needing psychological therapy. I was a trained researcher who became my own research subject as I tried to make sense of what was happening to me. I was an experienced manager who now struggled to manage the events taking place in my own life. And yet, throughout all this turmoil, my patients were always there in the background, remind-. ing me that there are many different ways to deal with loss and trauma and forge a way forwards.

Many of these patients, like me, were faced with life events that they hadn't been expecting – a child born with a disability or life-limiting illness, a sudden bereavement, divorce – all of these changes had left them feeling overwhelmed, unable to cope and at times as if they were losing their minds. This book is about these shared experiences and common 'mental health problems', which are often temporary but can feel as bad or worse than a physical illness.

This is the story of the people and experiences in my personal and professional lives that helped or hindered me in my struggle to defeat the dark forces of anxiety and depression. It charts the many ups and downs of that long struggle, and the lessons learned along the way.

I have altered some names and other identifying details in order to preserve confidentiality.

CHAPTER ONE

Tsunami

The mind creates a narrative, a story to fit the facts as we see them. And once created, the story may be very difficult to dismantle. Yet that story can have alarmingly powerful effects on our emotions and feelings.

MARK WILLIAMS ET AL,
The Mindful Way Through Depression

It had been a hard week. Paul had been away for much of it on business, and he was exhausted. I'd been at home, fire-fighting as usual, fitting in shopping, cooking, dog walking and chauffeuring around the edges of my full-on job as the head of a large Child Clinical Psychology service.

The only way we could find any time for keeping fit was to forgo weekend lie-ins. So, on Sunday morning, the alarm went off at 6.35 a.m., as usual. A quick cuddle, a cup of tea, and less than an hour later Paul and I were heaving up and down the swimming pool, me with the other breaststrokers in Medium–slow, and he with the stronger swimmers in Fast. I'd been lane-swimming every Sunday for almost twenty years, initially to escape from my colicky infant daughter, and subsequently to get thin (or keep thin, depending on how thin I felt on any particular Sunday).

Paul was a newer recruit, but had been coming swimming with me since we got together, eleven years earlier. He would probably have preferred to stay in bed longer, but he used to be sporty at school, and conceded that there was a need for this one dose of exercise in his otherwise sedentary life.

The daylight was already visible through the glass-and-chrome roof of the swimming pool, a welcome sign that spring was on its way. The snowdrops had arrived in our garden and the daffodils wouldn't be far behind. The usual crowd of regulars were in the pool. Paul and I had invented names for them, and it amused me to reflect on this to counteract the boredom of counting the lengths, up and down. The Greys, an obviously retired couple, were always there, slowing us down with their laboured swimming of twenty lengths precisely; the Hunk was a more appealing distraction, with his muscled shoulders and deep brown eyes, which occasionally caught mine as we swam past each other; Sit-up-and-beg seemed more concerned about keeping her hair dry than making any progress through the water, swimming as she did with her neck stubbornly erect and her eyes focused on a spot directly in front of her; I groaned inwardly as I noticed her making her way to my lane. Paul had told me that in Fast there was the Beached Whale, who rolled through the water down the centre of the lane, paying no attention to oncoming swimmers and sending out waves in all directions. I shifted my goggled eyes to the right and immediately spotted Paul's baggy old swimming shorts and solid legs powering their way to the end of the pool, but no sign of a whale. Perhaps he had had a lie-in.

I didn't feel particularly energetic that morning, and

I was glad when my forty lengths were done and I could head towards the communal showers. A queue had formed there behind a young mother and her sons. I waited my turn along with the others, all of us uncomfortable about removing our swimming costumes in front of two small boys. I was dimly aware that I was hungry, that Paul would be waiting for me, and that this had been an annoying start to the day.

*

The story so far is unremarkable: a predictable Sunday morning routine enlivened only by the personas we liked to invent for our fellow lane-swimmers. The next part of the story will be told and retold, worked and reworked a thousand times. Fast-forward four months, and I'm about to tell it to a woman I've never met before. She lives forty minutes' drive away: a pretty drive, if I were in the mood for it, across open countryside. As it is, I don't notice the scenery, so consumed am I by my recollections of that Sunday morning in February. There's no need to rehearse what I am going to say to the woman; as much as I might want to push them away, the thoughts keep forcing themselves back into my mind with astonishing clarity. I think of some of the autistic children I've worked with, who are obsessed with playing a certain section of a videotape over and over again. It's like that: my own tape repeats and repeats, even though I do nothing to make it happen. It unspools itself, unbidden, whether I want it to or not.

The tape begins with my delayed exit from the swimming pool changing rooms and into the car park. When I get to Paul's car, expecting him to be a bit annoyed that I've taken so long to get dressed, he isn't there. I'm surprised, because he's normally out before me, but then he sometimes has a shave, so that must be what he's doing. It's cold in the pale morning sun and I go back into the foyer of the leisure centre to wait for him. There's going to be a triathlon later on, so there are groups of people standing around in Lycra, chatting and sipping energy drinks. When Paul hasn't materialised after another five minutes, I feel a twinge of anxiety, but then I realise that I didn't actually see him get out of the water, so he might still be swimming. I climb up to the spectators' gallery high above the pool. The lane-swimming session is about to end, and there are only a few people left in the water, but Paul isn't one of them. Now I'm definitely worried. This is unusual, but perhaps he's having a shave after all, or a long shower – or maybe there's some kind of hold-up with the showers? I go into the changing rooms to investigate. I walk through the female cubicles into the family area, and on to the male cubicles, but I hesitate, because I don't feel comfortable walking into this all-male zone. There are men and boys going backwards and forwards between the cubicles and the showers and everything seems normal, so I feel reassured. I go back down to the foyer and ask the receptionist to send one of the male leisure assistants to check, just to be sure. I tell her that my husband is taking a long time to get dressed, which is unlike him, and I would just like to make sure that everything is alright. She's fine about it. She's beginning to call for a leisure assistant over her tannoy when a woman comes rushing, almost falling down the stairs. She's tall, with long, Pre-Raphaelite curls, and she's shouting at the receptionist:

'Call 999 and get an ambulance. Someone's collapsed in the changing-rooms.'

4

No, oh no. It's him, isn't it? My heart starts thumping wildly out of control. The receptionist is fumbling around with the phone. She's young, and she's probably never had to do this before.

The curly woman is agitated, repeating her instructions in a louder voice: 'CALL 999 AND GET AN AMBULANCE *NOW!*'

I go up to her. 'Is it a man who's collapsed?'

She's defensive. 'Yes, why?'

'Because I think it might be my husband.'

She's even more defensive, accusatory even. 'How do you know it's your husband?'

'Because I've been waiting for him and he's taking a very long time to get dressed.' 'What was he wearing?' she asks.

It occurs to me that this is a stupid question. 'Swimming trunks.'

'I'll go and see what I can find out.'

'I'm coming with you,' I say, about to follow her.

'No, stay here. I'll come back.'

Now I'm seized with terror. I'm still clinging to a tiny fragment of hope that it might not be him, but my pounding heart is certain that it will be. I have a strange sensation of my mind beginning to detach itself from everything that's going on around me.

The curly woman is back very quickly with a sponge bag and, as soon as I see it, I know it is Paul's. I recognise the brown and blue pattern straight away. I unzip it and there inside is his razor, his old-fashioned shaving brush, a round plastic bowl of shaving soap, a tiny bottle of shampoo and another of shower gel, picked up from overnight stays in hotels. Unmistakable.

I hear my disembodied voice asking: 'Is he dead?'

'No, they're working on him. But I must tell you that it's serious.'

'Are you a doctor?' I ask.

'No, I'm a nurse.'

'Can I see him?'

'No, it's best you wait down here.'

The reception area is filling up with triathlon participants, and a lot of people are aware that something is going on. I sense that people are staring at me, and I feel self-conscious with my wet hair and glasses: on Sundays, the hair-drying, contact lenses and make-up happen later, while Paul is cooking the poached eggs for breakfast.

A middle-aged woman comes up to me and touches my arm. 'Would you like me to sit with you?' she offers. 'I could get us a cup of tea while we're waiting.'

I'm dazed. I must be in some kind of shock, because I feel cut off from all the noise and activity going on around me. And yet I'm grateful to the woman: I need an anchor, something or somebody to cling on to. We sit side by side in reception. People are milling around. She goes and gets tea from the café. There are lots of leisure assistants in bright red shorts and yellow polo shirts. One of them comes up to us; he's only a teenager, but he seems concerned and asks if we'd like a bit of privacy. Later, I'll wonder if it's because I was crying, although I won't be able to remember if I was or not. He shows us to a small space under the stairs next to the sports injury clinic. There are bicycles and coats, but also a bench seat, and if the door is left open, we have a clear view of the stairs up to the changing rooms.

After a while, the curly woman comes down and announces that the ambulance has arrived. 'The paramedics are working on him. The plan is to stabilise him and then take him to A & E.'

A leap of hope: *if they're taking him to A & E, he must be alive.*

She leaves, and a little while later, a red-and-yellow leisure assistant is sent down to update us. He can't be more than sixteen, and he looks so incongruously cheerful that I find myself asking again: 'Is he dead?'

'Oh, no he's fine! He'll be going off to A & E soon.'

This time I don't believe a word of it, and sure enough, hot on his heels comes the curly woman again. One look at her stricken face is enough.

'I'm sorry,' she says. 'He died. He won't be going to A & E now. He'll be going to the mortuary. The ambulance will take him. You can go and see him there.'

No, oh please no. No, no. This can't be happening to me. It can't. It can't.

The nice lady has her arm around me and she's asking if I'd like to call anyone. I don't know. I can't think. She offers me her phone and I dial the first two numbers that come into my head. First, my sister Bryony.

'You're not going to believe this, but Paul just died.'

There's a strangled shriek. 'No, no, that can't be true.' She's trying hard not to cry. 'Where are you? We're coming.'

Then my ex-husband. Somebody must tell the children, because they'll be wondering where we've got to. He's a trained therapist himself, and I'm grateful for the calmness and sensitivity in his voice.

'Are they taking Paul to the mortuary in an ambulance?' he asks.

'Yes.'

'Do you want to go with him?'

I hadn't considered this, but as soon as he says it, I realise that I do. 'Yes, but they haven't said that I can.'

'Tell them that you want to. You might regret it later if you don't.'

He's right. At this moment, I still don't believe that this is happening to me, and I want to see Paul more than anything else in the world.

The paramedics have materialised here in the cupboard under the stairs. Two fit, muscled young men wearing green uniforms, just like in *Casualty*. There's no problem at all with me coming in the ambulance. They'll bring Paul out of the back entrance (*of course, he can hardly go out the way he came in, now that he's dead...*) and will then drive the ambulance round to the car park at the front.

The nice lady writes her phone number down on a scrap of paper. 'Give me a ring sometime, love. I'd like to know how you get on.' She hugs me tight, and then she's gone.

As I walk out through the foyer, I can hear an alarm going off, and there are people streaming down the stairs. I ask one of the leisure assistants what's going on.

'We've closed the pool as a mark of respect to your husband,' he says.

How strange that Paul will never know that a swimming pool was closed in his honour.

The ambulance is there in the car park, standing just behind Paul's black BMW (a company car, which, although I don't know it yet, his employer will take away from me the very next morning). The paramedics are waiting by the steps. They seem hesitant and anxious: perhaps they think they'll have a hysterical woman on their hands when I see my dead husband. My heart continues to thump in overdrive as I climb up to the ambulance door. I want to stop time right now and not go one step further. I've never seen a dead person before, and I know that as soon as I set eyes on him it will be confirmed; there will be no going back, my life will be changed forever.

And there he is. I let out a small gasp, no hysterics. He's lying on his back on the stretcher and he looks exactly as he does in the early mornings, in a peaceful sleep. That dear face. I touch his cheek. I kiss his forehead, very gently. It's still warm, though a little bit cooler than it should be. His hair is damp and tousled, from rubbing with a towel. I always love it like this, so much sexier than when it's combed and sleeked down for work. He's wearing his faded old jeans and grey V-neck jumper over the pale green shirt I got him from Cotton Traders. (*So, he was dressed when he died – or did somebody else dress him? I couldn't bear that.*) On the floor beside him is his dark green swimming bag. Inside that is the sponge bag, the ancient stripy towel he's used since boarding school, and his damp swimming trunks. The paramedics have relaxed, probably relieved that I haven't gone berserk. And it's true – even with my dead husband right in front of me, I'm strangely conscious that I need to behave, to show some decorum. They explain that we'll have to wait for the police to come before going to the hospital, as this is an unexpected death. We don't really know what to say while we're waiting, so there's a lot of small talk:

'Did you and your husband come swimming often?'

'Do you have children?'

'Do you get many deaths like this?'

This all seems quite surreal, with Paul lying dead between us. Fortunately, the police officer who has been assigned the job turns up soon. She's pretty and petite, with dark hair, and looks about the same age as my daughter, little more than a child. She's sympathetic and kind. She touches my arm. She just needs a few personal details; it's a formality with a sudden death, and there will, of course, have to be a post-mortem. I can feel tears beginning to well up when she says this (*Oh no – this body that I know and love will have to be cut open*), but there's no time to dwell on this thought, as she's already saying goodbye and we're about to set off for the hospital.

I've been in the back of an ambulance once before: three years ago, when my youngest son Simon, then aged ten, had to be driven two hundred miles from one hospital to another in the middle of the night for an emergency kidney operation. We had the blue light on then, but this time there's no need; the emergency is over, and the driver is going slowly and carefully. Even so, as the ambulance turns the corner out of the leisure centre car park, Paul's head flops to the side. This is the moment when I register that he really is dead. To my amazement, an experience that I know sometimes happens to trauma victims is actually happening to me: I can literally 'see' the times we've spent together, tumbling in front of my eyes … things like our wedding, our trip to Rio, roller-blading on the common with Simon, drinking Ricard with our French neighbours, Sunday walks with the dog in the New Forest, the 'naughty' fry-ups Paul would make for himself and the boys whenever I went out for an evening, walks along deserted Normandy beaches in the middle of winter, lying with my head in his lap watching TV – this great cacophony of pictures, sounds and smells. This is it then; these things will never happen again.

I don't take my eyes off his face. *Please Paul, please,*

please, open your eyes and everything will be alright again. Please. Please. But he doesn't. I keep looking for a breath, but his chest is motionless underneath his grey woolly jumper. I cradle his head all the way to the hospital, so that it doesn't flop, so that he can travel with dignity. I study every inch of his face: his blond eyelashes, his beautiful mouth, the grey stubble on his chin (*so he hadn't had a shave after all*), his pointy ears: they were a great asset at a fancy-dress party, if ever a hobgoblin or a devil was needed. I try and try to commit it all to memory, because I know that very soon, I will never see those features in the flesh again.

When we arrive at the hospital, tragedy quickly turns to farce. As it's a Sunday, the mortuary is locked and no mortician can be found. The paramedics are embarrassed and apologetic: they've rung for somebody, but it might take a while. Bryony and my brother-in-law arrive, and then my ex-husband. They're shocked, and I can tell that they're worried about me. We're all standing in the ambulance, looking down at Paul's body. There's no script for such occasions and the conversation seems pointless and banal. We say things like:

'He looks so peaceful, doesn't he?'

'How long ago did he die?'

'Did you get his swimming things?'

'Has anyone told the children yet?'

When the mortician arrives, she is indeed mortified, sincerely sorry that we've had to wait for so long in these difficult circumstances. She's tall and slim with long blonde hair, wearing a smart dark suit. Although she, too, seems very young, her manner is entirely professional. She gently takes control of the situation and suggests that we go to the hospital canteen for a coffee while she 'sorts Paul out'. She promises to come and fetch us as soon as she's done this, so that we can see him again.

The canteen is at the top of a slope, with a wonderful view across the Hampshire countryside. I remember this view from the time I was in the maternity wing just around the corner, giving birth to Simon. I was elated then; this time, I seem to be looking at the scenery through a giant glass bubble.

There are one or two junior doctors eating breakfast or drinking coffee and reading the papers, but otherwise the dingy canteen is deserted. The coffee comes from a machine, in polystyrene cups, and it's bitter and undrinkable. The others talk practicalities: someone must collect Paul's car from the leisure centre. My brother-in-law elects to do this. Do I have the keys? No, they must be in Paul's swimming bag.

My ex-husband still hasn't told our children, because they were asleep when he went round earlier. He says he'll go and do this now, so that they're prepared before I get home. Then there's our daughter, who's away at university, and Paul's four children. Someone will have to tell them. I say I'll do it. I'll ring them all later, and my parents, and Paul's sister and, and, and … the list goes on. Some far-away, capable part of me knows that I'll have to do it, but most of me doesn't feel like me at all.

The mortician comes back. She says that Paul is 'sorted', and we can see him. As we follow her along a path to the back of the hospital, I think, *I bet not many people know where the mortuary is in this hospital, but I do, and when I come back here in the future, I'll know what's behind that frosted glass door.*

There's a waiting room outside the chapel of rest.

Bryony and my brother-in-law stay in the waiting room while I go in. It's dark in the chapel. The room is sparsely furnished, and Paul is lying on a bed right in the middle. His hair has been combed, and he's been covered with a dark purple blanket, right up to his chin. I don't like this. He looks dead now, and when I kiss his forehead this time, it's much cooler. I don't stay long. I feel tearful and unbearably sad. I just tell him that I love him and I'll never forget him, and then I leave. Bryony doesn't want to go in; she says she wants to remember him as he was, vibrant and alive. But my brother-in-law does. He was very fond of Paul. He's in there for a long time. When he comes out his eyes are red, but I can see that he's determined to be strong and practical for me, and he returns at once to the question of how we're going to retrieve Paul's car and all get home.

The mortician appears with Paul's swimming things and a brown paper bag containing his 'effects': his watch, some loose change, the receipt from our entry into the leisure centre and the bunch of keys that we need, held together with a key ring showing a photograph of me taken years ago on the cathedral steps in Barcelona. (I recall that day very clearly. Paul was distracted by a beautiful young gypsy girl offering him a rose, while her accomplice stole his wallet, which contained all our holiday money. Now I wonder whether that was some kind of forewarning.)

The mortician asks me if I'd like to leave Paul's wedding ring on his hand, or if I want to keep it. This question throws me into a panic. I don't know. It hasn't left his finger since the day we were married, so should it stay there? Or should I have it to wear next to mine? I'm very agitated, but the mortician is calm and sensible.

'You don't have to decide now,' she says. 'Just ring me in

the next couple of days, and I'll save it for you if you decide you want it.'

I hear her explaining to my brother-in-law about the post-mortem and the coroner. She gives him the relevant phone numbers. I suppose she thinks he's more likely to take in this information than I am.

And then, suddenly, we're free to go.

We drive to the leisure centre car park, where my brother-in-law picks up Paul's car. A sense of utter desolation overcomes me as I see it still sitting there, still waiting for him, still empty. It feels totally wrong for my brother-in-law to get in and drive it away, and for me to be driven home by my sister.

As I open the kitchen door, I trip over *The Sunday Times*, which has been pushed through the cat flap. I notice that the egg poacher is on the stove: Paul must have put it there ready for breakfast. I think of him on a typical Sunday morning, the type of morning that usually followed our early morning swim. He is at the stove cooking poached eggs and preparing toast for breakfast whilst I dry my hair and put in my contact lenses. He has put on Steve Wright's Sunday Love Songs, and he is singing along loudly to the music in his rich tenor voice. Before meeting him, I would never have listened to a programme like that, but we have discovered that the music of the sixties and seventies is something that we both love, a shared history that forges a strong bond between us. After the cooked breakfast, we will read the papers and take the dog for a walk, and when we return, Paul will repeat the cooking activity for the boys – ever cheerful, never complaining, delighted as ever to be at home and away from the stress of the office. *Well, no poached eggs today – and what am I going to do with the rest of the day, now that our plans have been ruined? Come to think of it, what am I going to do with the rest of my life?*

Later, I'll recall only vague fragments of that first day: the boys' shocked and tearstained faces, a walk somewhere over frosted grass, the smell of food put in front of me that I couldn't eat, the violent hammering of my heart.

But by the evening, it is crystal clear to me that I have to have the ring. At least our two rings can stay together, even if we can't – and what would be the point of cremating it with him? I'm excessively preoccupied with this thought. I ruminate all night. *What if it's been thrown away? Or lost? Or stolen? It is gold, after all.* I phone the mortuary on the dot of nine the next morning.

The receptionist is cheerful and unconcerned. 'Yes of course, that will be fine,' she says. 'Paul's going to the funeral directors this morning, anyway', (*what a strange use of an active verb*), 'so you can collect it from there.'

I do, and I take it straight to the jeweller's to have it made smaller so it will fit my finger. I tell the jeweller that Paul has just died and the ring is too big for me. He seems horrified: he doesn't know what to say. Paul liked buying me jewellery and we'd been into this shop many times. The jeweller promises that the ring will be ready for collection by late afternoon. It is, and when I go back to fetch it, he refuses to let me pay a penny.

*

The next few days pass in a hazy fog. There are lots of people around, and I'm busy: phoning everyone in Paul's mobile contacts, choosing a coffin, arranging his funeral. My sister tells me later that I did all this with characteristic efficiency, and she marvelled at how I was able to. I can hardly remember doing it at all, but people tell me that I phoned them, and the funeral happened, so I suppose I must have done. I use Paul's phone to ring all his contacts, so each person who answers thinks it's him. They say: 'Hi Dad,' or 'Morning, Paul,' and I have to disappoint each and every one of them by being the wrong person, before I even say why it is that I'm phoning.

I go into work on the Monday and tell them that I won't be back for a bit. We have tea in one of the nurses' offices and I'm surrounded by caring and loving colleagues, hugging me and crying. I go shopping in Sainsbury's, I cook for the boys, I take them to their music lessons and I buy them fish and chips when I've had enough of cooking. I ring the coroner, and he tells me that Paul died of heart failure, and that his arteries were all clogged up. He's very matter-of-fact; he could be giving me cinema times or the dates of recycling collections. I suppose that deaths like Paul's must be two a penny to him. I can now collect the death certificate, and I do this the next time I'm in town. I have to get it from the registry office; the last time I was there was the day that Paul and I got married. The registrar writes down that I, as the informant, am the widow of Paul. I hate that. My official status has changed with one stroke of her pen: I'm a widow now, not a wife any more. She tells me that I'll need multiple copies of the death certificate, as many organisations need 'proof' of a death.

Back home, people keep hugging me and asking me if I'm OK. I don't know how to respond, so I say: 'Yes, thanks, I'm fine.' And I am, after a fashion, in daylight at least, because there's so much going on and so many people. I seem to have fallen into a way of behaving like an automaton. But the nights are terrible. I can't bear having no warm body to cuddle on the other side of the bed. Paul used to tell me that I would always reach out a toe or a hand to touch him in the night, even if I was fast asleep. He liked the fact that his presence gave me such a sense of security. Without him, I feel intensely agitated. I can't sleep and when I do, I have terrifying dreams and wake to find my arm or leg groping across to the cold, empty side of the bed, searching for him. The sobbing begins the moment I wake up and remember that he's dead: such desolation and misery as I never thought possible. I bang the pillow with my fists, bury my face in the sopping wet pillowcase, pull the duvet over my head to fend off the encroaching day. My GP gives me strong tranquillisers and sleeping pills which knock me out, but I hate that drugged sleep, which leaves me feeling groggy and exhausted for hours after I wake.

As the day of the funeral approaches, I become obsessed with the idea that I want to see Paul one last time to say goodbye. It's been ten days since he died. My youngest sister, Annie, has come to stay, and both she and Bryony are firmly against the idea. So, I ring the funeral directors' secretly and make an appointment for a 'viewing'. I tell everyone that I'm going shopping. I pick a bunch of snowdrops from the front garden as I go out. The nice young lady at the funeral directors' is as warm and friendly as ever. She says that she has dressed Paul in the clothes I took in a few days earlier, that she has done this with great care, and that he looks lovely. Do I want her to come in with me?

'No thanks, I'll be fine.' *This will be the last time Paul and I are ever together on our own.*

'He's just in there, then.' She points to a door off the reception area.

I push the door open and go in. The room is quite large, with a vase of plastic flowers on a table by the door. I don't remember any other furniture apart from the trestle table in the centre. On the table lies the open coffin I chose a few days earlier, and in it … I gasp out loud in horror, thinking for a moment that they have brought in the wrong person. I'm scared to go closer. I tiptoe across the room and, as I approach, I recognise the dark blue shirt that I bought him for Christmas at Debenhams, and I can see that it is indeed Paul, or at least a version of him. His colour has changed completely. He looks ruddy, yet waxy, and this time when I kiss his forehead, it's icy cold. I go to put the snowdrops in his hand, but his fingers are frozen solid and I can't move them. I'm completely freaked out. *How can this possibly be the warm, generous, vital person who lives with me?* This is dead meat. It looks macabre, grotesque, a scene from a horror movie: a carcass on a butcher's slab. I try to pull myself together and think calmly, rationally. *He must have been kept in a freezer*. That would explain the cold and the other changes in his appearance. I brace myself to kiss him one last time. *Goodbye my darling; I'll love you forever.* Then I leave and run all the way to the car park, tears streaming behind me. I know that my Paul is not in that body; he has long since left.

*

The thoughts that have been tumbling out in words come to an abrupt halt. I'm in a large, light room, furnished with calico chairs and a low couch covered by a dark green throw. There are patterned rugs on the floor and modern paintings on the walls. I'm sitting in a comfortable armchair by the fireplace and beside me is a low table with a box of

tissues on it. It's quiet, and although it's summer, the blinds
are down and it's shady and cool. The woman sitting diag-
onally opposite me has told me that her name is Jennifer.
She's about my age, fair-haired and serious. She says little;
when she does speak, her voice is warm and friendly, with
an accent I can't place. She has been listening intently to
my story, without interrupting or asking questions, and now
she asks me how I'm feeling. I say that it's been a relief to
be able to tell it all, from beginning to end. I realise that I've
needed to say everything, to lay it bare, to lay myself bare,
to somebody who may be able to help me to process this
terrible thing that has wrecked my life. But why? Why do
I have this strong need to unburden myself? To go through
the anguish of telling my story yet again? And why to her,
a complete stranger, of all the people in the world I could
have chosen? And then, suddenly, into my mind flashes
the memory of a client from way back at the start of my
training: a client who taught me one of the most important
lessons of my career. A lesson which explains why I am now
sitting in Jennifer's consulting room.

*

Kerry was my very first patient. She was extremely overweight. She struggled into the outpatient clinic, late
and flustered. Her glasses were steamed up, and as she
manoeuvred herself into the chair beside my desk, it was
clear that she didn't want to be there. I knew she'd been
referred for weight-management: her GP had written in
the referral letter that she had tried, and failed, all manner
of diets, and needed more support in tackling her obesity.
I was shocked to read that she was a year younger than me:
she looked like a middle-aged woman. In preparation for

this consultation, my supervisor had told me to take a history and explore Kerry's eating behaviour in detail – when she over-ate, how much she ate, what the triggers were and so on. This is how the 'behavioural' approach to assessing and treating problems works, and it was the first method that I would be trained to use. So, I introduced myself to Kerry and told her that this was what I planned to do.

Her reaction was hostile. 'Well, that will be a complete waste of time. I've tried loads of diets and nothing works. I can't see the point in coming here at all.'

'That's fine,' I said. 'Nobody said anything about going on a diet. All I want to do at the moment is try to understand what it is that makes you eat too much. Do you think we could have a go at looking at that together?'

Her posture relaxed slightly, and she muttered something which I took to be a reluctant agreement.

'Great. So, let's start with a typical day. Tell me what you do, starting from when you first wake up in the morning.'

Kerry's warm-up was gradual. To begin with, she was resistant to anything that she considered to be 'probing', but she kept coming to our sessions each week, and over time, we built up a picture of the huge amount of money that she spent on crisps and chocolate bars on her way home from work every day, and of her lonely life. One of the main triggers for her overeating was loneliness, and her belief that nobody wanted to spend time with her. She worked as a secretary and she lived alone, never socialising with colleagues from her office, although they did invite her. She had had a boyfriend, but it hadn't worked out and he had left her for someone else. She told me that she'd like another relationship, but she didn't think anyone would want to go out with a fat person. Between our sessions, my supervisor was pushing me to start Kerry on a diet. I'd collected more than enough background information and it was time to devise a treatment programme and get on with it. I had a strong sense that it was important to wait until Kerry was ready to take this step. Luckily for me, it was she who eventually took the initiative. She walked into the consulting room one day at the usual time, heaved herself into her chair and announced: 'I want to lose weight. I'm fed up with being like this. Can we start on a diet now?'

The next steps felt a lot easier. Together, we agreed a calorie-controlled diet and a reward system: Kerry would earn a point for every pound she lost in weight, and when she had ten points, she could exchange them for a present or reward of her choice – anything except food. I weighed her every week and the pounds began to come off very quickly. The tone of our sessions changed completely and she was always on time – indeed, often early – and animated, keen to make use of every second of our allotted hour. However, I was becoming aware that my placement was going to end soon and I would be moving into a different clinical area. I was reluctant to stop seeing Kerry while she was doing so well, but I knew she still had a long way to go. I talked to my supervisor and asked if it would be possible for me to go on meeting with her. He was a nice man and agreed that I could, since I would still be based in the same hospital, and he would continue with my supervision.

And so we carried on. Kerry knew nothing of the negotiations that had taken place behind the scenes; she continued to lose weight and to open up to me more and more about her life. We spent a great deal of time exploring her loneliness and her belief that she wasn't worth spending time with. I encouraged her to keep a diary of any negative thoughts that she had about herself, which we would then talk about and challenge. I also suggested that she should experiment with following up one of the invitations to go out for an evening with the girls from her office. She did, and she found, to her amazement, that she enjoyed herself. As her weight continued to decline, Kerry bought new, more fashionable clothes and exchanged her glasses for contact lenses. She went on holiday to Mallorca and brought me back a present: a mirror, which I still have, with a picture of the resort she'd stayed in engraved on it. It was gratifying to observe the gradual change in her appearance and demeanour as this increasingly attractive, confident young woman walked into the consulting room each week. And it seemed that I wasn't the only one who was noticing, when she admitted one day in the summer that a young man in the office had asked for her phone number. She giggled a lot as she told me this, and was embarrassed, but clearly delighted as well.

Meanwhile, though, discussions with my supervisor were happening again. I was nearing the end of my first year of training, and during the second year I would be based in a different location, many miles away. My supervisor was delighted with the progress Kerry had made; the graphs I had shown him of her weight loss sloped steeply downwards, and he was talking about writing up the case for publication. But he was clear that I would have to stop seeing her by the end of term. He would follow up with a few 'maintenance' sessions with Kerry after I'd left, and I could congratulate myself on a very successful piece of clinical work.

But I didn't really feel like congratulating myself. I'd

grown fond of Kerry, and although I, too, was thrilled with her progress, I sensed that she had become attached to me as well, and that it would be hard to say goodbye. I never imagined quite how hard. As she arrived for her next session, she was more animated than I had ever seen her, desperate to tell me about her date with the boy from the office, which had happened the night before.

I listened to her for a while, and then I dived in. 'Kerry, there's something we need to talk about.'

She looked vaguely surprised, but paused her story to hear what I had to say.

'We've been meeting for almost a year now, and you've done fantastically well, but you know I'm a trainee and my placement at this hospital is going to come to an end soon. Next term I'm going to be working somewhere else, a long way from here.'

'But you'll still be able to see me, right?' she said.

'No, I'm afraid I won't. I can see you for a few more weeks, but after that I won't be coming here any more. My supervisor, Dr S, can see you a few times, but we've almost reached the goal we set at the beginning of treatment, so it shouldn't be necessary for you to keep on coming every week.'

Kerry stared at me, saying nothing. I could see that she was shocked, but I was in completely uncharted waters, so I gabbled on some more about her fantastic progress and how much I'd enjoyed working with her. Then I asked: 'So, how do you feel about what I've just told you? About ending our sessions together?'

By this time, she had recalibrated her face and her answer came swiftly. 'It's fine. I'll be fine. I'm not sure about seeing Dr S, though. What's he like?'

I told her about my supervisor, who was a kind, sensitive man, but she wasn't really interested, and it wasn't really fine. I carried on seeing her, but from that moment on, her weight began to go up again. It was obvious when I plotted the graphs after our final session together: the slope was downwards until the point at which I told her I was leaving, and then it changed direction and continued on upwards. I took this to supervision, and tentatively asked my supervisor whether he thought that the change in Kerry's behaviour might be connected with her disappointment at me leaving her, and hence confirmation of her belief that she wasn't worth spending time with, but he was dismissive. He told me to look at the details of the treatment programme – the calorific content of the foods Kerry was now eating, the rewards we had chosen and whether they were still motivating – and to tweak these as necessary to keep her weight loss on a downwards course. But it didn't make any difference. I left, Kerry grew fat again, and that was that.

I reflected long and hard on this experience with Kerry, both at the time and in subsequent years, with colleagues who took a different approach to that of Dr S. I saw Kerry as needy rather than greedy, and I was sure that her attachment to me, and her strong desire to please me, were the keys to her dramatic weight loss early in treatment. I also felt that I hadn't handled my departure well with her, that it had been too sudden and she hadn't been properly prepared for it. I had no idea how to remedy this at the time, as my supervisor thought it unimportant, but I was left with a very strong sense that the relationship with the therapist is of crucial importance in helping a patient.

*

Huddled in Jennifer's armchair, reflecting on that early experience with Kerry, I'm acutely aware that the tables have now turned, and I'm the one needing help. Part of what had mattered to Kerry, and helped her, was the strength of the relationship between us. I know that I want that kind of relationship, too. I don't want medication that knocks me out and leaves me feeling groggy and disorientated. In fact, I don't want any quick fix – I'm too distressed and it won't work. I want a meaningful connection with somebody who will give me the time and space to think about what has happened to me and who will stay with me for as long as I need: *that* is the reason why I'm sitting here now.

Jennifer is a psychotherapist. Throughout my harrowing story, she has made no judgement and, unlike many of my friends, she has offered no advice; no coaxing or exhortations to 'feel better'; no promises that I will 'get over it' in time. She has shown concern for me and she has listened, *really* listened. So many people avoid talking about Paul altogether, and change the subject whenever he comes up. I feel comfortable talking to Jennifer; I feel that we have connected, and she's told me that she's in it for the long haul. When she asks me if I'd like to come back and see her again, I have no hesitation at all in saying that I would. And so, after that first session, I drive to her house at the same time every week, and sit and cry and tell her that I want to die.

Chapter Two

Aftermath

The immediate reaction to news of a husband's death varies [...] most feel stunned and in varying degrees unable to accept the news. [...] For a time, a widow may carry on her usual life almost automatically. Nevertheless, she is likely to feel tense and apprehensive; and this unwonted calm may at any moment be broken by an outburst of intense emotion. Some describe overwhelming attacks of panic.

John Bowlby,
Attachment and Loss, Volume 3: Loss

I don't recall much about Paul's funeral. I stood in the pulpit at the front of the packed church and held up the naff Valentine's card that I'd given him less than three weeks earlier. When you press a button on the front, a picture of a big red heart pulsates on and off, proclaiming: 'You are the light of my life.' I told the congregation that the light had well and truly gone out, and it was very, very dark. I don't know how I managed to hold it together in front of all those people. Shock, or adrenalin, or whatever it was, carried me right through the service, the cremation, the tea and the endless expressions of condolence. When I look back, I scarcely remember who was there. It felt as if a large part of me had detached itself entirely from everything that was going on.

*

The funeral is over, and all the visitors apart from Bryony have gone. A great black void opens up, and the acute anxiety I have felt since Paul died mushrooms into a paralysing terror. I can't see how I can manage without him. What will I do? What is my life now? Where has the future gone? Following the death of his wife, C.S. Lewis wrote: 'No one ever told me that grief felt so like fear.' That is exactly how it is. My heart hammers in my chest, and nothing will calm it. I try to read the newspaper; I make myself a cup of tea; I turn on the radio, but nothing works. I can't sit still. I pace; I cry; I pace some more. I wonder how I will ever look after the children or go back to work again, and these thoughts make my heart race even faster. I become obsessed with wanting to know how Paul died: I wasn't there, so how can I be certain he's dead? Did he feel any pain? Did he know he was dying? Did he think about me? Did he say anything? I need to go back to the leisure centre to find out. Bryony isn't keen, but she agrees to come with me.

We're met at the reception desk by a young man who is the duty manager. He takes us to his office upstairs. He's softly spoken and serious, but I sense that he's uncomfortable; I don't imagine that he has to conduct many meetings like this. He pulls out a file and opens it in front of him on his desk. Reading upside-down from the other side of the table, I can see that it's labelled 'Incident Report', and there is a printed outline of a male body with some marks drawn on it and a lot of text, handwritten in blue ink. He doesn't offer to show me the report.

'The man in the cubicle next to your husband heard him collapse,' he tells us. 'He looked under the door and saw him on the floor. He had to break the lock to get to him.'

'Was he alive when he was found?' I ask.

'I don't know for sure, but I think so, because the man who found him did CPR on him while they were waiting for the ambulance.'

'So the man, was he a doctor?'

'No, I believe he's a dentist.'

'Can I talk to him?'

'No, I'm very sorry, but we can't divulge his personal details.'

I realise that a door is being shut in my face. This nervous young man, who wasn't there, can't answer my questions, and won't allow me access to the one person who might be able to answer them.

'I'm sure your husband didn't suffer,' he offers, but this is hollow reassurance. How can he possibly know?

I try another tack, 'Can I see where he died?' If I can pinpoint the place, at least I will have clarity over one detail of what happened.

'Of course,' he says, and although I sense his hesitancy, he leads us down to the changing rooms. We see the evidence at once. There are strips of yellow and black tape plastered across the door of the cubicle, and a hole where the lock should be. We can't look inside because the door is taped shut. So this is it: the place where the man I loved so much ended his life. A nondescript changing cubicle in an ageing leisure centre. I never said goodbye to him. He didn't say goodbye to me either – or did he? I'll never know, and these missing elements will haunt me for years to come. At this moment though, a sense of desolation overwhelms me. I start to cry. My sister says a hurried thank-you-and-goodbye to the manager and steers me, sobbing, from the leisure centre to the car park.

Back at home, my mood vacillates between intense misery and wild panic. The house is full of flowers, and they keep on coming. People mean well, but I hate the sweet, cloying smell and burst of colour on every available surface. It makes the rooms look unnatural: a constant reminder that something is wrong. I have long since run out of vases and have resorted to jam jars and various ugly receptacles, covered in cobwebs, from the garden shed. I don't like this; I want everything to go back to how it was before. The postman arrives at the back door bearing a large cardboard box – more flowers, pale yellow orchids this time.

I scream and hurl the box at the wall on the far side of the kitchen. 'I don't want any more FUCKING FLOW-ERS – I want PAUL!'

My son, Will, who until then had been sitting quietly, eating a bowl of Shreddies at the kitchen table, looks up in alarm. Bryony, who is still here clearing up after the funeral, but also, I suspect, keeping an eye on me, is calm and measured in her response.

'Of course you do,' she says. 'Let's have a cup of coffee.' She puts the kettle on, retrieves the orchids from their resting place beside the dog's bowl and puts them between a vase of freesias and a pot of winter violets on the work surface. There's a card in the box, which she hands to me. It's from the carer of Amira, a ten-year-old girl whom I've known for a long time.

*

When a child is referred by two consultant paediatricians simultaneously, it's a fair bet that there's a good deal of anxiety surrounding the referral. I had started to specialise in working with children and families as soon as my training was completed, and I was based in the Child Development Centre of a big local hospital. Amira had come to the attention of the paediatricians when she was two, because she had feeding difficulties. This in itself was unremarkable, but her short history was devastating. When she was a baby, her mother had tried to stab Amira in the stomach with a kitchen knife, after hearing voices telling her that her baby was evil. Amira had survived the attack with emergency surgery. Her mother had been incarcerated in a psychiatric hospital, and now her father was attempting to bring her up single- handed. The doctors could find no physical reason for Amira's poor eating, so she was sent to see me to try to get to the bottom of it. I knew that she would be coming with her father and a Punjabi interpreter.

The room we met in was far too large. It was usually a venue for training sessions or larger meetings, although it doubled up as a clinical room for some of the doctors. The only other option was a stuffy office with three oversized armchairs and no table, which was even worse. I tried to make the space as welcoming as possible by removing the roll of blue paper from the examination couch in the corner, shoving the blood-pressure apparatus into a drawer and putting out some toys for Amira to play with. When they came into the room, I was struck by how small Amira was. She was like a tiny doll, with silky black hair and huge brown eyes. She was holding the female interpreter's hand. When I greeted Amira, and pointed out the toys on the table, she showed only a fleeting interest, and chose instead to sit on the interpreter's lap, clutching the picture book she had brought with her. She stayed like this for most of the session. She seemed anxious, and unusually quiet for a two-year-old. Her father must have been in his twenties, overweight and wearing a baseball cap and bright white trainers. He spoke only through Mariam, the interpreter, and gave an unemotional account of what had happened to Amira, and her current difficulties. He seemed tired and disengaged.

I asked about Amira's eating. 'Can you tell me what Amira eats, for a typical meal?'

'Nothing.'

I knew that Amira's weight, although low, was just within normal limits, so this couldn't be the case. 'She must eat something, or she would've starved by now,' I said.

'Well, maybe a couple of spoonfuls of rice.'

'Anything else? Vegetables? Meat?'

He clearly understood this, and shook his head vigorously, saying something in his own language.

'He says she doesn't like meat or vegetables,' Mariam translated.

I decided to try a different angle. 'What about in between meals? Does she have snacks?'

'Crisps, when she's in her car seat.'

'Anything else? Sweets?'

He seemed very reluctant to answer this question.

After a silence, Mariam supplied the information. 'He's got a sweet tooth. He eats a lot of chocolate. He gives Amira chocolate, too.'

A picture was beginning to emerge of a child who had little routine around mealtimes, and probably gained most of her calories from unhealthy snacks. This was confirmed when I questioned Amira's father more about the mealtime arrangements. 'Do you and Amira have your meals together?'

'No, I feed her, then I eat later.'

'Does she sit at a table?'

'Yes, but she wants to get down. It's not easy to keep her there.'

'Are there any other distractions when she's eating? For instance, do you have the TV on?'

'Yes, she likes to watch cartoons.'

'Do you feed her anywhere else, apart from at the table?'

'No.'

At this, Mariam cried out in exasperation. 'Yes, you do, you know you do!' Amira's father stared at his feet as Mariam continued, in English: 'I've seen him running around the apartment after her, trying to get her to eat. He tries to spoon rice into her mouth when she's in bed – even when she's in the bath.'

Further discussion revealed that Amira's father had no experience at all of managing young children, and was struggling to cope without his wife. I asked him, with Mariam's help, to keep a diary of what, where and when Amira ate anything at all over the next couple of weeks. After that, it was relatively easy to cut out snacks and introduce a regular routine around mealtimes, in which distractions were minimised and a wider range of foods was gradually introduced. This worked well, Amira's father grew in confidence, and within a few weeks, the feeding difficulties that Amira had presented with were resolved.

That could have been the end of the story, but a year later, Mariam requested a further appointment. I wasn't really surprised. With such a distressing history, it seemed unlikely that everything would be sorted out with a feeding programme. This time, only Mariam and Amira came. Both of them were immaculately groomed and wearing starched summer dresses. We met in the over-large room once more, and, once again Amira, now three, sat steadfastly on Mariam's lap and showed only a passing interest in my toys. Mariam told me straight away that she and her husband had decided to adopt Amira. At this point I knew very little about Mariam's own background, or whether she had children of her own. I certainly wondered why a couple in their fifties would decide to adopt a three-year-old, with the inevitable loss of freedom that such a move would entail. Mariam told me that she and her husband had one daughter, now grown-up and living in Australia.

'So, it must have been a big decision to take on a three-year-old at your stage in life?'

Mariam seemed tense, perhaps unsure as to how much she should divulge in front of Amira. 'Yes, my husband and I are both in our late fifties. But we couldn't leave her in the situation with her father.' She lowered her voice. 'I know he used to leave her on her own in the flat sometimes, when she was asleep. I saw him drive off in his car. He was only really interested in getting another woman. As soon as we took Amira, he went straight back to Pakistan to find another wife.'

It didn't seem appropriate to go into this any further in front of Amira, although in subsequent meetings with Mariam on her own I did discover a lot more about the background to Amira's adoption. At the time, I focused on trying to engage Amira, and on exploring why Mariam had brought her back. Amira could now talk, but she used her speech sparingly, and she was wary of my attempts to play with her. I tried, unsuccessfully, to interest her in a teddy bear and a puzzle, and then I brought out a bag of plastic farm animals.

'Ooh look, it's a sheep,' I said, handing the miniature sheep to Amira.

'Sheep,' she repeated, and took it from me.

I produced a second sheep. 'Here's another sheep,' I said. 'She'd like to say hello to your sheep.'

'Sheep,' she repeated again, and took the second sheep from my hand, but made no attempt at any sheep greeting. By now her eyes were firmly fixed on the bag full of animals.

'There's lots of other animals here,' I said. 'They all live on a farm. Shall we see if we can build it together?'

I tipped the contents of the bag out on the table. Amira was able to name several of the animals as I picked them up, but all of my attempts to start a game were ignored.

'Ooh look, the dog's chasing the chicken! Shall we make the chicken hide?'

No response.

'Oh dear, I think the horse has hurt his leg. Shall we make him a bed so he can lie down?'

She stared solemnly at me, and made no attempt to join in. Instead, she picked up one of the pieces of plastic fencing and tried to join it to another piece. I helped her with this, and she then proceeded to construct an elaborate array of 'fields', into which she sorted the various animals – cows in one, sheep in another and so on. She was careful to separate the black sheep from the white, and the chicken from the ducks, and this activity kept her absorbed for a long time, during which Mariam told me about the current difficulties.

Amira had started at a local nursery, but she wasn't joining in with the other children. Her play was solitary, and she seemed frightened and disturbed by the noise and rowdiness of the others, often putting her hands over her ears and crying. At home, she was compliant, but she seldom played with her toys, preferring to follow Mariam around the house. She seemed anxious and jumpy a lot of the time, and she had developed some strong fears, which to Mariam seemed quite irrational: for instance, she avoided a set of china plates on the mantelpiece and an old radio in the corner of the kitchen.

It was clear that Amira had significant problems: problems that we would wrestle with over a number of years. This session marked the beginning of a long association between me, Amira and her adopted family. Amira showed many of the early signs of autism, but was she autistic? Was she suffering from an attachment disorder as a result of her traumatic early history? Was she predisposed to suffer from severe mental health problems because of her mother's psychotic illness? Or was it some combination of these? Whatever the answers to these questions, the main issue for Mariam was that she had taken on a young child in later life – in itself a significant sacrifice – and now found herself bringing up somebody very different from the 'normal' child she had imagined. We would spend many hours thinking about the challenges that this presented, and trying to understand what lay at the root of Amira's difficulties. Mariam would latch on to me for emotional support in much the same way as Kerry had, and as I, in turn, would latch on to Jennifer.

At this moment though, back in my kitchen at home, I'm holding a handwritten card from Mariam, detached from its discarded orchids and forwarded to me from work, which reads: 'Why is it that the worst things happen to the nicest people?' I'm touched, and thoroughly ashamed of my own self-indulgent behaviour. How could I possibly justify my hysteria when Mariam had embraced her difficulties with such calm?

*

After that I make an effort, I really do. Eventually my sister leaves and the boys are back at school and college. I try to get a grip, but I can't stop crying. It starts a few moments after I wake up from my sleeping-pill-induced sleep, at the point at which I always remember that Paul is dead, and carries on all day. It has a rhythm all of its own: at times, it's a quiet, monotonous whimpering, and then I'll open a cupboard without thinking and see his clothes, or the sweeteners he put in his coffee, and I'm overcome by convulsive sobbing.

Events seem to conspire against me. I come down one morning to find that the house phones have stopped working: the line has gone completely dead. This throws me into a panic and I find myself ringing my father in Devon on my mobile and screaming hysterically at him. He is a calm and measured man, seldom given to displays of emotion or reacting to them in others, but he registers my alarm and offers at once to drive up and help me sort it out. This calms me down minimally, but I still have to wait several hours for him to complete the journey. During this time, I chew my nails and pace up and down the kitchen like a caged animal. When he arrives, we go straight to Currys, buy a new set of phones, come home and plug them in, and the problem is solved. It's so easy. Why couldn't I do it?

At the time, I'm just grateful to Dad for helping me; with hindsight, I'm struck by the symbolism of the dead line and the abrupt cutting off of communication.

Soon after this, when Dad has returned to Devon, I'm in the kitchen getting lunch when water starts to pour through the ceiling and down the chimney breast. We live in an old house, which needs a lot of maintenance, but it has never been an issue before with Paul's extensive DIY skills. Panic comes flooding back at this new emergency and I stand rooted to the spot, staring at the point on the ceiling where the water is now gushing through, and screaming at it.

The children come running. 'What on earth's the matter, Mum?'

I can only point, and continue screaming. They, at least, have some common sense, and fetch buckets and washing-up bowls to catch the water. Then they phone their father, my ex-husband, who is round in five minutes and rings a plumber.

What is the matter with me?

*

I've read that the death of a spouse is the most stressful of all life events: according to scales calibrated to measure such things, it scores 100 out of 100 possible points. The pain is so unbearable that much of the time what I really want to do is to follow Paul – to die. I think about this all the time. I'm desperate to see him again and this is the only way. I clutch at straws. Annie takes me to see Linda, a spiritualist friend of hers. She lives in a modern bungalow and has frizzy blonde hair. She is wearing pink, she has long, decorated fingernails and she sits on a sofa surrounded by crystals ... crystal bowls, crystal balls; spherical and heart-shaped crystals suspended on plastic thread from the ceiling and every available window. The whole room has the appearance of an Aladdin's cave made out of glass, and it grates uncomfortably on my sombre mood. But Linda is warm and kind, and after asking me some preliminary questions, she invites me to lie on her couch for a session of 'guided imagery'. I'm doubting inwardly but I'm here, I'm paying, so I might as well get on with it.

The couch is warm and comfortable; Linda's voice is soft and calm. She's talking about taking me across a bridge from this world to the next. I am to imagine everything I can see, smell, feel, touch. I'm resisting – this seems pointless – but at the same time I'm trying, trying hard to follow what she says. And then, quite suddenly I'm transported. Paul's parents are sitting side by side on a dark wooden seat in a garden. I'm walking over a gilded footbridge towards them. The light is golden, and they're surrounded by a blaze of tropical technicolour flowers and exotic vines. They both look well and happy, and they're smiling at me. Paul is standing behind them, his outstretched arms holding the back of their seat. He's wearing the dark blue shirt he wore in his coffin and he looks utterly miserable. I want to hug him. And then as suddenly as it appeared, the vision is gone and I'm back in the world of pink crystals. I feel both elated and desolate. Was that a manifestation of my mind or a real communication from Paul? The experience unsettles me, and it doesn't take long for me to return to thoughts of killing myself. It's the only way I can think of that will reunite me with Paul again, and there is an added urgency now that I see that he needs me.

A longstanding friend and work colleague phones to

find out how I am. I don't tell her that I'm shaking all the time, but she does detect a wobble in my voice, and asks me to come round for coffee. I drive the ten miles to her house and by the time I arrive, rain is sheeting down. She lives in a large mansion on the edge of a common. On this occasion, I register that we're sitting in her study, which is surprisingly untidy compared to the immaculate state of the rest of the house. I wonder vaguely why we aren't in the enormous kitchen as usual, but then realise that her husband will be around somewhere. I don't imagine that she's one of those women who hide their husbands away from the recently widowed, but then I remember that she's a doctor, so perhaps this is more of a consultation than a social visit. She asks me gently how I'm feeling, and that's it: the floodgates open. I cry and cry and wail and cry and simply can't stop. I'm so distressed that I've lost all control. I'm going mad. I'm a wild animal, raging, clawing, desperate. She stays calm. She says I need help. She makes strong coffee and we sit and drink it and eventually the torrent subsides. She says that I can't drive home alone; it's still raining heavily and now it's dark, too. I insist that I'll be OK, but she is adamant and sits in the passenger seat as I retrace my route back up the motorway, her husband following close behind in their car to transport her home again.

My ex-husband, too, is alarmed and arranges for me to see a psychiatrist. I drive to a private clinic on a bleak housing estate surrounded by wasteland, on the outskirts of a soulless dormitory town. The psychiatrist is benign and affable. He writes with an old-fashioned fountain pen. He asks me about my sexual history and I wonder why that is relevant. He asks me what makes me most anxious at the moment, and when I tell him it's all the DIY tasks I can't do without Paul, he tells me that he himself is a dab hand with a screwdriver and offers to come and help. He then immediately and regretfully withdraws the offer – I am, after all, his patient. I'm beginning to find this encounter uncomfortable, and I've just had my first taste of what it's going to be like to be a middle-aged widow. He diagnoses moderate depression, prescribes antidepressants, and says he thinks that some therapy might help. He writes a long letter to my GP and I take the pills, but the near-constant crying and shaking don't diminish. I'm alarmed at my departure from the sensible, controlled self that I'm used to, and I fear that I'm going out of my mind. Perhaps the psychiatrist has a point, and it would help to talk to someone about how bad I'm feeling. I cling to this thought and follow it, and that is how I come upon Jennifer, who is always there for me, at the same time every week.

*

In my early meetings with Jennifer, I sometimes cry for the whole of my allotted fifty minutes and say very little, but she is always listening and always concerned. She asks me how I met Paul, and, bit by bit, I begin to pull some coherent thoughts out of the haze of panic.

— It's funny thinking back to that first meeting with Paul, because I would never have imagined that we'd end up together. I remember being struck by two things about him: one was that he was short – well, short-ish – and overweight, but he certainly didn't look like I'd expected him to. I knew his wife: she was an attractive woman, and I assumed that she'd be married to an equally attractive man. The other thing I noticed was that Paul was incredibly nice.

We'd been invited to a dinner party at his house. I was breastfeeding Simon, who was three months old, and I needed to feed him and settle him down to sleep. It was Paul who took me upstairs, found me a comfy chair to sit in and made a little nest in the middle of a bed for the baby, with pillows on either side to make sure he didn't roll off.

– So, you noticed his sensitivity. He was aware of your needs, and the needs of your baby?

– Yes, definitely. I was really touched. And during the evening, I felt that there was some sort of connection between us. One of the other people at the dinner party was very high up in the Health Service, and he was going on and on about the people he mixed with in the government, really showing off. Everybody else was listening to him with rapt attention, but Paul wasn't. He had a photo album with pictures of his house in France. The others had a quick look, but I was the only one who was really interested, and Paul seemed delighted. I remember he came and sat down on my side of the table and we went right through the photo album, from beginning to end.

– So, you were sensitive too, to something that mattered a lot to him?

– Yes. I hadn't really thought about it like that, but I suppose I was. I think that something about that emotional connection, or sensitivity, or whatever it was, must have made a lasting impression. That and the fact that neither of us was impressed by a show of arrogance. At any rate, five years later, we were both divorced from our previous spouses and married to each other.

The old feeling of guilt surfaces as I tell her this. Jennifer says nothing. I'm expecting her to pass judgement, like so many others have, but she doesn't. She seems far more interested in hearing more about what Paul meant to me:

– Tell me about him.

Where to start?

– He was an optimist, good fun, even impulsive at times. I remember once when he asked me to turn up at Heathrow after work with my passport and I discovered he'd booked tickets to Rio! That was so amazing – he was bursting with excitement about showing me all the sights… and yet it ended in disaster because I slipped a disc and had to be airlifted back home after only three days. Paul was so calm; he took it all in his stride…

– So you miss having someone to share your experiences with. But it's interesting that you've chosen to tell me about another catastrophic situation. Paul was there to help you then; he made you feel safe in a crisis. You could depend on him if things went wrong. You are in another crisis now, so how can you feel safe? Who can you depend on?

It's a good question, and the answer is far from clear, but I'm aware of feeling better for having talked to her, even though I'm the one who does most of the talking. She doesn't say a lot, and when she does speak, her words are economical – a distillation of what matters to me with the clutter removed; a voice given to a fear I couldn't name. She says these little things, and I feel listened to and understood. I cry, and she's never phased. This matters, because I don't want to alarm the children by crying in front of them. I need somewhere else to offload. She never judges me, avoids topics or changes the subject. She never gives me advice or tells me that everything will be alright. But what seems to matter more than anything is that she is always there, reliably there, every week at the same time; always ready to listen, really listen, to whatever I want to tell her. She gives me her email address, and asks my permission to write to my GP to tell him how bad I've been feeling. I feel contained, enveloped by her warmth and caring. She is my anchor in the raging storm that has engulfed my life. Even her downstairs cloakroom, with its lavender soap and soft white hand towels is a haven of calm. I like talking to her about Paul. She's not wary of the subject like so many other people who avoid it completely, in case they upset me, or because they don't know what to say. They don't realise that it's all I think about, all day and all night: all I want to talk about. She does; she knows.

*

At home, away from Jennifer's consulting room, the desolation and anxiety continue, and I sometimes wonder whether talking to her about Paul makes me even more disturbed by his absence. I know that the boys expect me to be upset, and although I try not to cry in front of them, their eyes register alarm and fear at this drastic change in their normally capable and contained mother. I resolve to confine my crying to times when I'm alone. This is often when I'm in the car, although I quickly discover how easy it is not to notice pedestrians or traffic hazards when driving in a highly emotional state. After coming close to knocking a woman over on a zebra crossing, I abandon the car and become obsessed with walking instead. I need to get away from the house with all its painful associations, and on our doorstep is a bridleway leading out into open countryside. Jess, the Border collie Paul gave me seven years ago as a puppy, is my constant walking companion. I talk to Paul all the time, out loud, as if he were with us.

'Where are you, Paul?'

'Can you see us?'

'Please, please send me a sign, just so I know you're OK.'

I hold my hand out beside me. 'Please, please hold my hand, just for a minute, so that I know you're here.' But nothing happens, and I have no sense of his presence.

By now, it's springtime. The verges are sprinkled with daffodils in full bloom. Although it's warm, the sky is grey with clouds and an early morning mist lingers. Jess and I are walking along our road, heading towards the bridleway and the freedom of open country. I'm distraught again, and the tears are streaming down my face.

'Where are you, Paul?'

'Why did you die?'

'Please, please send me a sign.'

I glance upwards, and although my vision is distorted by tears, I glimpse a single white feather floating gently, slowly down in front of my face. It hovers from side to side and lands silently on my foot. I'm astounded.

'Is that really you, Paul?'

I pick up the feather and put it in my pocket. Jess and I walk on into the woods. One hand is in my pocket, fingering the feather. But very soon, doubts begin to surface.

'If that really was you, Paul, send me another feather, just so that I can be sure.'

Before long, I spot another white feather, nestled amongst the pine needles on the path in front of me. After that, I find white feathers constantly on my walks with Jess. Sometimes it takes a while for them to appear, but by the end of the walk they always do.

A few days later, Paul's four children come for Sunday lunch. I'm in the kitchen waiting for the vegetables to cook, and I'm talking to one of Paul's sons. It's a cold day and all the doors and windows are closed. We're leaning on the island in the middle of the kitchen, talking about Paul.

'Do you ever have the sense that he's with you?' I ask.

'No, never.'

'I don't either, but I've been seeing these white feathers, and they often turn up when I'm thinking about him or talking to him.'

'That's weird,' he says.

'Yeah, I know. I wonder if they could be some kind of sign from him, some sort of communication?'

At that precise moment, a tiny white feather appears from nowhere on the ceiling and flutters gently down to land on the surface of the kitchen island between us.

Paul's son gasps and jumps backwards, knocking over a stool as he does so. It spooks me, too, but at the same time I notice that it calms me down fractionally. Does Paul somehow know that we're all here having lunch together? Can he sense our distress? Is he trying to reassure me?

*

From then on, as the days go by, feathers keep on appearing in the background. Sometimes I'll see one caught amongst the leaves of a hedge as I walk along the road; sometimes one will cling to the aerial on my car, or to one of the windscreen-wipers; sometimes I will rediscover one that I put in my handbag days earlier. I can't explain why I'm drawn to them; I just have a vague sense that they are linked with Paul in some way, and that they are a calming influence.

Four months before he died, Paul and I had bought a motorhome: a huge, six-berth beast, with left-hand drive. We called him Leo, inspired by his number plate, and we planned to use him for holidays in Europe, and for a Big Trip when we eventually retired. Paul loved Leo. He spent hours installing a quality sound system, and I would often find him out in the front garden late into the evening, happily listening to his CDs and tinkering with the wiring, or organising the contents of the cupboards for the trip to Spain we had planned for Easter. By the time Paul died, we'd had just three outings: two to the New Forest, and one to Dorset.

In the weeks following Paul's death, Leo looms up at me every time I look out of the kitchen window, and I know that I have to sell him. I don't think I can manage such a huge vehicle on my own, and anyway, without Paul, my interest has evaporated. But how do you sell a motor-home? I have no idea, and my heart races with anxiety just thinking about it. A search online isn't illuminating, as I'm unsure of Leo's specifications, nor of how much money I should ask for him. And then I remember the couple we bought him from. We only met them once, at Fleet services on the M3, but they were friendly and we'd shared a bottle of wine, squeezed in with their young son around Leo's tiny table, toasting holidays past and future. I decide to email them to ask for advice, and they respond immediately. They are shocked to hear what has happened to Paul, and they offer not only to help me with the sale, but to contact the Welshman who was also keen on Leo at the time when Paul and I bought him, to see if he is still interested. He is, and very soon I find myself inviting the Fleet services couple and a man from Abergavenny over for lunch.

The chosen day happens to be Simon's fourteenth birthday, but we agree to delay the celebrations until the business is over. As it turns out, I don't have to do anything apart from making sandwiches and cups of tea. Fleet services man hooks up the bonnet and explains the intricacies of Leo's engine, while his wife demonstrates the storage, sleeping and cooking facilities. The Welshman is impressed, and before long he is accompanying me along the High Street as I transfer many thousands of pounds, stashed in a brown envelope, from his bank to mine, this being the quickest way of doing it in the days before internet banking.

Later, as I watch Leo's taillights disappear through the front gate, I am overcome by an acute sense of desolation: there goes not only Leo, whom Paul loved, but also great swathes of the future we had imagined together. All that is left, on this drizzly day, is the patch of dry gravel where Leo has stood untouched for the past six weeks. As I stare down at it, I catch sight of a small white feather trapped between two stones. I pick it up and stroke it and put it in my pocket. It is just enough to stem my tears and awaken a glimmer of enthusiasm for presents and birthday cake.

*

I don't mention to Jennifer that I've been seeing these feathers, perhaps because I don't want the illusion to be shattered. I don't know what they mean, but I don't want them to stop. Although it seems crazy, they bring with them some strange sense of closeness to Paul and a fractional easing of the near-constant anxiety that I feel. I do continue to tell Jennifer more about my life with Paul, and one day I tell her about my butterflies.

– A couple of weeks before Paul died, Simon went to Portugal for half-term with his best friend's family. I was out for supper the evening he got back, so Paul went to collect him. He sent me a lovely text, which I still have somewhere on an old Nokia phone; I remember exactly what it said: 'One tired boy safely home. A huge tuna mayo sandwich devoured and he's tucked up in bed, fast asleep xxxx.' Simon had brought me a present from Portugal and he gave it to me the next day, wrapped up in tissue paper. It was three different-sized porcelain butterflies: one sunshine yellow, one turquoise blue and one a deep, earthy red. I've had loads of presents from the children over the years, bought in tacky gift shops, which I would have put in the bin if they hadn't been from them, but these butterflies were actually gorgeous. Paul and I had several discussions about where to put them, and we settled on the narrow strip of wall over the French doors in the kitchen. The day before he died, Paul was up the stepladder with his toolkit, hanging each butterfly on the wall.

I start to cry as I think of those three butterflies still hanging there, and I tell Jennifer that I'm seized by anxiety at the thought of ever having to take them down.

Jennifer says: They are a very powerful reminder of Paul, and perhaps also of your three children, and how much he helped you with them. The thought of removing them is unbearable, just as Paul's removal from your life is unbearable.

*

The next week, I turn up at Jennifer's house to find that her doorbell is broken. There's a note beside it asking callers to ring a different bell on the back door. As I walk round the side of the house, I notice a trampoline in the garden. So she has children! I'd never even considered this before. I feel a stab of – what? Envy, that her children have such a warm and caring mother? Jealousy, that there are other people in her life whom she cares about apart from me? But there's also a reassuring sense of identification with her: I now know that she is a mother too, and she even has the same trampoline as us.

I don't say anything to Jennifer about the trampoline, but there is something about it that makes me feel a stronger link with her, and I notice that I'm beginning to look forward to seeing her each week. She never suggests a topic of conversation. It's entirely up to me to decide what to talk about, yet whatever this is, she manages to find a way of linking it to my current preoccupations in a way that feels helpful. For instance, I tell her about my Spanish friend Mari, who lives near Barcelona and comes to stay for a month every summer. Her husband, Pepe, was killed in a car crash eighteen months before Paul died. Paul and I, and the boys, were in Spain staying with them at the time. It was a huge shock, but Paul took control of the situation in his usual calm way, looking after Mari and the rest of us, and managing everybody's distress with the minimum of fuss.

– Paul was there for Mari. He really cared about her. We both did.

– And you wonder who is there for you, who will care about you now that Paul is dead?

– As soon as she heard that he'd died, Mari was on a plane to England. Neither of us could ever have imagined that it would happen to me, too, just eighteen months later.

– So Mari is there for you now?

– Yes, she is – but she's in Spain.

Jennifer sits quietly and doesn't say anything more, but later, I realise that, of course, she is here for me, too – right here, in the middle of my crisis.

Not long after that, I have a dream which I tell Jennifer about. I'm in her consulting room with her when two young girls, who I assume to be her daughters, come in and sit on the floor and start playing. They are very sweet, but even though I get down on the floor and play with them, I'm annoyed. Jennifer wonders if I'm cross that there are other people apart from me who take up her time: her family perhaps, or other patients who come into her consulting room? And it's true – there is something comforting about having her full attention during the time I spend with her, and I don't like to think of sharing her with others. I realise that I'm becoming attached to her. I depended on Paul in so many ways, and now I'm depending on Jennifer to help me to process what has happened, and to get through it.

*

A few days before Paul's birthday – the first since he died – I'm beside myself again, catapulted back into the sea of despair. How can you go on living when the love of your life is suddenly gone, wiped out, just not there any more? When the person who believes in you is no longer there to support you? How can the loss possibly be borne?

I know that I have family, and friends, and Jennifer, but is it enough? This emotional seesaw, swinging between despair and fragile hope, is exhausting. I tell Jennifer that Paul's last birthday was on 7 July 2005, the day the terrorist bombs went off in London. He was working in the West End that day, and he heard the explosions. He was unhurt, but was it a forewarning of the catastrophe awaiting me seven months down the line?

There's another catastrophe just around the corner now, although I don't know it yet.

CHAPTER THREE

Grenade Moments

The grenade moment. Life has been trundling along and then, bang, with no warning, it explodes.

CATHY RENTZENBRINK,
A Manual for Heartache

One weekend not long before Paul died, he and I went to visit my daughter Emily, who was in her first year of university. We stayed in a cheap hotel in the city centre, in a room on the fourth floor. In the middle of the night, the fire alarm went off. Thinking that we were about to be evacuated, I leapt out of bed in a panic, wrapping the top sheet around me. I remember Paul saying, 'It's alright for you,' and laughing, as he lay naked on the bed with no covering. Fortunately, it was a false alarm, but later I wondered whether it was another forewarning. Apart from the fire incident, we had a lovely weekend with Em and her friends, pottering around the antique and junk shops, eating in student cafés, and walking in the park.

A few weeks after Paul's death, Em and I were having lunch in one of those cafés again. It was heaving with young people and the windows were steamed up and dripping with condensation. I couldn't stop thinking about the fact that Paul had been with us the last time, but now he wasn't, and never would be again. I abandoned my resolve not to cry in front of the children, as I just couldn't control the tears. When we left the café, my overwhelming sense of grief and loss had not diminished. We walked to the end of the road and crossed over into the park on our way back to Em's hall of residence. As we stepped on to the grass, I looked down and saw that it was strewn – literally carpeted – with white feathers. I was taken aback. In this place that I now associated with a sense of foreboding, did Paul somehow detect my distress? Was he trying to reassure me? The feather sightings came thick and fast in the early weeks after his death: was he somehow trying to connect with me when I was at my most distraught?

*

Now Paul has been dead for seven months, but the sense of foreboding seldom leaves me. I'm sitting at the kitchen table, having supper with two of his sons. It's early October and the evenings are drawing in; we're eating by candle-light. It's not the easiest of evenings, as they have come expressly to talk about Paul's estate – never a straightfor-ward topic where step-families are concerned – so the atmosphere is already tense.

The phone rings.

'Hello, it's me.' It's one of my sisters, but since my sisters and I all sound the same, this is not especially informative. I establish that it's Annie, phoning from the car. Dad is driving her and Mum home from a hospital appointment.

'Mum's here,' she says. 'She's had some investigations done about her cough. She wants to talk to you.'

My heart thumps. This is unusual. Mum never rings

from the car, and she loathes talking into mobile phones.

'Hello, Vanessa.' Always my given name, never my nickname; always that slightly accusatory tone.

I brace myself.

'I've been diagnosed with lung cancer,' Mum says. 'It's terminal. I could live for a few extra weeks if I have treatment, but I don't want any. I'm going home.' My mother always comes straight to the point. She is eighty-eight, and a doctor, and she speaks her mind – often to the consternation of those around her. She and I have had a tense relationship for years, and I don't know how to react.

I hear myself saying, 'Oh no, that's terrible. Are you sure? How bad is it?'

She must have picked up on the distress in my voice, because she's reassuring: she's an old lady, she's had a good life, she doesn't want to suffer the pain and indignities of cancer treatment. She has no doubts at all that she has made the right decision.

I say I'll drive down to see her at the weekend. As soon as I put the phone down, I burst into tears. There is shock, regret at the sorry state that our relationship has often been in, and the surfacing anticipation of another loss. Paul's sons are embarrassed, not sure what to do, and they soon make their excuses and leave. I'm glad to see them go, so that I can cry uninhibited. And thank goodness, the awkward discussion about money has been curtailed, at least for now.

For the next eight weeks, Bryony and I do the four-hour drive to a remote hamlet on the north Devon coast every weekend. In the car, we talk about Mum, and how difficult it has been since she and Dad retired and went to live in the West Country more than twenty years ago. Over the years, Mum had often vowed to get a train up to see us on a regular basis, saying she missed us, but it had seldom happened – and when it did, she was usually exhausted and bad-tempered. Nor had she shown much interest in her grandchildren, never coming along to school plays or concerts or sports days to offer grandmotherly support. Although there are obvious practical difficulties about travelling between Devon and the Home Counties in your seventies and eighties, Bryony and I had often felt hurt by her behaviour, and abandoned.

In her final illness, however, Mum has turned over a new leaf. Gone are the bad moods and the constant berating of Dad for the things he has or hasn't done. To begin with, she sits in a chair in the breakfast room, but before long she's in bed most of the time, holding court in her bedroom. She's smiling, jovial even, as she lies propped up by pillows, and people come and go; she always did love being the centre of attention. So many people – neighbours and friends from Devon, old colleagues from work and a few characters from our childhood – come to say their last goodbyes. And all the time the dog is jumping on and off her. We sprawl across her bed, drink wine, listen to Radio 4 and plan her funeral service.

As she gets weaker, we wash her and brush her hair and moisten her lips with cold water. There is one harrowing evening, when she tries to walk to the bathroom on her own and falls over. We hear the crash from the kitchen and run through to find her sprawled face-down in her nightdress: I'm shocked to see how tiny and fragile this often angry, powerful woman really is. She tells us that she doesn't want us to be distressed at the end; that we must make sure that she has adequate pain relief. My sisters and I are all agreed when we think the time has come to ask the district nurse for a morphine pump. It's a moment of great closeness between the three of us as we stand in a huddle in the kitchen, arms entwined around each other, and make that decision. None of us thinks that Dad should have to make it. That night when we drive away Bryony and I know that we won't see Mum alive again.

The phone call comes three days later, at 6.30 a.m. Dad says that Mum died in the early hours, and he's been waiting for a respectable time to ring. Bryony and I are there by coffee time. The bedroom door is open, and Mum is lying on her back in bed. The dog still keeps jumping on and off her. I go in and touch her face and it's already cool. Her features look sharpened, severe. Annie has lit a candle beside her bed. Mum stays there all day. The district nurse comes to wash her and lay her out. Annie helps, but I can't face it. Throughout the day, as we come and go for meals and coffee, and take the dogs for walks, she lies there with the door open for all to see. In the evening, after dark, the undertakers come. They're in an ordinary estate car, and they have the strong West Country accents of the local farmers. They put mum in a black plastic body bag, zip it up and carry her out to the waiting car. I find this horrifying, like putting rubbish in a bin bag for collection. I stand sobbing in the middle of the dingy, unmodernised kitchen. The last few weeks have been good, and we have said a loving goodbye. Mum gave her daughters the gift of dying a dignified death, and that is surely something to aspire to. But there are no white feathers, and I don't cry about her death again for a very long time.

*

Mum dies just before Christmas. It's also my first Christmas without Paul. I think back to Christmas eve last year. Paul has been up since 3 a.m. in order to complete the vast food shop before the cars are backed up to the mini-roundabout outside Sainsbury's, and he is now boiling a gammon ham and making sure that there are enough clean glasses to serve drinks when my parents arrive. He does all this without being asked, and cheerfully, for he is on holiday and likes nothing more than being at home with me and the children and their assorted pets. When his in-laws turn up he is welcoming and hospitable and ignores my mother's attempts to freeze him out by answering questions in monosyllables and burying her face in a book. On Christmas day, as the children crowd onto our bed to open their stockings, I discover that Paul has done a stocking for me too. He dismisses my squeals of delight, saying that it's just a joke really, but amongst the metal puzzles and chocolate coins there are CDs, books and a bottle of my favourite perfume.

This year, not only has Paul gone, but there will be a three-week break from therapy. I sense that Jennifer is alarmed. She's going away, but she urges me to email her at any time if I'm feeling bad. I do, but only to let her know that Christmas has been OK. I'm beginning to feel a bit better some of the time, a bit more in control. I ascribe this, in part, to the knowledge that there is someone I can go to who will accept all the appalling grief and misery that I'm experiencing without question. She is a receptacle, a container into which I can pour all this raw emotion, and so keep it away from the children and my friends, who understandably just don't know what to do with it. It's not so much about what she says, because she doesn't say a lot, but about the fact that she is there, every week, no matter what I throw at her. And I can talk about Paul as much as I want. I still have a strong need to do this, and it's a relief to know that there is somebody who will listen, who doesn't feel the need to tread carefully around the subject. She reflects back to me much of what I feel about Paul, and there is something about this process that is grounding and calming.

The New Year doesn't begin well. Simon and I are invited to a party by the mother of one of his school friends. I dare myself to go, even though I'm sure that I won't know anyone there. The young people quickly disappear upstairs and it's an OK evening, talking to strangers in an unfamiliar kitchen. But when midnight comes, I'm alone, surrounded by everyone who has someone to kiss or hug. I feel desolate and start to cry in front of all these people I don't know. I can't help it. I can't bear it. I just can't see how life can be worth living without someone to hug. I'm relieved to get back to my weekly meetings with Jennifer; I can't hug her, but I'm quite sure that she cares.

One night, I dream that I'm on a train with Bryony. I think we're going somewhere like Oxford, and I'm excited. But the train doesn't stop at the right station, and soon I begin to worry, because I don't recognise the names of the stations we're going through. Eventually we get to Derby County, and I know we've come much too far. All my luggage has disappeared, and my handbag, too. I panic and tell Bryony I'm going to find the guard. But I end up in a compartment right at the end of the train, and I realise I can't get out. It's just a hole really. I can hardly breathe.

I tell Jennifer about this dream.

– It frightened me. But I don't really know what it means.

– I wonder if it's a metaphor for your life? You start off on the journey feeling optimistic, but things that are important to you disappear along the way.

– But I end up panicking.

– Perhaps you are worried about your own death. After all, Paul died, and your mother. In the dream, there is no escape from death.

Yes, that makes sense. And now that these things have happened in my life, death is much more real.

As spring arrives and the first anniversary of Paul's death passes, a friend suggests that I should try internet dating. She means well; she thinks that I'll be happier if I'm distracted by another relationship. I mention this to Jennifer. She doesn't tell me directly what she thinks, but I sense something cautious and protective as she says that it is still very soon after Paul's death, and 'there are a lot of frogs out there'. Years later, I will remember that particular phrase.

Something is happening with Jennifer since the Christmas break. She's going away again, this time unexpectedly. She tells me she has to go abroad, to her country of origin. This is also unexpected, because psychotherapists don't usually disclose anything about their personal lives. It makes me anxious, but I still have her email address and now that I feel more in control, I can manage a week without seeing her – until it happens again … and then again. She always goes abroad. She doesn't tell me why, but my mind goes into overdrive with fantasies of an elderly parent who is dying or dementing.

After several weeks of to-ing and fro-ing, for her physically and for me mentally, she drops her bombshell.

– We both know that it can't go on like this. I'm going to have to move back home and close down my psychotherapy practice. But I won't go until you've found another therapist.'

I'm stunned. Just as I'm beginning to take tiny, tentative steps into the world again, I'm going to lose Jennifer, too. So, *this* is how Kerry felt when I abandoned her. No wonder she didn't know what to say. No wonder she started eating again. First Paul, then Mum and now Jennifer: it's too much. I don't know what to say either. I'm panic-stricken. I find it almost impossible to concentrate on what Jennifer's saying, but she's telling me that she'll give me the names of other therapists I can visit. She says I should see several, and take my time until I find somebody I'm comfortable with. She writes down some names and telephone numbers and, although I want to hurl them back in her face, I take them without a word and begin my search: what choice do I have? Inside, though, the panic wells up and my sleep becomes troubled and erratic again. The detached feeling that I had in the leisure centre when Paul died returns to remind me that I don't believe this is happening to me. But it is, and I know I must get a grip, and so I grit my teeth and set off in search of a replacement.

The first woman I speak to is frosty and distant on the phone, but Jennifer has told me that she has an excellent reputation, so I dutifully drive to her large, detached house and climb the wooden steps to her consulting room on the top floor of a garden annexe. The room feels chilly. She sits miles away from me and invites me to tell her why I have come. I begin to recount the details of the past sixteen months, with little emotion this time as I feel both nervous and intimidated. She wears an unchanging, grim expression and she says absolutely nothing. I feel discouraged, and eventually angry, because I know that I will be paying a lot of money for this consultation and the benefit of her 'expertise'. After more than an hour, she speaks. She says, 'It sounds as though a tsunami has overtaken your life.' Her voice is whiney and she delivers this pronouncement with a flourish that suggests that she thinks she has said something profound. And that is it. She goes on to talk about fees and available times, but I'm hardly listening, so desperate am I to get away from her.

A few days later her bill arrives, but I'm so incensed that I ignore it. A couple of weeks after that, she sends a duplicate bill, this time accompanied by an abrupt note asking me to pay up. I do, but I enclose a letter telling her that I think her consultation was a complete waste of time and money, and that I don't need to be told about the patently obvious tsunami-like nature of my recent life. Needless to say, I never hear from her again.

I feel acutely aware that Jennifer wants to go, so what am I going to do? I carry on seeing her, but our sessions take on a desultory tone and I find I have little to say. Inside I feel numb and furious, but I can't express this. The well-brought-up side of me triumphs, and I tell her that I feel guilty for being the one who is preventing her from going.

The next woman I visit is different. She doesn't work from home, but from a rented consulting room near the university where I often teach. She's called Jocelyn. She's a similar age to Jennifer and she seems mildly distracted. This impression is reinforced by her hair, which escapes in erratic wisps from the tortoiseshell clasp at the back of her head. She reminds me of my A-level economics teacher, whose hair was piled willy-nilly on top of her head, in what my best friend Liz and I gigglingly referred to as a *'Ptitsi Nyest'* (a 'birds' nest' – a facetious combination of English and Russian, which we were studying at the time). But she's friendly and really quite chatty for a therapist – more so than Jennifer. I feel, resentfully, that I must let Jennifer go to her ailing parent. And so, with a heavy heart, I agree to move to Jocelyn.

At the end of our last session together, as I stand up to leave, Jennifer asks if she can touch me. She takes my hand and says something about wishing me luck for the future. She's wearing a black dress and all I can think is, *How can you do this to me?* What I actually say is goodbye and thank you, and that is that.

*

Jennifer is wishing me luck for a future which seems to have been all but obliterated. As the psychoanalyst Stephen Grosz observes: 'The future is not some place we're going to, but an idea in our mind now ... a fantasy that shapes our present.' As versions of my future containing a husband, a mother and a caring therapist recede in turn, I'm reminded again of my patient Amira and her adopted mother, Mariam. Amira was eventually diagnosed with autism, but Mariam's future changed overnight from the moment Amira came into her family. At work, I met with parents in similar situations all the time. For years, long before I was widowed, I ran a support group for parents of preschool children who were newly diagnosed with autistic spectrum disorders (ASDs). Mums and dads came in and out of the group when their children were attending our special needs nursery. The parents covered a wide age range and came from many different backgrounds, but what they all had in common was a diagnosis which, one way or another, would change their lives forever.

The group met in a dingy basement kitchen, which doubled up as a staffroom at lunchtime. The only windows looked out on to a corridor which linked one part of the Child Development Centre (CDC) to another, so we had to keep the blinds permanently drawn to block out prying eyes. I ran the group with a colleague, and before the parents arrived each week, we did our best to make the room as welcoming as we could, arranging the chairs in a circle and setting out biscuits and a tray of cups for tea and coffee. We would buy the drinks and biscuits on our way into work, since the NHS would not run to such extravagance. It did, nonetheless, provide the room and facilities, and the china we found in the cupboard under the sink was surprisingly pretty: dainty teacups and saucers with an orange and yellow floral print, which seemed out of place in the otherwise austere surroundings. I think back now to some of the stars, and wreckers, of that group, and their different reactions to the situation in which they found themselves.

Carrie was a bubbly young mum with two small boys. She would drop her older son off at his preschool before trundling up the hill to the CDC with her laden buggy, always arriving a little out of breath. Her younger son, Toby, was strikingly good-looking, with a smattering of freckles across his nose and a thatch of unruly blond hair. His eyes were a piercing blue, but they had a vacant expression and veered off to the right or left if you tried to make eye contact with him. Carrie always turned up for Toby's assessment sessions on her own. She told us that her husband worked in London and couldn't take time off to come with her. She knew that Toby was being assessed for autism, but she denied this possible outcome from the outset.

'Toby,' she told us repeatedly, 'is fine. He's always been a quiet boy, but he loves playing with his brother and we don't have any problems at all with his behaviour. And he doesn't flap his hands or spin around like autistic kids do.'

Toby was indeed an amenable child, and the Centre staff quickly developed a soft spot for him. He settled easily into the nursery, but it soon became apparent that his play was solitary and repetitive, and he only ever approached an adult if he needed help with something. He wasn't interested in playing with the other children or in joining in with activities arranged by the teachers; provided he was left to his own devices, he was happy.

Following several weeks of assessment, our team concluded that Toby was autistic, and a colleague and I were delegated to break this news to his parents. Although Toby's father had been invited to attend the appointment, Carrie turned up on her own, as usual. She seemed as cheerful as ever, although I noticed that she was clenching and unclenching her fists repeatedly. We went over the details of the assessment we had done, and explained what we had been looking for in each of the tasks we had carried out with Toby.

As we got closer to the point of giving a diagnosis, though, Carrie tried to pre-empt what she feared we would say. 'You can tell me anything, but just don't tell me he's autistic,' she said.

'I know it's not what you want to hear,' I replied, as gently as I could, 'but we have to be honest with you.' We went on to give her the autism diagnosis and our reasons for arriving at it.

Her face drained of colour. She sat rigid in her chair, her fists now held in tight balls. 'No,' she said. 'That's not right. That can't be right. You must be mistaken.'

We talked some more about what we and the nursery staff had observed. When my colleague was in mid-sentence, Carrie suddenly snapped. Her face crumpled, she lurched forwards, and wailed. I have a vivid recollection of her, seated with her head in her hands, her long fair curls cascading forwards, discarding one sodden tissue after another, unable to speak. She cried for a whole hour without interruption. Any further meaningful dialogue was out of the question, so we arranged to see her again the next day. This time, she was calmer and able to talk at length about the loss of the life she had imagined with Toby, the Toby she now felt had disappeared.

'He's such a happy boy,' she said. 'That's what I just can't get my head around. I always thought he'd go to school with his brother and have friends and he'd grow up and go to university and get married and have children of his own. Now all of that's gone.'

No amount of reassurance from me or my colleague that Toby was still the same Toby, and could still have a bright future, had any impact, and over the coming days, Carrie remained distraught and tearful. She hadn't told her husband about Toby's diagnosis, and this too was something that she found profoundly difficult to address.

'He won't accept it. He just won't. I don't know how to tell him – I can't. I can't do it.'

The challenges of sharing an ASD diagnosis with other people, both inside and outside the family, was a topic that often came up in our parents' group. We felt sure that Carrie would benefit from the support of other parents who had found themselves in a similar situation to her, and we encouraged her to join the group. She wasn't keen at first, but after a couple of weeks she agreed to come, and it was during her first group meeting that she met Jan. Jan's son, Charlie, was a little older than Toby, and he had been diagnosed with an ASD some months earlier. Jan herself was a short, stout woman with cropped black hair and a round face that was always smiling. Her reaction to Charlie's diagnosis had been very different. She accepted it straight away with remarkable equanimity.

'I knew something was wrong with him, so it's a relief, really, to know I wasn't imagining it,' she told us. 'But quite honestly, it doesn't make any difference. Charlie's still exactly the same boy as he was before you told me this, and I love him just as much.'

We could never have engineered a better introduction to the group than the one that Jan gave Carrie. Carrie was trembling with anxiety, and she started crying as soon as she got into the room. We introduced her, and told the group that her son had recently been diagnosed with autism. The other parents offered words of reassurance, but it was Jan who moved over, sat down next to Carrie and put her arm around her.

'I cried and cried about Charlie,' she said (we hadn't known this). 'But it was a long time ago, when I first noticed that something wasn't quite right with him. For ages, I tried to pretend that I was wrong, that he'd grow out of it, but deep down, I knew he wouldn't. When I compared him to other people's children, I could see that he was different.'

Carrie's sobbing subsided as Jan said this; she was listening. 'What was it you noticed?' she asked.

'Hmm, well it's quite difficult to put your finger on it,' Jan said, 'but what sticks in my mind is one time when he was about two and he was playing with his cousins … or, at least, his cousins were playing with toys and having a lot of fun, and Charlie just toddled away and sat in front of the TV. When I thought about it after, I realised that he never really liked playing with other kids.'

'I thought Toby was deaf,' Carrie revealed. 'He never seemed to notice when I called his name, so I thought he couldn't hear me.' She paused, tears welling up again. 'Now I know he isn't deaf – he's autistic. That's why he's not interested in me calling him.'

This was a very brave admission for her to make in front of a group of people she'd only just met, and Jan was right there to encourage her further.

'I know, it's really hard. But the thing is that Charlie hasn't changed at all, just because he's been given a diagnosis. He's still my lovely boy. He's at nursery now, and he'll be starting school in September. He's getting help and he's definitely making progress.'

'You mean he's going to a normal school?' Carrie asked.

'Yes. He'll have a helper who'll be with him for several hours every day, but he'll be in a normal class with normal kids.'

We had tried several times to have this conversation with Carrie, but it made all the difference to hear it from another mum who was in the same boat. I could see the first glimmer of something more hopeful as she lifted her head and started to imagine a different future for Toby. It was the beginning of a long and supportive friendship between the two mums, and they both made a positive and enthusiastic contribution to the group until they left when their boys started school.

It wasn't always that straightforward. There was a time when the group became difficult to manage, when the media was full of stories about the possible link between the MMR vaccine and autism. There was one couple in particular whose anger about this was pervasive. They were well educated, always fashionably dressed, and Olivia was their first child. Although classic autism is far less common in girls, they accepted that Olivia was autistic, but they had done their homework on autism and they claimed that she'd been fine up until she had the MMR vaccine.

'There was nothing wrong with Olivia until she had the MMR jab,' they would say. 'She was a normal baby. She smiled at us, she waved bye-bye, and she was starting to talk.'

They had videos of Olivia to prove this, and they insisted that we look at them and share them with our colleagues in the assessment team.

'The day she had the MMR, she got a temperature. And then she got more and more ill, and she went floppy. It's *obvious* that the vaccine did it. Those bastards! How dare they say it's safe when they know damn well it isn't?'

They were determined to sue the manufacturers of the vaccine, and they wanted us to back them up. Their anger dominated the group. They would march in, week after week, demanding support for their cause, and berating the other group members for their lack of initiative.

'Come on you lot, you *know* we're right. What's the matter with you? How can you let your kids be harmed by these shitheads and not want to do anything about it?'

The rest of the group seemed both cowed and bewildered by this noisy intrusion into their normally calm Friday mornings, and my colleague and I were in a difficult position, caught somewhere in the middle of opposing viewpoints. We knew, and had often discussed in the group, that parents frequently give a history of loss of skills in some areas before their child is diagnosed with an ASD, and that the MMR vaccination is given at the age when speech is beginning to develop rapidly, so any delay in language development is easy to attribute to the vaccine. I had encountered many other parents who felt that the MMR was to blame for their child's setback in development, but not in this group setting. On the other hand, the purpose of the group was to provide the parents with support, whatever their point of view, so we had to let Olivia's parents have their say.

Eventually, during one particularly difficult group session, my colleague gave voice to something we had both been thinking: 'I wonder whether your anger at the vaccine manufacturers has been displaced somehow – that it's really an expression of the anger you feel about Olivia's autism diagnosis?'

They reacted to this with fury. 'How dare you say that? You're all the same. You're all part of a huge NHS cover-up. All you ever do is close ranks.' With that, they stormed out of the room, crashing the door shut behind them.

The next week, they returned, perhaps surprisingly, but perhaps my colleague's remark had been assimilated to some degree. They seemed fractionally more engaged, although they were still cross with us. It was the rest of the group, and Jan in particular, who came to our rescue.

She said, 'You are where you are. How is it helping Olivia to be so angry? You can't change what's happened. Be kind to yourselves, and to her. You have to drop this and put your energy into making the best of things for her.'

After this, their hostility didn't disappear, but they did begin to focus more on Olivia, and to integrate a bit better with the other parents. And they continued coming to the group every week until Olivia started school.

Jake was another child whose parents believed he had been damaged by the MMR vaccine. I first met them when they brought Jake in for an assessment. At the time, he was barely two years old. He toddled unsteadily into the room and made a beeline for the radiator. He had a small stone clenched in his fist, and he ran this along the surface of the radiator, backwards and forwards, again and again, producing a grating sound which set our teeth on edge. I tried to distract him by offering toys, but even the ones that lit up or played music had no effect. His parents were resigned.

'He doesn't like toys,' they said.

I asked if there was anything he did like, and his mum produced a packet of crisps from her backpack. One slight rustle of the foil was sufficient to bring Jake running across the room. Those crisps, then, became the key to assessing him. He was given a crisp only in return for cooperation: sitting at the table, looking at me, looking at a toy, and so on. It was still a difficult session: Jake was far more inter-ested in his own pursuits than in anything I or the toy box had to offer, and the results of the assessment suggested that he was not only autistic, but had a significant learning disability as well. His parents took this calmly. They were a jolly, affectionate couple. They loved Jake to bits, and they were going to protect and nurture him at all costs.

'We know he's autistic,' they said. 'That's no surprise. We know it's the MMR. It doesn't make any difference to us. He's our son and we love him.'

They started coming to the parents' group and their contribution was always positive – if at times somewhat overwhelming, as they both loved to talk. We learned that they ran a local butcher's shop, so their easy patter had no doubt been honed by years of chatting to customers. They joined Olivia's parents enthusiastically in their crusade against the MMR vaccine. Jake's father knew people 'in high places' and he was going to launch a petition on behalf of them and all other families who had similarly suffered. They were supportive and encouraging towards other parents in the group who were upset, or having difficulties with their children's behaviour. They never had a single cross or disparaging word to say about Jake. And then one day they marched into the group and announced that they'd discovered a cure for autism.

It wasn't unusual for the parents to talk about, and even try out, various remedies that they'd been told about, or more often read about in the newspapers or on the internet. Most of these had little, if any, scientific backing, and they often consisted of strange diets or dietary supplements that could, it was claimed, ameliorate autistic symptoms. It was understandable that the parents would want to try anything that might help their children, and even Jan wasn't immune to this. She admitted one day that she'd been supplementing Charlie's diet with fish oils for several months.

'I don't think it's made much difference,' she said, 'but it's not doing him any harm, so why not?'

Jake's parents, though, were adamant that they'd found something really big, something that really would make a difference. They'd read about ABA (Applied Behaviour Analysis), an intensive home-teaching method that broke skills down into small components and then built them up by teaching them over several hours each day. Proponents of the method claimed that it was able to 'cure' autism, and there were plenty of examples in the literature of children who had been able to attend mainstream schools with much improved social skills following treatment. I didn't want to dampen their enthusiasm too much, but I did voice some doubts. I knew that the literature contained many counterclaims, too, but Jake's parents dismissed these outright. They were determined to forge ahead. And so, a few weeks later, when they had engaged a teacher and got going on the programme, I went to visit them at home to find out how they were getting on.

By this time, I was widowed. Jake's parents didn't know this. They were aware that I'd taken a 'sabbatical' from work for a few weeks, but they had turned their attention to setting up Jake's home programme, and had stopped attending the parents' group anyway.

Entering their home was a shock. They lived in a nondescript house on a council estate full of similar houses, but that similarity ended at the front door. Inside, the living room was stripped of furniture, apart from a bulky TV sitting on a solid cabinet in one corner of the room. The TV was turned on, the volume down low. There was a threadbare sofa and a couple of armchairs, and that was all – no carpets, no pictures, no table of any kind. The wallpaper was ripped in places, and there was heavy scribbling over the lower part of the walls. The radiators had deep scratches across them – presumably Jake had been at work with his favourite stone. Jake's parents were warm and welcoming, and if they noticed my surprise at their sparse living conditions, they didn't comment on it. They were keen to show me the boxroom they had turned into a home-teaching space for Jake. It, too, was devoid of furniture or decoration, except for a child's red plastic table with a low plastic chair on either side. This was where Jake received his home teaching for thirty-five hours each week. That morning, his teacher had taken him to a local nursery to talk about integrating his programme into attendance there, so he wasn't at home when I visited.

We moved into the living room and sat down with cups of coffee, a rare treat according to Jake's mum, as they couldn't risk hot drinks when he was around. They went on to elaborate on what their lives had been like over the months since I'd last seen them. Jake's mum did most of the talking. She was matter-of-fact, now and again deferring to her husband for confirmation of what she was telling me,

'Jake's behaviour has got worse,' she said. 'He doesn't listen to us, and if we try to get him to do things, like going to bed or getting ready to go out, he has a huge tantrum. We try to be firm with him, but he kicks and scratches and he's bitten us several times. It's harder to stop him now because he's getting stronger. And the most difficult thing is…' She hesitated, glancing at her husband, then continued. 'He's started putting his hands in his nappy and smearing his poo on the walls.'

I had no idea that things had become so hard for them. They had never described Jake's behaviour as being so challenging in the parents' group, and yet neither of them seemed particularly concerned. I was starting to ask them more about the circumstances in which Jake's most difficult behaviour occurred when his dad cut across me.

'You don't need to concern yourself with any of this,' he said. 'His home teacher's going to deal with it. Part of Jake's programme is about managing his behaviour.'

His wife supplied confirmation: 'He's going to learn to

talk, and to do puzzles and things like that, and to cooperate with us. We're doing the programme too, so we know what his teacher's doing with him.'

Their enthusiasm was so great that it seemed inappropriate to raise any major doubts about what they were telling me. Meanwhile, I was vaguely aware of the TV, still on in the background. Jake's dad suddenly stood and turned the volume right up. A two-minute silence was about to be observed for the first anniversary of the 7/7 bombings in London.

'I hope you don't mind,' he said. 'I think it's important to remember all those people who died – and their poor families.'

We sat in silence. I was overwhelmed with emotion, and within seconds, tears were coursing down my cheeks. I kept my head bowed as the tears splashed on to the notes on my lap, causing the ink to run off the edges of the page. It was Paul's birthday; today was the first one I had lived through without him, and as Jennifer knew well, a day I had dreaded. I felt so desperately sorry for Paul, for myself, for the victims of the bombs, for Jake and his parents, for the huge challenges in their lives and the loss of the little boy they had anticipated having. And yet, they were remarkably calm and upbeat about their situation; they genuinely believed that they could find a way through to the son that autism had taken from them. Were they wildly unrealistic? Was there anything I could take from their optimism?

I had started to read books about grief very soon after Paul died. As I digested information about the stages of grief that some experts believe bereaved people typically go through, it dawned on me that there were parallels with the reactions of the parents in the support group to their child's autism diagnosis: there was initial denial and shock, shown by many of the parents, particularly Carrie, who was overwhelmed by the enormity of the loss of the future she had envisaged up to that point; there was sadness, experienced by all the parents to varying degrees; there was anger and resentment for some, notably Olivia's parents, who were also determined to find someone or something to blame for the loss of their perfect daughter; there was a universal loneliness, sometimes expressed as envy of the parents of 'typical' children, and sometimes as a sense of distance between themselves and friends and family unable to understand what they were going through; and, in rare cases, an early acceptance and desire to get on with life.

When I was running the group before I was widowed, I had read about reactions to diagnosis, and I tried to bring as much sensitivity and empathy as I could to the experiences that the group participants brought. But I knew I would always be perceived as a professional who didn't have a disabled child of her own. My knowledge of autism and local services was useful to the group, but it was the parents sharing a common experience who were able to provide true support and guidance to each other. After Paul died something shifted, and my experience of the group's anguish and sense of loss was no longer drawn from the pages of a textbook, but rooted deep within me. I too had felt, and continued to feel, profound shock, sadness and loneliness, as well as envy of friends who still had a normal married life. So was there anything I could learn from the parents about finding a way of accepting what had happened? Could I myself move forwards, as many of them had done or were trying to do?

CHAPTER FOUR

The Dating Dilemma

*The bereaved commonly suffer a deep and persisting
sense of loneliness which remains largely unalleviated
by friendships. The loneliness of social isolation can be
mitigated by friendships and social activity, but emotional
loneliness can only be alleviated by involvement in a
mutually committed relationship, without which there is
no feeling of security.*

JOHN BOWLBY,
Attachment and Loss, Volume 3: Loss

I start by trying to forge a relationship with Jocelyn. To
begin with, it feels odd to drive to a different place at a different time of day, and I badly miss my weekly trek across
the countryside to Jennifer's house. Jocelyn's consulting
room is in an enormous subdivided Edwardian house, and
it is bright and airy, with high ceilings and big windows.
Just inside the door is a table holding a substantial vase
of fresh flowers. I notice that these change each week. I
love flowers and these are beautiful, but I imagine that it
is the management rather than Jocelyn who chooses and

changes them, as she has told me that she doesn't live here. The couch in Jocelyn's room is covered with a deep maroon patterned throw, and has plain woven cushions on it. The chairs are modern, minimalist, and beside mine is a low table with the obligatory tissues. Jocelyn sits opposite me and we talk. Gone is the stark emotion of those early sessions with Jennifer, and although I feel comfortable talking to Jocelyn, I'm strangely disengaged. Her wispy, escaping hair remains a distraction, and now that I have an opportunity to observe her more closely, I see that she is wearing a thick layer of bright red lipstick. As the weeks go by, this sometimes changes from red to luminous pink, and is often smudged, giving a vaguely clown-like impression. Around her neck, she weaves scarves or pashminas in muted colours, but it's to the other end of her body that my attention is repeatedly drawn. Her shoes are flat and round-toed with a strap across the middle, just like the Start-Rite shoes that I, and much later my daughter, wore to primary school. But these are not navy blue or black regulation school wear. They are hand-painted, brightly coloured, with little flowers and figures dancing across the toes. And she has more than one pair: sometimes the background is green, sometimes yellow ochre; the figures may be pink, or red, or purple, but always dancing with the vitality and gay abandon of a young child's painting. I'm mesmerised by these shoes; they remind me of the research I did with children's drawings many years ago. I find myself wondering whether real children painted the figures, how old they were, how they made the paint stick on to leather?

But I digress – and that's rather how it feels with Jocelyn. I don't mind talking to her, but I don't ever feel the need to reach for a tissue. I tell her about Paul, about my mother, about Jennifer going away, and she listens, but I sense that she's bored ... or perhaps it is I who am feeling boring, still going on about all of this as time marches forwards. Or is it that I'm unwilling to entrust myself to a therapist again, after what happened with Jennifer?

I tell Jocelyn that my son's music teacher texted me to ask me out for dinner, and she suddenly seems much more interested. I tell her that I'm being stalked by someone who keeps turning up at the crack of dawn and leaving flowers and red wine outside the back door, and she seems positively riveted. I mention the internet dating idea and she's on the edge of her seat. There's no trace of Jennifer's concern: she seems keen and encouraging, insofar as it is ever possible to divine what a therapist really thinks.

The reality of my daily life, though, clashes uncomfortably with Jocelyn's blatant enthusiasm. By now, it's well over a year since Paul died and, as his presence recedes, the unbearable loneliness grows. I hate the endless evenings watching TV on my own, and the empty weekends when my friends are all tied up with their husbands. On a very ordinary weekday evening, Paul and I would settle down to watch TV after supper. Paul would lie on the sofa and Tick Tock, Simon's cat, would already be in his favourite spot next to Paul. A thriller would be about to start, and I would position myself with my head in Paul's lap, where I could bury my face when the tension got too much for me. We would lie contentedly like this for hours, Paul, the cat and me, with only the occassional interruption to fetch coffee or another glass of red wine. But the thing I miss more than anything is being the central person in somebody else's life. Paul knew what I was doing most moments of most days, and there were many times during the working week when we would ring each other just to check in and say hello. I would sometimes feign annoyance if I was busy, but I loved it really. Now that never happens. My phone is silent unless one of the children has an emergency. My friends get in touch weekly or monthly, but nobody really knows, or cares, what I do from moment to moment. This upsets me a great deal, but when I try to talk to Jocelyn about it, she offers little by way of understanding or comfort. Instead of staying with the uncomfortable feelings, she encourages me to challenge them by getting up, getting out and filling the vacuum. Her behaviour gives her away: she says little when I supply her with negative ruminations, but encourages me when I mention possible social engagements, particularly ones that might involve a man.

My sisters and some of my friends also suggest that it might be time to 'find someone else', and one friend in particular strongly recommends internet dating. I'm wary. I can't imagine that I could ever find a replacement for Paul, because I still love him as much as ever. The fact that he died hasn't changed my feelings about him. And the thought of dating again, after a gap of so many years, fills me with a sense of horror. I wonder whether my friends are urging me on for my own benefit or theirs? It must be a drag for them to see me depressed and tearful so much of the time, so surely it would be a relief to have somebody else take me off their hands? Jocelyn, too, seems convinced that I would feel better if I sought out another relationship. I'm not at all convinced, but in the face of so much pressure, I feel that I should at least make an effort. I think about the bravery of the patients in my group, who dared to go out into the world again in the face of loss and disappointment, and I decide to give it a go.

*

The friend who recommends the internet as a source of dates tells me that the choice of website is important. In order to meet somebody who is educated and of the right (i.e., left) political persuasion, she suggests *Guardian* Soulmates. I remain unconvinced and nervous, but one Saturday evening, when Simon is out and I'm at home, as usual, with the TV, the dog and the cats for company, I tentatively switch on my laptop. I type in that I'm a woman looking for a man no more than five years older than I am, and living within thirty miles of my home town. The response is instantaneous. Pages and pages of men are suddenly arrayed before me. At first, I'm struck by how old they all look, but then of course I haven't dated anyone for years. I'm also surprised by how unattractive many of them are. How could that one possibly think that anyone would want a date on the basis of such an unflattering photo? But there are a few who look OK, and when I click on their profiles, I find that some of them can write grammatical English, and sound OK too. I begin to read through the more alluring profiles in detail, only to find that, after viewing five, I'm blocked from seeing more until I subscribe.

Despite my misgivings, I'm sufficiently intrigued to take it a step further, and I put some care into creating my own profile. Later, I will learn that most women are economical with the truth when describing themselves, but at this stage, I'm so naive as to be completely honest about everything: my age, my situation, my interests. After all, if anything is going to come of this, I want to find a genuine soulmate. I have to invent a pseudonym, so I call myself 'Three Degrees'. I do, in fact, have three degrees – and the reference to the 1960s pop group will not be lost on anybody my age who shares my guiltily lowbrow taste in music. I find a flattering photo of myself and press 'submit'. The response is astounding. Every day there are new messages for me and very quickly my reservations disappear. I find that I'm hooked, spending hours of my time each evening online. Some of the messages are blatant invitations to meet for sex, and some are from men who are so hideous that I can hardly bring myself to reply. I respond to all but the sex invitations.

I compose carefully worded replies to the ones who look the most appealing. It is strangely intoxicating to feel the object of interest again, and I find myself rushing in from work and heading straight for my laptop. It takes up a lot of time once you get into correspondence with several people who want to tell you their life stories and hear yours, and I'm a slow typist, particularly when I'm trying to compose the best possible version of myself. I stop watching TV, and Simon believes that I'm bringing home masses of work to do in the evenings, since I've perfected the art of switching from Soulmates to PowerPoint at a split second's notice.

After a few weeks, GoldenTouch10 suggests that we meet. This throws me into a panic. It's been harmless fun flirting on the internet, but the thought of actually coming face-to-face with the reality of one of these photos is disconcerting. I ask Bryony what she thinks. She and I have shrieked with laughter at the photos of many of the men on offer, but she thinks that GT10 looks OK. By now I have learned that his real name is Craig and he works in

IT. He suggests a drink, possibly supper, in a country pub. The safety guidance tells you to meet for the first time in a public place. This seems public enough, and it's summer and will be light, so I agree.

On the appointed day, I can't settle to anything. I tell Simon that I'm meeting a friend for supper (true), and with the predictable lack of interest of an adolescent boy, he murmurs something which sounds vaguely like assent and returns to his Xbox. I tell Bryony to keep her mobile on and beside her all evening. As I drive across the countryside, I'm tormented by doubts: *What am I doing? How could I possibly have thought that this was a good idea? What will Paul think of my disloyalty? (I'm really, really sorry Paul – it's only a drink.) What if he's awful? What if I actually like him?*

By the time I drive into the pub car park, I'm shaking with anxiety. GT has said that he will wait in the pub doorway, and as I drive past, I see him. He looks reasonably like his photo, but he's shorter than I imagined – and what on earth is he wearing? It appears to be a dark brown V-neck jumper with three horizontal stripes round the middle, one white, one black and one yellow. And I know in that instant that I could never, ever be attracted to a man who wears a jumper like that. I consider turning around and driving away, but having agreed to the meeting, I know that I must face him, so I park, introduce myself and walk into the pub and one of the most boring evenings I have ever spent.

There's nothing wrong with GT; he's perfectly pleasant and keen to have supper after the first drink, but we have nothing in common and I just don't know what to say to him. I decide to make use of my professional listening skills and ask him to tell me all about himself. In my experience, there are few men who shy away from such an invitation to hold forth, and he doesn't disappoint. After regaling me with endless tedious stories about the IT company for which he works, he mentions that he's actually involved with a woman.

'Really?' I ask. The uncharitable thought that occurs to me is how? But I keep that to myself.

'Yes,' he says. 'I'm sorry, I probably should have mentioned it before suggesting that we meet.' He looks chastened.

All I experience is relief. 'Don't worry,' I say. 'I've only been widowed for just over a year. I'm not looking for a proper relationship yet.'

Now he seems relieved, so I ask him to tell me about his girlfriend. He takes a large slug of beer, and that is when it all becomes unexpectedly weird.

'I met her at a personal growth group I saw advertised on the internet,' he says, adding: 'It's something else I do to meet women.'

The psychologist in me is always alert to opportunities for personal growth, so I ask him to tell me more about the group.

'It's very experiential. We meet once a week in different people's houses, and every few weeks we have a weekend retreat away somewhere.'

I'm intrigued. 'So what do you actually do on these retreats?'

'Well, we start with everyone taking their clothes off. It's incredible how much better you can tune in to your body without any clothes on.'

I certainly wasn't expecting that. There is something so completely incongruous about the idea that this boring man in his bumblebee jumper should find himself in a room full of naked cult enthusiasts that I almost laugh. But I manage to keep a straight face, weather the remainder of the evening, pay for my supper and head for the car park.

As I pull out my car keys, a feather flutters to the ground: I must have picked it up and pocketed it on a walk and forgotten about it. I get into the car and drive off, relieved to have got away from GT10, but at the same time unaccountably upset. I find myself sobbing as I drive. The feather has unsettled me, and in its wake, a maelstrom of unwelcome thoughts pour into my mind: *Were you there Paul? Did you see him? I know he's awful. I wouldn't ever go out with anyone like that. I miss you. I love you. Why did you have to die?*

The reality of my situation hits me with renewed ferocity: I'm not interested in boring, strange men like GT. Paul is the only man I want – but he's not here, and he's not coming back.

By the next day, I've recovered, and GT is on the internet early. He really, really enjoyed the evening with me – and guess what? He's finished with his stripper girlfriend. He wonders if I'd like to have dinner again tomorrow?

I think not. So far as I'm concerned, he definitely doesn't have the golden touch.

*

After this inauspicious beginning, I steel myself to go on other dates, too insignificant to warrant detailed description, but sufficient to supply material with which to amuse and gratify both Jocelyn and my friends. I find that I can generate these anecdotes with ease, and my audience is pleased that things seem to be going well.

My internal reality, however, continues to be much less

positive, and I'm reminded of a child I worked with several years ago. In her case, the glowing reports I was delivering were to my professional colleagues. I was involved in a research project looking at communication between visually impaired children and their parents. Emma was two, and she had been blind from birth. I was assigned to visit her at home in order to make a short video of her interacting with her mother. She lived in a leafy suburb in a big detached house, which her mother, Cathy, kept immaculately. I had met Emma and Cathy once before, when they came to our clinic for an initial, rather formal assessment, and we wanted to supplement this with a more detailed picture of their communication skills in familiar surroundings.

In common with many blind children, Emma's motor development was delayed, and she was not yet moving around independently. She was significantly overweight, and when I arrived at the house, I found her sitting in the middle of the living room floor, rocking backwards and forwards and grizzling intermittently. Cathy looked as though she might have dressed up for my visit: she wore fashionable glasses over her carefully made-up eyes, glossy red lipstick and a tight pencil skirt which accentuated her slender hips. I noticed a box of toys on a low table, some distance from where Emma was sitting.

The research guidance stated that I could not give any advice at this point, and so I delivered the standard instructions to Cathy: 'I'd like you to play with Emma for a short while in the way that you normally do. I'll give you some warm-up time, and then I'll film you both for about fifteen minutes. After that, we can talk about how it went.'

The session didn't go well. Cathy sat on the sofa near

the box of toys and held them out in turn to Emma.

'What's this, Emma?' she would ask, or, 'Look at this Emma. It's nice, isn't it?'

Emma showed little interest in any of the toys, and apart from stilling briefly to the sound of a squeaky plastic duck, she continued rocking and grizzling. Cathy seemed stiff and uncomfortable, and breathed an audible sigh of relief when the fifteen minutes of filming was finished. She was candid about her discomfort.

'I don't know how to play with her,' she said. 'I do try, but there isn't much that she's interested in, apart from food, and that just makes her fatter.'

This admission led us easily into a conversation about ways of developing positive and meaningful interactions with a visually impaired child, making use of many of the insights we had gained in our research so far. I encouraged Cathy to 'think herself into' Emma's sightless world, trying to imagine the sorts of experience that Emma was most likely to be aware of, and hence show interest in. I gave her advice about specific techniques she could use when playing and communicating with Emma, and left her with a printed handout of practical guidance and a promise to phone her weekly to find out how she was getting on.

The regular telephone feedback was a pleasure to receive, and from week one I was reporting positive results back to my team. Cathy decided early on to wear a blindfold for half an hour each day, so that she could get some sense of Emma's dark world. She learned straight away that it was only objects that Emma could touch or hear or smell that were part of her immediate experience, and this had a direct impact on what she chose to talk to Emma about. Cathy lapped up suggestions. If I asked her to *tell* Emma what she was holding, rather than asking her what it was, she complied at once. When I suggested that she use specific words like 'round' or 'spiky' to describe things, rather than 'nice', she developed a rich vocabulary of adjectives to describe Emma's toys and common household objects.

Six weeks later, I did another home visit and witnessed a remarkable transformation. This time, Cathy was wearing an old tracksuit and she got down on the floor at once to play with Emma. Emma herself was no longer rocking or grizzling, but stilling in anticipation of a play session with her mother, and reaching out at the sound of a familiar toy. Indeed, she was making great efforts to grasp noisy toys that Cathy placed just out of her reach, and I could see that she was edging closer towards independent locomotion. I made another video to document her progress, and congratulated Cathy wholeheartedly on the fantastic effort she had made, and was continuing to make.

It was when Emma had been put to bed for a nap and we were sitting down with cups of coffee that Cathy told me how she really felt. She started crying, and along with her tears, the frustrations and disappointments of the past two years poured out of her.

'When I was pregnant with Emma, I was happy. I had everything to look forward to. You can't imagine how shocked I was when they told me she was blind. Disappointed would be a massive understatement. I didn't want a baby that wasn't perfect – and yet I felt so guilty for having those thoughts.'

'And now?' I asked her.

'Now I've got a bit more used to the idea, but every day is hard. Like the playing – if I had a normal child, I'm sure I'd know instinctively how to play with her. I don't want to have to learn new ways of doing it. People expect me to get on with it – professionals like you, too – so I do, but deep down I resent it. It doesn't seem natural.'

These words of Cathy's echo in my mind as I consider my own attitude to the internet dating. Dating in the normal way felt natural; this feels anything but. People encourage me – my friends, my sisters, professionals like Jocelyn. They want me to succeed, to 'deal' with my situation and move forwards. Superficially, all seems to be going well and I can provide a positive commentary for their consumption, but inside I ache with sorrow at the loss of the partner I actually want. Cathy and I have much in common: we're both guilty of telling stories that aren't the real story, and we will both need a lot longer to adapt properly to what has happened to us, and to feel comfortable with the situations in which we find ourselves. I don't want to go on dates with strange men any more than Cathy wants to adopt an unfamiliar way of playing with Emma, but at least we're both trying.

*

Even so, I'm disillusioned with dating, and I decide to stop searching. I don't initiate any more contacts myself, but emails continue to alert me if anyone makes contact with me. After a while, I find myself corresponding with Tarragonman: he has been persistent, in spite of my half-hearted replies to his communications thus far. He reveals that his pseudonym refers not to a fondness for herbs, but to the tiny house he owns in the hills outside Tarragona in Spain. His name is Peter, but I can call him Pedro. I have to admit that he writes beautifully. He has a degree in English Literature from a top university and he's a lecturer. And he's a widower. I allow myself a flicker of hope. We exchange longer and longer emails and I find myself logging in every day to read his next instalment and compose my reply. We tell each other a great deal about our lives, and it occurs to me that I'm growing attached to somebody I have never met, and yet feel that I know intuitively. I think of the early days with Paul: I got to know him well long before we became an item. Could this Pedro actually develop into another soulmate? I tell my sister Annie about him. She's excited. She so wants me to be happy again and she has a 'good feeling' about Pedro. I do too, and when, after what seems like months, he suggests that we meet, I find that I actually want to.

We are going to a concert in Oxford, and I wait for him in the doorway of Blackwell's. It's a bright winter's morning and I'm nervous, shivering with both anticipation and the cold. I've seen his photo on the internet and I know that he has thinning blond hair and glasses, so I recognise him instantly as he hurries along the pavement towards me. As he approaches, he speaks: *'Buenos dias, señora!'*

In that instant, my edifice of hopes and dreams comes tumbling down. The voice is high-pitched, whiney. Not at all the cultured baritone I had imagined. I'm devastated, but I compose my face, smile and join him to walk to the concert. It's a string quartet, playing exquisitely in an elaborately panelled room, and I find the music soothing and settling.

Afterwards, we have lunch. He's nice, but the illusion has been shattered. We have plenty in common, but I learn that he has lived in the same house and worked in the same college ever since graduating, and I have a depressing sense that his life has stood still, that he hasn't grasped the opportunities proffered by its auspicious beginning.

Still, he likes art, opera and walking, and so do I, so I see no harm in meeting again as companions to enjoy our shared interests.

Over the ensuing months, we go to the Cortauld and Tate Modern, the London Coliseum and Covent Garden, and we tramp for miles across the South Downs and the New Forest. I quite enjoy his company, but more than that I enjoy the activities and having someone to do them with again. He, on the other hand, seems to be getting keen. I can see it in his eyes. I remember how Paul used to look at me when we were falling in love.

Pedro says he likes me, 'And if there's something else developing, I'll keep it under wraps for now.'

This alarms me, because I have no romantic feelings whatsoever about him. He tries to hold my hand; I tell him I just want to be friends. He takes me to see his house, which for me reinforces the state of dilapidated stuck-ness that I now associate firmly with him. He's lived there for thirty years, and I'm pretty sure that none of the dark wood furniture or equally sombre décor has been altered since he moved in. I invite him to my house in return. My father is visiting and they get on famously, chattering about the old ILEA, Red Ken and the lamentable state of further education. Pedro makes a huge effort with Simon, virtually shoving him into the garden to kick a football around. My boy knows how to behave and doesn't resist, but afterwards he's scathing.

'Mum, you know I hate football. Why did I have to play with him?'

'I think he was just trying to be friendly,' I offer, but I feel guilty about dragging Simon into something I feel lukewarm about myself.

'I hate people who make you do things just because they think it's cool. Why didn't he ask me if I actually *liked* football first?'

I can't answer this, but Simon's distaste tunes me in to some more of the things that I find unattractive about Pedro: how skinny he is, how he pushes his food around his plate and never finishes it all, how his varicose veins protrude from his shorts when we're out walking.

Then Simon asks: 'You're not going *out* with him, are you Mum?'

I reassure him that no, I certainly am not, that we're just friends, but it bothers me that Simon so obviously dislikes Pedro, and I begin to think that I should re-evaluate what I'm doing. The trouble is that I'm so starved of male company that I find it hard to stop seeing Pedro, and yet I'm growing more and more uncomfortable about our divergent agendas.

Pedro invites me to his home town again. He takes me to a French bistro run by a friend of his, and I have the uneasy feeling that we're being treated as a couple. After dinner, he invites me back to his house for coffee. It's midsummer, still warm and light, and by now I know him well enough to think this will be fine. I sit on the sofa as he makes the coffee, which takes a while as he has an espresso machine that only makes one tiny cup at a time. He comes back with a tray and puts the coffees on the table beside me – and then he pounces.

I'm completely unprepared (although, with hindsight, of course it was the obvious next move). My disquiet is rapidly followed by a growing fear: for once, I haven't told Bryony where I'm going, and Simon only knows I'm having another supper 'with a friend', so nobody actually knows where I am. Pedro is ardent, pressing me, begging me to stay. I'm scared. Into my mind race all the stories I've read about the dangers of internet dating, accompanied by a most unwelcome memory of a book I once read about a serial killer who used to groom his victims by advertising for a girlfriend in the small ads. I know that I must keep calm and not aggravate him or hurt his feelings. So I tell him that Simon is expecting me home, that he doesn't like being in the house alone at night, and that he's going away on a school trip next week (true) so I could come back then (also true, but extremely unlikely – in fact, not a hope in hell). This seems to placate him, and after a few more excruciating minutes of fumbling and murmuring, he lets me go.

I don't think I've *ever* driven so fast. I throw myself into the car and on to the motorway and I don't begin to calm down until I'm in my own kitchen with the door bolted behind me. And that is it. Pedro is angry, says I have led him on, says I shouldn't be on a dating site if I'm not looking for a relationship. *But I didn't say I wasn't – just not with you* (although I don't actually say that). Years later, in a Christmas card, he tells me that he has met someone else and remarried. I'm pleased for him. I really am. It's what he wanted. He just wasn't right for me, and sadly, I never got to see his house in Tarragona.

Jocelyn listens to all of this with a faint smile of amusement. I can picture her clearly, sitting opposite me, hair askew, lipstick smudged, shoes dancing, in rapt attention. Although it was I who finished with Pedro, I've been knocked off balance by the experience.

– I feel sullied, I admit to Jocelyn. I couldn't bear him touching me. It felt like a betrayal of Paul.

She says something about needing time to get used to the touch of another man, but to me it feels like a one-sided conversation: she is either unaware of the uneasy mix of hope and despair that lurk behind my dating stories, or she is unwilling to address it. But I find the dating too unsettling to manage on my own. I decide to pack it in, and the next time I switch on my laptop, I delete my dating profile.

*

After I've been seeing Jocelyn for several months, my brother-in-law dies. He's fifty-six, and an alcoholic. Bryony phones to let me know, in a curious reversal of the phone call I made to her from the swimming pool two years earlier. She tells me that the news was delivered by a police officer, who was on her doorstep when she got home from work. My brother-in-law had led a troubled life, but I was fond of him. He adored Paul, and he and his mates from work have helped me out in numerous practical ways since Paul died. Ten days later, I'm at his funeral. My now fifteen-year-old youngest son informs me that this is the fifth family funeral he has been to in less than five years (both of Paul's parents, Paul, his granny and now his uncle). He has been to only one wedding.

My panic level increases again after my brother-in-law's death. I'm disturbed in particular by the thought that now there really is nobody at all to help with DIY. Where will I get my next consignment of gravel for the front drive from? And how will I find another tree surgeon who will do a day's work for a couple of beers and a few cups of tea?

But something else is wrong, too. I tell Jocelyn.

– I don't *feel* anything at all. I was very fond of my brother-in-law, and I depended on him. But I feel nothing about his death – no pain, no grief, no anything.

I'm worried about this, as it seems unnatural, especially as my sister and her children are so upset.

– Do you think there's been so much loss in my life that I've been inoculated against feeling it?

I don't remember Jocelyn's reply, but later it occurs to me that the dating activity might also be a kind of inoculation against the overwhelming sense of loss following Paul's death. Jocelyn seems to want to help me to build up stronger defences, but will it work? I don't know. Seeing her, however, has become a habit, part of the working week, and a small part of me still thinks that I should try to follow her relentless encouragement to be positive. So I continue driving over to the university every Tuesday morning and then going to work.

*

Removing myself from the internet cattle market, where lonely men and women display their wares for all to see, is a relief. I'm talking to a friend about this one evening. She was divorced for many years, but then met a man through a dating column in *The Telegraph*.

'You don't *have* to advertise yourself, you know,' she says.

'Well, how else would you find somebody?'

'This paper works differently,' she explains. 'You look at the ads that men have placed, and if you like the look of one, you dial the number at the end of the ad and you can hear a recording of them talking about themselves.'

This is interesting, given my recent experience with Pedro's voice: I could have eliminated him before we even met. My friend is keen to demonstrate how straightforward it is, and since we're at her house, she easily locates a copy of the paper and we try out a few of the numbers. Soon we're listening to hesitant regional accents, confident ex-public-school boys and everything in between. My friend encourages me to take the paper home and try it out for myself, and so I do. I find that I can snoop on as many men as I want (at great expense, I later discover, when the phone bill arrives) without having to advertise myself at all. I can leave a message for men I like the sound of and then dial into my own box number to discover any messages that have been left for me in return. I'm not sure why I'm doing this, but at least this time I'm in complete control of the process, and there is no danger of any unsolicited contact.

After a few days, Simon asks: 'Mum, why do you keep picking up the phone and not talking to anyone?'

So, I start to use my mobile instead (at even greater expense) in the privacy of my bedroom, and to my surprise I find that it's quite exciting. I've had a message from a divorced doctor who tells me in a friendly, educated voice that he would love to have a chat and leaves his mobile number. I ring him that evening, when Simon is safely ensconced in his bedroom 'doing his homework' (i.e., on Facebook). We talk for ages, and then he suggests meeting for a meal in another country pub. We don't have photographs of each other, so I describe my height and hair colour and tell him that I'll be wearing a watch tied on with a velvet ribbon (my longstanding solution to a metal allergy aggravated by the buckles on watch straps). He responds by saying that there's something he must admit to, because some ladies find it off-putting. *Oh no! What on earth is coming next?* But it is only that he has a beard. I don't mind this, as I did, after all, do much of my early dating in the 1960s and '70s, when beards were ubiquitous.

We arrange where to meet and I'm nervous all over again, this time in case I don't recognise him. I needn't have worried. As I'm parking my car, an ancient, rusting Volvo estate drives up beside me, and out of it steps a man as ancient as the car, with the longest beard I have ever seen. This is no neatly trimmed goatee, or even a slightly unruly Mrs Tiggy Winkle. It reminds me of the beard worn by one of the characters in *The Twits* (a Roald Dahl book that my children loved me to read to them): a beard which harboured all manner of horrors, from stale food to nesting birds. I'm appalled. I realise that photos do matter, after all, but it's too late to escape and another unappealing evening looms ahead.

Gerald is certainly eccentric, if not firmly on the autistic spectrum. He's wearing a threadbare tweed jacket with a rusty pin on the lapel and scuffed leather patches at the elbows. He talks … and talks, and talks, mainly about the obscure branch of medical research that he's interested in. When I ask him how long he has been divorced and the answer is twenty-eight years, it completes the picture of an odd man who has lived alone for a long time and has lost his social skills, if he ever had any in the first place. He doesn't ask me a single question about myself, not one, until I'm so hungry and desperate that I excuse myself, go to the loo and ring Bryony.

'Help!' I say. 'He looks like the Ancient Mariner and he never stops talking about himself. We haven't even had supper yet.'

She laughs. She thinks it's hilarious. But she's sympathetic as well. 'For goodness' sake, tell him you're hungry and get something to eat. I'll ring back in an hour and say a water pipe's burst, so you need to come home.'

This seems like a good plan, so I go back, we eat, and as the meal drags on and I'm fast becoming an expert in the chemical structure of neurotransmitters in my own right, I notice that the pub has emptied and we're the only customers left. The barman, a toned and tanned Australian, stands opposite me and behind Gerald. He must have registered my boredom and discomfort, because he starts making faces at me and clowning around behind Gerald's head. I'm in serious danger of laughing out loud when, mercifully, my phone rings. It's my sister, bearing news of a water-related emergency. We pay the bill and walk towards the car park. To make conversation, I remark on how bright the stars are away from the pollution of city lights. I wish immediately that I hadn't said anything, for this turns out to be another area of special interest for Gerald, and he stops us in our tracks to begin a lecture on the minutiae of the constellations. Thankfully, the danger of impending flood damage gives me a sufficient reason to interrupt his own riveting flow, and at last I'm secure in my car. Loud music and fast driving along empty country lanes help to dispel some of the awfulness of the evening, but next day there is a text: Gerald really enjoyed my company and wonders if I would like to come to a lecture he's giving on the chemistry of neurotransmitters?

When I tell Jocelyn about Gerald, her smile of amusement spreads. So far as I can tell, she welcomes my return to dating and the entertaining anecdotes that accompany it. But my grim reality behind the fun still has Paul at its centre. Outwardly, I appear cheerful; inside, I feel flat and desolate. I miss Paul constantly. I long for the security of the life we had together. I know that with the dating, I'm trying to locate that security, but the more I look, the more depressing I find it, and the more I miss him. I keep thinking about stopping the dating again – and now I'm beginning to think about stopping with Jocelyn too.

I mull over all this yet again one afternoon when I'm sitting in the garden. It's a hot day, Simon is at school, and two of the cats are sprawled out on the patio, soaking up the unseasonable warmth. I'm preoccupied with the thought that dating is such a struggle. It's been a disappointing experience so far. I've felt anxious about every date, and any hopes I've harboured about any of the men have been dashed as soon as I meet them. This leaves me feeling upset and disillusioned, and I wonder whether I'm doing myself more harm than good by carrying on. It knocks your confidence to feel that you're repeatedly failing at something. And yet, there's still a part of me that thinks it would be nice to meet someone else. I remember what Jennifer said about there being lots of frogs. I've certainly encountered plenty – but there must be some princes too, surely? As soon as I have this thought, it feels disloyal to Paul: what would he think if I met someone else? I recall us having one of those frivolous conversations long before he died, which went something like:

Me: 'If I died before you, would you find somebody else?'

Paul (sensing a trap): 'I don't know. Would you want me to?'

Me: 'No. I wouldn't want you to be lonely, but when you died and she died and we were all in heaven, how would you choose between us?'

Paul (exasperated): 'Don't be ridiculous! I hope you'd find someone else if I died first.' (Neat deflection.)

Me: 'Do you?'

Paul: 'Of course I do. I love you. I'd want you to be happy.'

On that evidence, he had given me permission to find a replacement. As I'm pondering on this thought, my eyes are drawn to the large lavender bush in the flowerbed bordering the patio. Paul and I planted it together a long time ago, and over the years it has grown woody and ragged, and it overhangs the edge of the patio by several feet. Even so, every summer it sprouts a forest of green stems, each one crowned with a spoke of lush purple flowers. The scent is intoxicating, and it is smothered with bees and white butterflies, drinking in its nectar in the sunshine. As I watch their comings and goings, I notice that one of the butterflies isn't a butterfly at all, but a white feather clinging to a purple frond. I watch as the bees hover around it, moving from stem to stem, oblivious of its presence. The conversation with Paul is still in my head, and I think that perhaps this is his way of trying to reinforce his message that I would have his blessing.

Later that day, when I find another voicemail in my box, it makes it slightly easier to decide to give the dating one more try.

*

Mark sounds upbeat and cheerful, so I ring him and we chat easily on the phone. Bryony is staying with me, and she decides to listen in on the extension. I'm terrified that she will laugh or snort or otherwise reveal herself, but she doesn't, and at the end of the call, her first impressions are positive. We both agree that he sounds friendly and genuine, but we are both equally puzzled by his admission that he doesn't drive. It seems odd, but his explanation is that he used to work in London, so didn't need to, and anyway, his wife (now dead) loved driving and was happy to do it all.

We arrange to meet at a pub which is right next to a train station. By now, we've spoken several times on the phone and I think he has a lovely voice. I'm quite hopeful again (as is my sister) and looking forward to meeting him. I decide to catch a train, too, so that I can have a drink. I arrive early, and wait at the top of the subway steps. When his train arrives, I scan the passengers climbing up towards me and admit a couple of flutters of excitement as good-looking men approach me ... but then walk past. The flow of passengers slows to a trickle and I'm thinking that perhaps he has missed his train when I hear my name. He has seen me first, and is striding towards me.

'Hi, I'm Mark,' he announces. He's wearing a wide smile, and what I'm very much afraid is a shiny gold tie.

'Hi,' I say, and I smile bravely, trying hard to hide my disappointment that the tall, handsome hunk I had fantasised about turns out to be shorter than me, with thinning hair and a sagging face. He's wearing pale linen trousers and a black-and-white check sports jacket, which I judge to be an unfortunate accompaniment to the golden tie.

Once we're inside the pub, I discover that he is a real gentleman. He takes my jacket, pulls back a chair for me to sit on, insists on buying me a drink and goes off to collect menus. He takes great care over selecting a good bottle of wine, and of course we drink it all, because neither of us has to drive. Over dinner, I learn that his wife died seven years ago and he has two grown-up sons. He has tried to make the most of his life as a widower and has been on many dates, but has not yet found 'the one' he is looking for.

He's easy to talk to and seems to be genuinely interested in my story. At the end of the meal, he grabs the bill and dismisses my protests outright.

'No,' he asserts. 'I insist on paying.'

'But I'd rather pay my way,' I say. 'We've only just met, and I don't want to feel that I owe you anything.'

He is adamant. 'You don't owe me anything at all. It's just that I *cannot* allow a lady to pay for her own dinner.'

I protest again, weakly this time. 'Please – I'd rather make a contribution to the evening.'

But there's no persuading him. 'No, I'm sorry, I can't let you,' he says. 'And anyway, I've talked to my sons about it, and they're fine about me spending money on taking ladies out.'

So, he has discussed dating with his sons! I file this piece of information away for future scrutiny.

We walk companionably back to the station, where he tells me how much he has enjoyed the evening, and that he would really like to see me again. I've enjoyed myself too, and so we agree to meet at the same pub in a couple of weeks' time.

When I get in, Simon is watching TV, legs stretched out on the coffee table and the debris of a Domino's pizza beside him on the sofa. My heart is pounding in my chest as I ask, too brightly: 'Guess where I've just been?'

There's a barely noticeable flicker of interest as he says, 'Where?', his eyes still firmly fixed on the screen.

'Out to dinner with a man,' I say, heart pounding still faster as I await the anticipated outburst.

'Oh, right,' he says. 'Was it good?'

I'm amazed. 'Yes, thanks, I had a nice time. Don't you mind?'

'No, why would I? I think you should definitely go out with someone.'

'You mean you wouldn't think it was awful?'

He finally shifts his eyes from the TV. 'No Mum, of course not. I know you've been lonely since Paul died. I think you'd be happier with someone. I know you're old, but you're not that old, and you don't look nearly as old as some of my friends' mums.'

Well, that was certainly a lesson in the power that guilt can muster to distort your view of the world.

Mark is a nice guy, but we don't have a lot in common and I don't find him at all attractive. After a few dates, I tell him this (well, not so bluntly) and he is as perplexed about my admission as I am about his inability to drive. He informs me that people always used to tell him that he looked like Paul McCartney. I gather that this piece of information is meant to impress me, but my response, which I keep to myself, is that it must have been a long time ago. Later, my sister helpfully adds that he would hardly want to look like Paul McCartney does now, with his dyed hair and hanging jowls. Mark's principal interests are steam railways and horse racing, neither of which appeals to me at all. He also likes dining out, as I've discovered from the outset, and drinking. After a while, I begin to realise that he drinks a great deal, and I wonder whether this is why he chooses not to drive, or whether his inability to drive led to excessive drinking. He doesn't own a computer and can't use the internet, which, along with the driving issue, gives the impression of a man who is limited in some ways. Our meetings are beginning to feel uncomfortable and I want to step back, but the more I try, the more eager he becomes. He wants to sleep with me. He says it would be nice, and that he has slept with all the other women he's dated. He even tells me that he got chatting to a woman at a bus stop and took her home to bed. (I'm not sure what message this story is meant to convey, but I will certainly have my wits about me the next time I'm waiting for the Park and Ride.)

Eventually I have to spell out directly that I want no more than to be friends, and for a while he's cross and, like Pedro, accuses me of leading him on. After a few sulky weeks with no contact, he bounces back, and we remain friends and exchange Christmas cards and the occasional text.

*

After Mark, I lose interest in accessing my message box. There was nothing wrong with him, but I can't summon any enthusiasm for meeting another boring man. My mood plummets, and before long I'm faced with another grim realisation: it is a thousand days since Paul died. I've been working this out on my walks with Jess, and today is the day. How can I possibly have lived for a thousand days without him? It's such a long, long time. To everyone else, it's just a normal day. Simon goes to school and I go to work. I see a patient, go to a meeting and try to deal with the usual tide of emails, but the screen is blurred; I can't think properly. Every time I go to the loo, I cry. I take to sitting in there because it's quiet, a refuge from the banality of normal working life.

Inevitably, it's not long before the cleaner is knocking on the door: 'Are you alright in there?'

I come out and she notices my tear-stained face. She gives me a hug and shepherds me into the kitchen, where she makes us a cup of tea. She's a warm, motherly woman and I can talk to her. Her husband died in his early forties, leaving her with two children to bring up and very little money. She works all hours to make ends meet, despite being overweight, with chronic asthma and painful feet. We have a cup of tea and a cry together, and afterwards I think that I'm a lot better off than she is – and not just materially.

When I get home, I'm still feeling upset and disorientated, and so I email Mari in Spain. Mari's determination to move on after her husband Pepe's death was relentless. Through her, I learned that *match.com* operates in more than one country, for she had picked up dates in Madrid, Barcelona, London, or anywhere else she happened to be. These had provided us with many a Rioja-filled evening of hilarity, but in the end, she found Toni, a gentle man who is a teacher living in the next village to her in Catalonia, and they have been together ever since. So, it is to her that I pour my heart out on this awful thousand-day anniversary, knowing how much she, too, adored Paul. She responds with a letter to him.

Dear Paul,
Vanessa is still counting the days: (today 1000)
that you left without saying goodbye.
  One thousand days today,
  One thousand nights tonight
  One thousand and one cups of tea tomorrow
  You will never bring to her in bed.
  But you still live in her mind.
  There she is: sad and alone
  Wanting to beat the fight,

And the loneliness that you left her behind.
Please, Paul, make her understand that you will
never come.
It wasn't your fault, but you must do something
more effective than sending those white feathers.
You, ever so polite,
Left without asking
Left and never said why
Left and she is still waiting.
Please, Paul help her if you can.
With lots of love, Mari.

I cry and cry when I read this. I know Mari wants to help me, but I still have no clear idea of the way forwards. I email her back, and tell her that I've lost faith in dating. She responds at once, telling me that I must carry on. 'How can you fill the vacancy if you don't advertise?' she asks.

CHAPTER FIVE

Interlude: Sensory Threads

The training programme values the reflective scientist-practitioner model as a basis for clinical psychology. There is a strong emphasis on integration of theory, research and practice in all aspects of the programme. (It) aims to train clinical psychologists who are skilled in evidence-based psychological assessment and intervention (and) produce applied research of the highest quality and impact.

KING'S COLLEGE LONDON
Doctorate in Clinical Psychology

I'm struck by Mari's supposition that the white feathers are ineffective. Are they? Or do they carry some psychological significance that serves a purpose? I think back over everything that has happened since Paul died. I can see that reflecting on the parallels and overlaps between my experiences and those of my patients has helped me to take small steps forwards, but I still don't know what to make of the feathers. My patients can't help me there. But perhaps some other aspect of my work as a clinical psychologist can? I remember that, as well as being a clinician, I'm a trained researcher. In fact, the strong emphasis on producing research is something that sets clinical psychology apart from many other health professions. Could this be the key to understanding what the feathers mean? I learned early in my training that the tools of a researcher are useful for making sense of the world, and as I progressed with my career, I began to realise that pretty much any question was amenable to investigation by research, provided you took your time to frame the question carefully and went about researching in an ordered way. It's worth a small digression back to my beginnings as a researcher to illustrate this point.

Consider this house:

It was drawn by a seven-year-old girl. Why has she attached the windows in the corners, and drawn the chimney at a funny angle? Is it because she doesn't have the drawing skills to produce something better? Or is it because she 'knows' that windows are 'on the edge' of a house, and the chimney goes 'on the roof', and she's satisfied that her drawing conveys this knowledge? My hunch was that the latter was more likely; children invariably seem to be so pleased with the drawings they produce. As I started visiting primary schools and collecting examples in the very early stages of my own research on children's drawings, I became more convinced.

A good example is the drawing below of a zoo by Martin, also aged seven:

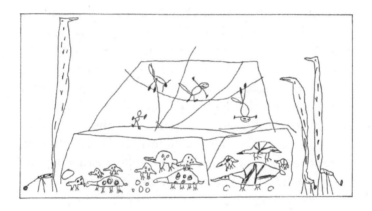

Martin clearly knows that giraffes have long necks. There are other animals, possibly monkeys, identified by their ability to balance and hang upside-down. Two other types of animal are distinguishable by spots, and a combination of stripes and pointed noses or beaks. But is Martin prevented by his limited drawing ability from producing something more accurate, which would help us to identify all the different animals in his picture properly? An influential theory of children's drawings around at the time claimed that the 'errors' children made could indeed be ascribed to such production problems. If I wanted my alternative explanation to be considered seriously, I would have to gather good evidence. So, I wrote a research proposal, managed to find funding and then spent long hours in London primary schools running experiments. In one I managed to show, in a carefully controlled way, that children did indeed prefer drawings that looked like the ones they produced themselves, compared to more 'adult' versions. In another, I set out several cups and put children under pressure to draw accurately by hiding a sweet in a particular cup which had its handle turned away, so that it couldn't be seen from the child's point of view. Each child's task was to draw this cup really well, so that the next child coming in would be able to find the sweet. To my amazement, and excitement, almost all of the younger children drew cups with clearly visible handles! They 'knew' that cups have handles, and it was this that they needed to communicate above all in their drawings. They *could* draw more accurately (a cup without a handle is easier to draw than one with a handle), but they chose not to.

I was gaining good evidence in support of my 'knowledge' theory of children's drawings, but I still needed a direct test. I thought back again to some of the early drawings I had collected. I had asked the children to copy things, too. Jamie, the five-year-old boy who was asked to copy the real-life model (A) below (a wooden house and tree with a wooden train hidden at right-angles behind the house in such a way that only the end of the string for pulling the train along could be seen), produced drawing (B):

(A) Wooden model for copying

(B) Drawing of model produced by Jamie, aged five

His drawing is a fairly radical departure from what he could actually see. He has set the house in a garden with grass and a path, added a doorknob, letterbox and chimney, depicted smoke coming out of both the house's chimney and the train's funnel, and drawn a complete train, even though the model train wasn't visible to him. All of these features are evidence of things he knows about the objects concerned.

But could I show that children would incorporate knowledge into their drawings about an object with which they were completely unfamiliar? I made a 'nonsense' object out of polystyrene and asked children to draw it both before and after they had had an opportunity to handle it. It was an easy object to draw, but the findings were striking: the children drew less accurately after they had handled the object, so keen were they to include their new-found knowledge in their drawings. So, I found the evidence I needed, which enabled me to develop my own theory of children's drawings, publish my findings and make my contribution to this area of study.

*

That was over thirty years ago, when I was doing a PhD, but my interest in research stayed with me throughout my career as a clinical psychologist, and inspired me to investigate a whole range of questions that I encountered clinically in different work settings. I questioned whether the drawings of particular patient groups might be useful in clinical assessment; I wondered how the parents of blind children like Emma might help them to communicate better, how sleep problems could best be managed in children with special needs, whether autism could be diagnosed reliably in two-year-olds. Each time I had a question, I carried out research to try to find an answer, and made my contribution to the evidence.

Back in the present, I have a question about the white feathers which continues to nag me. All the while, in the background, as I go to work, go to Sainsbury's, go out on dates with disappointing men, the feathers keep appearing and I keep thinking that they're a sign from Paul. But are they? When I tell friends that I think they might be, they are often sceptical (if not to my face, I can see it in their eyes), so I ask the vicar, who took Paul's funeral service and still comes to visit me, what he thinks. His response is reassuring. He tells me that he has been told enough stories by recently bereaved people to convince him that there is communication with the 'next world', but that it is indirect – often in the form of signs seen in nature, such as a rainbow or a feather. I find this interesting: are these feathers really some kind of communication from beyond the grave?

I decide that I must do some proper investigating. The research psychologist in me needs to look for the evidence when something can't be explained easily. The wherewithal for doing this has been drummed into me for decades. I can't carry out a large-scale experimental study, but I can at least try to evaluate the evidence from different sources. I start with the internet. I Google 'white feather' and I'm amazed at what I find; there are forums, chat rooms, literally hundreds of pages devoted to people's descriptions of white feather experiences following the death of a loved one. I had no idea that this stuff existed.

Here are a few examples:

Janet from Harrow: 'I lost my daughter earlier this year and kept asking for a sign. One day I opened the door and looked outside hoping, and there was a white feather on top of a plant pot.'

Alex from Yorkshire: 'A small white feather blew into my car today as I was driving along. As it's the anniversary of my mum's death, I believe she is sending me a message to let me know she is OK in the afterlife.'

Donna from Wakefield: 'I lost my mum three months ago and I miss her a lot. Today I asked her for a sign that she was OK, and shortly afterwards a small white feather appeared at my feet. I believe that she sent it to me.'

Beryl from Glasgow: 'I lost my husband a few weeks ago. Before he died, we discussed that I would like some white feathers from him, just to let me know that he is around. The day after the funeral, I was lying in bed and I felt a push on my shoulder as if to say: "Get out of bed". So I got up and went downstairs, and in the room where I kept his photo and a candle, there were two white feathers on the carpet.'

Sam from Leeds: 'My father-in-law passed away in June, and while visiting him at the cemetery, two white feathers fell at our feet. It was a very comforting sign.'

Emily from Brighton: 'Two days after my grandpa died, I found out I was pregnant. I was gutted I didn't get to tell him my news, but one day when I was standing in Mothercare, a white feather fluttered down right in front of me. People later told me it must have blown in through the door, but the shop was in an enclosed shopping centre. Another feather came out of the packaging when I unpacked my Moses basket. Another was nestled in the folds of a shawl that my grandma gave me. It was such a lovely feeling: Gramps was letting me know he knew about our baby.'

Sam Hayward used her experience of finding white feathers after her husband's death as inspiration for a novel about a bereaved woman. She found her first feather soon after her husband died: 'It was a few days after the funeral and I was still in shock. I was sitting on the sofa and picked up one of our favourite wedding photos from the book-case. I just stared at it and reminisced. When I went to put it back, there was a bright white feather lying where the photo had been.' After that, she found feathers in all sorts of places, including on her bedside table, in her car and on her leg. 'They usually appeared when I was feeling desperately low or at times when I needed reassurance.' She saw them as messages of comfort from her husband.

I start searching for books, too, and I learn that white feathers are the calling cards of angels. Gloria Hunniford's daughter, Caron Keating, died tragically young as a result of breast cancer. Following this loss, Gloria outlined her own beliefs about white feathers in the foreword to a book about angels, writing: 'Caron firmly believed that when you find an isolated white feather in an unusual or obscure place, it's an angel's calling card. Now, when I find one, I say to myself, "that's Caron's calling card".' She elaborates on this in the book she wrote about Caron after she died: 'I'm not talking about when you find five or six [feathers], where obviously a bird has been, I'm talking about a single perfect white feather that I have found in the most unlikely of places.'

Some of the examples she gives are finding a single white feather on the landing when her house had just been cleaned; watching a lone feather fall from a cloudless blue sky on to her son's hand when they were talking about Caron; and discovering a white feather on a covered train station platform when she was taking Caron's sons out for a birthday treat. She describes getting 'a very comfortable feeling every time I see a white feather. It certainly doesn't freak me out any more, because I believe my daughter is there … when I see white feathers in splendid isolation, and I see them all the time, I pick them up and put them in my pocket and say, "Hello, Caron … Hello, Caron," and … it gives me the strength to go on.' As she often finds feathers when she is with Caron's children, she believes that Caron is acting as a guardian angel to the whole family.

I soon discover that there are hundreds more pages on the internet devoted to the white feather/angel connection:

Kerry from Derby: 'My nan used to say to me that if you found a white feather and someone had recently died, it meant angels were looking after them and they wanted you to know. My grandad died in July and I saw feathers on the day of his funeral, and when we buried his ashes. I still see them now, and it is a comfort to know that the angels are looking after him.'

Tracy from Edmonton: 'I suffered my third miscarriage last week and, as you can imagine, I was devastated. Yesterday a white feather

floated down from nowhere and I knew it was
my guardian angel.'

John from Ramsgate: 'I have always believed in
angels. Not long after my father died, I found
a feather in my garage. I knew it was from him,
letting me know that he was around and OK.'

*

I'm both pleased and disappointed by these revelations.
On the one hand, they offer further evidence to support
my view that feathers might provide a link with the dead,
particularly since I made my own connection between Paul
and the feathers before I knew that any of these accounts
existed. On the other hand, the scientist in me recoils from
accepting the sentiments expressed in emotive anecdotes
with no evidence to back them up. I decide to investigate
further, by asking people who have suffered a significant
bereavement whether they, too, have had any such experiences. What I discover is interesting: no more feathers, but
a variety of sensory experiences of different types, which
seem to be commonplace.

My sister Annie, whose son died of a brain tumour
aged ten, told me that she and our mother were sitting in
the graveyard, some months after his death, when a robin
came and hopped on his grave. They both thought at once
that it was him. Another time, when she was talking about
her son, she smelled wood smoke, even though there was
no obvious fire. This happened again, many times, always
when he was uppermost in her mind. Less than a year after
he died, she dreamed that she was driving down a familiar
hill near where she lives in Devon. It was early morning

and it had been raining hard. The roads were shimmering in the glow of the sun. Her son walked across the road in front of her, swishing a stick the way he always used to when walking through nettles. He smiled at her and said: 'Don't worry about me, Mum. It's fine where I am. I'm fine.' She was reassured by this dream for a long time afterwards.

Julian Barnes writes a lot about his dreams of his much loved wife, whose decline and death happened rapidly after she was diagnosed with a brain tumour:

'In dreams she arrives looking and acting very like herself. I always know it is her – she is calm, and amused, and happy, and sexy and so, as a result, am I. The dream falls swiftly and regularly into a pattern. We are together, she is clearly in good health, so I think – or rather, since this is a dream, I know – that either she has been misdiagnosed, or she has made a miraculous recovery, or (at the very least) that death has somehow been postponed for several years and our life together can continue … some nights, after turning out the light, I remind her that she hasn't been in my dreams recently, and often she responds by coming to me. Sometimes in these dreams we kiss; always there is a kind of laughing lightness to the scenario. She never reproaches or rebukes me, or makes me feel guilty or neglectful. [The dreams] are always a source of comfort.'

A friend had already booked tickets to fly to her house in Greece when her mother died. The funeral wasn't for a week and so she decided to go on the holiday, but she felt guilty about it. She was sitting in her garden in Greece one evening when a barn owl alighted on a tree close to her. It was snowy white and sat very still, looking at her. She stared into its eyes, and after a while it flew off, right over the top of her head, so close as to ruffle her hair. She knew that the owl was her mother, who was OK, and that it was alright for her to be in Greece.

Another friend was out shopping soon after her mother died. She went into M&S, where she and her mother had often enjoyed shopping together. As she walked through the door, she felt somebody take her hand. She knew it was her mother, and she stayed in the shop for as long as possible so as to prolong the experience. She didn't want to leave, because she knew that her mother would let go of her hand if she did. That was exactly what happened as she went out of the door. She never had this experience again, but was greatly comforted by it at the time.

A friend of a friend knew somebody who was terminally ill with cancer. The dying woman was very close to her and promised that, if there was life after death, she would communicate this to her somehow. She was an irreverent woman with a sense of humour. Soon after she died, her friend awoke to the sound of an enormous raspberry being blown in her ear. She knew at once who had delivered it.

There are other examples on the internet:

Emma from Surrey: 'When my mother died, we had to clear out her house. I used to do a few hours at a time, as I found it so upsetting. I'd have the radio playing in the kitchen on the station that my mother had left it on. Nine or ten times when I was in the kitchen taking a break, the song 'Smoke Gets in Your Eyes' came on the radio. It was my mum and dad's song; they danced to it at their wedding and my dad used to sing it and dance my mother around the kitchen when I was a little girl. Many people would say it was a coincidence, but it's not a recent song, so it's very unusual for it to come on so many times, and it helped me.'

Linda from Richmond: 'Soon after my father died, he made his presence known one afternoon when we suddenly smelled the ointment he used to apply to keep mosquitoes away. Strangely only my mum and I could smell it, although there were other people in the room. Another time, a gold-coloured moth flew into the room my mum and I were in. My mum was sure that it was my dad visiting us again.'

In an interview about the death of his wife, Felicia, Leonard Bernstein said:

'I am frequently visited by a white moth or a white butterfly. Quite amazingly frequently. And I know it's Felicia. I remember that when she died, her coffin was in our living room and just a few of us were there – the family and a rabbi and a priest, because she'd been brought up in a convent. We were playing the Mozart Requiem on the phonograph. Everybody was absolutely silent. Then this white butterfly flew

in from God knows where – it just appeared
from under the coffin and flew around,
alighting on everybody in the room – on each
of the children, on the rabbi, on the priest, on
her brother-in-law and two of her sisters, on me
… and then it was gone … though there was
nothing open. This has also happened to me
here, sitting outside in my garden … white.'

My professional self is keen to investigate
further, and I decide to carry out a survey of
people who have been bereaved to try to find
out how common these experiences are. I
send out questionnaires to twenty-five people,
and find that a quarter of them report 'signs'
following the death of a loved one.

'One morning, I was at work and I was thinking
very intensively about S [husband who had
died recently] as I crossed over into the main
hospital. As I turned the corner into the
corridor, there on the ground in front of me was
the most beautiful, large white feather. I felt
a bit shocked and I wanted to pick it up, but
there were lots of people around. I thought it
must have been a sign from S.'

'One of D's "things" was Sudoku, and after he
died, an electronic Sudoku game suddenly
switched itself on. Also, at the crematorium,
a tree fell into the river a few feet away from
me. And two crows came down the chimney at

Christmas – we'd had the fireplace put in while
he was ill at home; he felt the cold and we
enjoyed sitting by the fire.'

'After my brother-in-law died, at his post-
funeral breakfast, a magpie looked through
the window at my sister and I. After my sister
died [a few years later], I came home and two
magpies appeared. I always say hello to them.'

'After my daughter Clare died, I was walking
home carrying groceries when a butterfly flew
in front of me and got my attention. It flew
across the road to our building and hovered in
front of Clare's bedroom window.'

My sister, Bryony, is sceptical about such things
and jokes that, after her alcoholic husband
died, she used to see a disembodied can of
Foster's floating towards her. Others on the
internet are sceptical about these 'signs' too.

Catrina from Sutton: 'The truth is that these
feathers fall off birds that are flying in the sky.
You don't see the birds because they've flown
past before the feathers fall. Feathers are falling
all of the time, but before a bereavement, we
just never notice them. The truth is that death
hurts and we all take comfort in different things
because that's how we deal with it. If there is
a particular song that I hear loads and loads, I
could say that it was sent to me by my relative,

but the hard fact is that it played before my relative's death, I just didn't notice it before because it didn't have significance.'

However, the rejoinder to this is:

James from Liverpool: 'But if feathers just come from birds, how come they fall inside my house when all the doors and windows are closed?'

*

Behind these differing views is the vexed question of whether or not there is life after death. Is it possible that Paul really is sending feathers to me from somewhere? Did my friend's mother really take her hand and guide her around M&S from the 'other side'?

In my survey, only eighteen per cent of the participants firmly believed in life after death, and the rest were equally divided as to whether they didn't believe at all or were 'on the fence'. There is a plethora of books on the subject which purport to 'prove' that there is heaven or life after death or another world, many of them based on people's 'near death' experiences, and for a while I devour them, because I really want it to be true. One of the most convincing is by Eben Alexander, an American neurosurgeon who fell into a coma after suffering a rare form of meningitis. He wasn't expected to survive, but he did, and he went on to describe in great detail the 'journey into the afterlife' that took place when he was unconscious, which he took to be proof of the existence of heaven. This had a profound impact on him, especially because his professional training allowed him to dismiss a whole host of alternative explanations for his experience. Even so, every time I encounter a dead rabbit or bird on a walk with Jess, I'm tormented by doubts. Dead really does seem very dead indeed. So why do I keep on talking to Paul, especially when Jess and I are out walking, with the evidence of death in nature all around us? Am I expecting him to reply? I'm not, so it seems a bit crazy, but the vicar reassures me that it is something that bereaved people do all the time, particularly when visiting the place where the body is buried or the ashes scattered, and whether or not they believe in an afterlife. Julian Barnes is a well-known unbeliever in life after death. I decide that talking to him, knowing that he too has lost a much loved partner, might help to illuminate this issue. He is kind enough to agree to be interviewed, and he tells me, almost five years after the death of his wife, that he talks to her constantly.

'I talk to her about the house, I talk to her when I'm driving, at first, I used to talk to her every night just before I went to sleep, tell her what I'd done that day. I go to the grave … it was very important to me that I had the luck that she could be buried close to home and I used to go several times a week. I needed a place to go where some evidence of her was in order to talk to her … and I still do. Over the first six months to a year, I very badly needed to go to that place in order to tell her things … and tell her how I was. I still go to visit her about every two weeks … and before I go away anywhere, I go and visit her and tell her where I am going. When I say to [the woman] who cuts my hair,

and who does believe in life after death, that
I've just been visiting my wife, she will say: "Oh
well, there you are, you do think she's there."
And I let that go, but I don't for a moment
actually imagine that anyone is listening to me.'

So, I ask him the same question that is bothering me
about my 'talks' with Paul: what is he doing talking to his
wife if he doesn't believe that anyone is receiving the communication? He explains:

'I'm, as best as I can, continuing the life I had
with her. Just because somebody has died, it
may mean that they are not alive, but it doesn't
mean that they don't exist. She exists very
strongly in my memory and I need that memory
to be as active as possible. So I not only talk
to her, but sometimes I will ventriloquise her.
I will use her voice back to me ... often about
trivial domestic incidents. I'll say: "Do you
think I should do this?" and she'll say: "Yes, of
course you should," so it's a form of continuing
companionability. Ford Madox Ford said, "You
marry to continue the conversation." To an
extent, you should try not to let death interrupt
that conversation, even though you know you're
doing both sides of it. Though it's also true that
there are limits to this ventriloquism. That,
if faced with something new or of a different
order, my ventriloquism runs out. In a new
situation, her voice doesn't come through and
I can't develop it further. I can predict how she

would react in some situations: for instance, I bought a very nice painting the other day and I know she would have liked it ... and I have ventriloquised her congratulating me on buying the picture ... but if it was something outside the life we had together, I don't know if I would be able to do it.'

I can relate to this: although I have never tried to ventriloquise Paul, I very often ask myself what he *would* say or do in the many situations that require a reaction or a response or a decision, such as whether I should go out on a date or go to a New Year's Eve party without him.

*

There are many people who believe that this process of 'communication' can be taken a step further: that it's possible to achieve two-way communication with the dead person, albeit indirectly, through a spiritualist or psychic. The need to do this can be overpoweringly strong: remember my visit to Linda of the frizzy pink crystals in the early days after Paul's death? When I ask Julian Barnes what he thinks about spiritualists he is dismissive:

'I think that's complete hokum.' I am sceptical, but not entirely convinced; after all something happened as I lay on Linda's couch, even if I can't yet provide a clear explanation for it.

Bryony tells me about a spiritualist who has a regular show on some daytime TV channel. This woman apparently has the most amazing powers, and is able to tell people things about their dead relatives that she couldn't possibly have known any other way. She's coming to a venue near where I live to do one of her live shows, so this will be a good opportunity to look for more evidence. I buy tickets, and my sister and I set off to be amazed.

The auditorium is large, and although it's a weekday evening, the seats are completely sold out: clearly the desire to communicate with the dead is very strong indeed. Our seats are right in the middle of the stalls, and I feel vaguely anxious: I'm not sure whether it's because I hope the psychic will get in touch with Paul or because I hope she won't. Bryony sits beside me, rigid with apprehension, and I wonder why on earth she suggested this. She says she's terrified that the psychic will make contact with her dead husband, and that if she does, I must speak to him, because Bryony just can't. I tell her not to be so stupid: what would I say to him? I can hardly pretend she's just popped out for a minute if he's here watching us both from the other side! In the event, it seems that he isn't, although Bryony does grab me in terror at one point when the psychic announces that she's in contact with someone called Bill – her dead husband's name.

The psychic – let's call her Cindy – is bubbly and middle-aged. She marches on to the stage in a flurry of flashing lights, razzamatazz and loud music. The way it works is that she receives a 'communication' from the other side, which she relays to the audience in the hope of locating the appropriate respondent. It goes something like this:

Cindy: 'I'm seeing a dog running right across the floor, over to that side.' (She indicates the left side of the auditorium). 'Does that mean anything to anybody?'

Lady in audience: 'Yes.'

Cindy: 'Give the microphone to that lady.'

Lady in audience: 'My dog had to be put down last week.'

Cindy (to the lady): 'I've got a man here, and I'm not sure if the message is for you. Does the name Dan mean anything to you?'

Lady in audience: 'No.'

Cindy: 'Does the name Dan mean anything to anyone else?'

(Several hands go up. One boy is jumping up and down.)

Cindy: 'Bring the microphone over here.' (To the boy:) 'Yes, sir?'

Boy in audience: 'My uncle was called Dan.'

Cindy: 'Did he pass quite recently?'

Boy in audience: 'Yes, he was killed in a car crash, about six months ago.'

Cindy: 'Did he have a dog?'

Boy in audience: 'Yes. The dog died yesterday after eating rat poison.'

Cue cries of 'Ooh!' and 'Aah!' and 'Wow!' from the audience, and rapturous applause.

I'm not convinced, by this or any of the other scenarios that unfold during the course of the evening. After all, what are the chances of somebody knowing someone called Dan, with some connection to a dead dog, in an audience of over three thousand people? I find myself agreeing with Julian Barnes, who says: 'I don't despise people for going to a spiritualist; I think they are deluding themselves.' He adds: 'After World War One, spiritualism rocketed because there were so many people who had lost sons, lovers, husbands, and desperately wanted to get in touch with them. The spiritualist movement, sometimes benignly, sometimes malignly, benefited from this.'

Well, that is certainly consistent with all the merchandise

on sale in the foyer both before and after Psychic Cindy's performance.

The point is, though, that for those who do believe, the psychic provides a link with the person they have lost. As Julian Barnes explains, 'The grief-struck use whatever means they have at their disposal to remain sane, not kill themselves and maintain what contact is possible in their universe with the dead person.'

The psychoanalyst Stephen Grosz was reduced to tears twenty years after his mother's death when he heard that his sister had 'spoken' to her via a clairvoyant. He writes: 'We turn to clairvoyance when we need our dead and can't accept death's finality. We want to believe the clairvoyant can bring the dead back into the land of the living.'

The link that this 'contact' with the dead person provides via the psychic is comforting, as are the sensory experiences or signs that many other bereaved people report, and the continuation of talking to the person who has died, and even engaging in 'dialogue' with them, in the sense of either ventriloquising or imagining their replies. All of these experiences are reported as being positive (the dead person does not rebuke; the feathers are seen as angels, not demons), and a comfort to the person left behind. They appear to be common both to those who believe strongly in an afterlife and those who are sceptical: so what do bereaved people themselves make of them, and are their views shaped by whether or not they believe in life after death?

Julian Barnes is very clear that when he dreams about his wife, 'I don't believe this is her coming to me ... I believe that no part of us survives death. We just break up and go off in all directions and are redefined in terms of carbon atoms, elsewhere in the world ... I don't believe

there is a spirit element that survives. I don't believe …
I don't believe full stop. I believe that these dreams are
self-generated, by my situation and by my needs. Within
the dreams I can feel comforted by what she says, until the
point when I realise, within the dream, that she's dead. I
like having these dreams until the point where the cold
water is thrown over them, by my own beliefs coming out
within the dream.'

Annie's dream about her dead son walking across the
golden road provided her with comfort, too, and both of
these examples fit in with Freud's early understanding of
dreams as hallucinatory fulfilments of a wish: in Julian
Barnes's case, the wish that his wife were still alive; in
my sister's case, the wish for her son, following his tragic
death, to be OK.

My father is another unbeliever in life after death:
'Death is it,' is his unequivocal view. After Mum died, there
were no feathers, robins, dreams or any other sign, and he
made no attempt to communicate with her. Her death as
an elderly lady was not a surprise; it was inevitable and
he was expecting it. She had had a long life and a 'good
death', and her time had come. He wasn't miserable after
she died – it was a natural phasing out – and he was able to
be matter-of-fact and objective about it. However, Dad is
a deep-thinking man, widely read in philosophy, theology
and psychology, and he adds that he is intrigued by the 'certain' and 'vivid' experiences reported by others whose views
on life after death differ from his own. He regards these
as psychological manifestations of the effects of loss and
separation, and thinks that you have to know the person
in order to understand how they experience the aftermath
of loss in their particular way.

The vicar's view, unsurprisingly, is different. His personal belief is that the spirit continues when the body dies, although he's quick to point out that there are vast differences in belief between Christians, let alone between Christianity and other religions, and so he doesn't think that it's possible to construct a point of view that is representative of 'Christianity'. His own view derives from personal experience and from talking to bereaved people. He tells me the story of a pair of brothers, who were very close: let's call them John and Jim. As children, they used to sleep in adjacent beds and hold hands as they went to sleep. Later in life, Jim was not ill but he had a sudden heart attack and died. John woke up feeling Jim holding his hand, yet it was not until later that day that he learned that Jim had had a heart attack. In the vicar's view, this can't be explained rationally: there has to have been an emotional or spiritual connection between the two brothers that survived after the death of one of them. When John himself was dying, some years later, he described seeing his dead brother, Jim, waiting for him at the foot of his bed. This was comforting and John died a peaceful death. Many people, particularly those with religious beliefs, are convinced that they will be 'reunited' with their loved ones after death. I remember hearing the father of one of the Lockerbie victims saying on the radio that it would have been 'unbearable' for him to carry on after his daughter's death if he did not have the strong belief, indeed certainty, that he would see her again in heaven.

The vicar has more to say about spiritual life after death, based on his experience of being with people who are dying. He tells me that the person who is dying often seems to be able to control the time of their death, which suggests to him that even death itself can't be purely physical. He adds that if someone is able to 'control' the time of their death, perhaps they can also take some control of communication from 'the other side'. Bereaved people typically describe the communication as being indirect (feathers, robins, barn owls; a sound, a smell, a dream) rather than actually seeing the person who has died. He adds his own examples: a bereaved woman who often experienced a strong smell of pipe smoke in her cottage, long after her husband had died; and people reporting that a dead person has 'moved' an object in their home from one location to another. His conclusion about this is that 'people build scenarios that give them comfort', and that 'heightened awareness in the bereaved person soon after the death of a loved one may increase the likelihood of communication occurring'.

This raises the question of whether the experiences reported by the recently bereaved change over time, as they become less recently bereaved? It seems that they do. Julian Barnes describes how, three years or so after his wife's death, he had the same kind of dream in which he and she were doing things together, being happy, when: 'Instead of my realising she was dead, she realised she was dead, and that seemed to me to perhaps put an end to the dream narrative.' More recent academic writing about dreams, having the benefit of understanding of the physiology of sleep and dreaming which was not available to Freud, suggests that dreams may perform a restitutive function, to increase comprehension and allow realities to be grasped at a deep emotional level. This seems to be consistent with Julian Barnes's changing experience.

In my survey, only people who had a firm, or at least

possible, belief in life after death experienced signs of communication from their dead loved one. And these 'signs' were all reported within the two years following the death, often on the day of the death itself or very soon after. Bryony describes how, on the day of her husband's death, she parked her car in the corner of the car park of the school where she worked. As she walked away, she heard a whooshing and cracking sound behind her as a fir tree crashed down on to her car. It wasn't until later in the day, when she got home from school, that she discovered her husband had died. Reports in the survey of similar phenomena occurring long after a death were non-existent, and most people said that they lessened over time.

*

Fast-forward to more than four years since Paul died, and I'm walking alone through a deserted gorge in southern Crete. It's midsummer, very hot indeed, the ground is parched and sandy, and the few scrubby trees provide little shade from the sun. The sides of the gorge tower above me, giant slabs of rock with the occasional bush or mountain goat clinging to the almost vertical slope. It's hard work negotiating the steep, uneven path in this heat, but I'm rewarded two hours later when I emerge on to a tiny, secluded beach, inaccessible by any other route. I swim in the deep-blue water and sit for a while in the welcome cool of the little chapel on the edge of the sand. Before setting off on the return walk, I light a candle for Paul and leave it burning in the sand-filled receptacle, where I notice that many have put candles before me, despite this being such an isolated place. I talk to Paul most of the way through the gorge and back, telling him what I've been doing, asking him how he is, and (as ever) why he died – but, this being more than four years on, I don't cry any more, and I don't search desperately for feathers, although I do still see them, often. In this hot, dusty place, though, there is little sign of any animal life, and so I joke to Paul: 'Huh, well you certainly won't be able to send me any feathers here, will you?' I feel almost smug in my certainty that this would be an impossible feat, and as I carry on walking, I actually say to him: 'You see, I told you so.' As I turn a corner in what must be the driest, deepest and most inaccessible part of the gorge, I see a carpet of white feathers strewn on the sand in front of me.

My sister Annie, more than twenty years since her son's death, looks back at the episode of the robin in the graveyard and reflects that it was probably wishful thinking to believe that it was her son. She says, 'Perhaps there are signs in nature happening all the time, but in the extremity of grief you are more open to them, more likely to notice.'

The death of a loved one is unbearable, and the need to find some source of comfort, some way of maintaining a link with the person who has disappeared from your life is entirely understandable. For me, the feathers are highly significant: it's as if there is no way to bear the loss, and so the feather (or robin, or dream, or smell of pipe smoke, or barn owl) becomes the way. I'm reminded of Donald Winnicott's writing on the subject of 'transitional objects', the sometimes strange objects that babies and young children use as comforters. One of my sons had his 'raa', a cloth which he sucked while simultaneously stroking the side of his nose with his finger; my nephew had a Snoopy dog, whose ear fulfilled the same function as the 'raa'; my niece had her 'bakdin', a hand-knitted woollen blanket that went everywhere with her. Winnicott believes that these attachments begin when the infant makes a link between the sucking related to feeding and the simultaneous caressing of a bit of sheet, blanket, wool etc.: 'Out of this affectionate fondling activity,' he writes, 'there can develop a relationship to something which happens to be lying around, and this object may become very important to the infant.' Babies latch on to these objects in the same way as they 'latch on' to their mother's breast. The sensory properties of the object – its texture and smell – are of vital significance to the child. Although not all infants develop such associations, their appearance is viewed by Winnicott as being a healthy aspect of the child's emotional development: part of a developing sense of security, and evidence that memories of relationships are beginning to be built up. He writes: 'It is not the object itself that is transitional; it represents the infant's transition from a state of being merged with the mother, to a stage of being in relation to the mother as something outside and *separate*' (my italics). The infant endows the object with subjectively created properties, and uses it as a source of comfort, particularly at times of stress and separation from the mother.

For the time being, I have come as far as I can with evaluating evidence from a variety of sources, and I believe that this is what may lie behind the significance of the white feathers: the bereaved person, in a highly emotional state following the death of a loved one, and finding the separation from them unbearable, may weave a link between the person they have lost and an object (or sound, smell or touch) that happens to be around when they are thinking of the dead person; hence my latching on to the appearance of a white feather during a painful walk when I was consumed with thoughts of Paul and my futile attempts to communicate with him. These 'sensory threads', which are different for different people (just as transitional objects are different for different infants), provide a link and a source of comfort, a means of making the separation a little more bearable, and perhaps a healthy aspect of the gradual detachment from the person who has gone. As time goes on, the memory of the dead person inevitably fades; C.S. Lewis, in writing about the aftermath of his wife's death, poignantly describes this as being 'like snowflakes settling down on my memory of her until her real shape is hidden'. Likewise, the sensory thread may be elongated, pulled in a different direction ('feather' episodes or dreams become less frequent; their quality changes) but it will not be lost or forgotten, just as children do not forget their early objects. As Winnicott observes: 'Children often surprise their parents by remembering bits of cloth and weird objects which the parents had long forgotten. If an object is still available, it is the child who knows just where, in the limbo of half-forgotten things, this thing still lies, perhaps right at the back of a bottom drawer, or up on the top shelf of a cupboard.' My son could always find his 'raa' in the chaos of his bedroom, long after he started school; I am alert to the appearance of a feather anywhere, and I always want to pick it up.

The question remains as to why there are sensory threads binding us to some people who have died, but not to others? Neither Annie nor I experienced robins or feathers when our mother or other significant people died, and our father experienced no sense of a link of any kind after Mum's death. Only a quarter of the bereaved people in my survey reported such experiences. However, those who did also all reported a very strong sense of loss at the time of death, describing their feelings using words and phrases like: 'distraught', 'beside myself with grief', 'lost', 'incapable', 'frightened', 'I have had my heart ripped out', 'I don't know how to survive this'. It seems that the strength and quality of the attachment to the dead person must be important, too. And, as time and therapy carry on, I will find out even more about the strength of my attachment to Paul.

CHAPTER SIX

Moving on Again

---

*A large body of research shows that the quality of the
therapeutic alliance is one of the most crucial mediators
of change in any therapy. Client/therapist matches are a
vital, yet still poorly understood factor in bringing about
therapeutic change.*

ANTHONY ROTH AND PETER FONAGY,
What Works for Whom?

Back in the real world, I conclude that Mari is wrong about
the feathers being ineffective, but she may have a point
about needing to advertise the partner vacancy. I'm as
reluctant as ever to go on any more dates, but I heed her
advice and summon the energy to dial into my message box
one last time: if this is no better, that's the end of it.

I have a message from a man called Nigel, and before
long I find myself talking to him. He has a warm, friendly
voice and tells me that he owns a string of health food shops
and is separated. We arrange to meet in a pub I already
know. He describes himself as curly-haired and of medium
height and build, and I spot him sitting at the bar as soon as
I open the door. He greets me with a wide smile and a warm
hug, and we're soon sitting down and chatting as if we've

known each other for years. He is friendly, interesting and interested, and this easy reciprocity could not contrast more starkly with Gerald's one-sided monologue. Our conversation meanders around families, friends, interests and the joys and perils of blind dating, and after a couple of glasses of wine, he tells me how attractive I am. I smile to myself as I register the thought that perhaps, at last, I have met somebody I could 'click' with. The conversation moves on to jobs, and he tells me that he's in the process of selling his health food shops.

'Why?' I ask, and it's then that everything goes pear-shaped.

'I've got cancer,' he says.

What? I didn't see that coming at all: he doesn't look ill. I'm stunned into silence – I have no idea how to react.

'I've had a lot of chemotherapy,' he continues, 'but it's spread. There's nothing more that can be done.'

So, this is late-stage, terminal cancer. Words continue to elude me, and I sit there, dumbfounded, trying to absorb the shock.

He goes on: 'My oncologist says I've got weeks, at most. My solicitor's told me to put my affairs in order.'

'But you look so well,' I offer, pathetically.

'I know,' he says. 'And I feel well, too, since I stopped the chemo. Who knows? Maybe the cancer will miraculously disappear – you do hear about that sometimes.'

He adds that I'm the only date he's told, because I'm such a nice person. By now, though, the mood of the meeting has changed irrevocably, and such flattery falls on deaf ears. I feel alarmed, panicky; desperately sorry for him, for Paul, for myself. I'm keenly aware of the irony that, in trying to devise distractions from the repercussions of death, I've been brought face to face with it again. In the car park, we hug tightly and Nigel says, 'We could do this again – we really could, couldn't we?'

But we both know that we won't.

My profound discomfort at Nigel's revelation reminds me of a distressing case I worked with years ago. It was relatively early in my career, before I had children of my own. I was based in a Child Development Centre attached to a well-known children's hospital, and the eminent paediatricians would sometimes refer tricky patients to our mental health service with little more than a request to 'see what you can do with this child'. One such referral was Bobby and his family. Bobby was ten, and he had Duchenne muscular dystrophy. I knew that this was a progressive, inherited disease, in which the muscles gradually waste away. It mainly affects boys, and in those days, the life expectancy of a boy with Duchenne was mid-twenties at best. I was to see Bobby with a child psychiatrist colleague, a pleasant man I had worked with several times before.

When we met the family for the first time, Bobby had already lost his ability to walk, and he was in a wheelchair. He was a pale boy, with brown hair and freckles; a little overweight, but polite and responsive to any questions we asked him. His younger sister, Sarah, was five years old and similarly pale and polite, but she seemed shy, and more reluctant to engage in conversation. Both parents were teachers, and they were probably in their late forties. His mother appeared caring and keen to engage. His father was bearded and serious, and I noticed that he always wore a rucksack, which gave the impression that he might, at any moment, take off for a hike across the surrounding countryside.

The conversation flowed, largely due to the fact that my colleague was a warm and friendly man, undaunted by the scenario that presented itself before us. A typical exchange would be along the lines of:

Psychiatrist: 'So, what do you like doing as a family?'

Mum: 'Walking. We always walked before we had children and we've carried on the tradition with them.'

Psychiatrist: 'So how do you manage now, with Bobby's difficulties?'

Dad: 'I used to put him on my shoulders when he was smaller, but now he's a bit too heavy, so we push him in the wheelchair. It's quite easy to find walks with a tarmac surface.'

Psychiatrist: 'And how about you, Bobby? Do you like going on walks?'

Bobby: 'It's OK. I like it when we go downhill, 'cos then I can go really fast.'

Psychiatrist (laughs): 'And you, Sarah? Do you get to push Bobby's wheelchair?'

Sarah: 'Yes, sometimes. I like going downhill too, but Mummy says I have to be careful.'

We spent a lot of time talking about the practicalities of everyday living, and ways in which the best possible quality of life could be maintained for Bobby. We also talked a fair bit about discipline. This is often a challenging topic for the parents of disabled children, because of the understandable conflict between the need to set normal boundaries on behaviour, and the tendency to overprotect or overindulge, particularly when a child has a life-limiting illness. I contributed to these discussions whenever I could, but much of the time I sat in horrified silence. I felt that there was a massive elephant in the room: that this child was going to die, that we were all thinking it (or, at least, the adults were – I didn't know what the children had been told), but nobody was talking about it. It felt as though we were engaged in some awful mutual pretence to shield us from the painful reality of what we were actually facing. Little did I know that, some years down the line, my own nephew would die at the age of ten. At that stage of my life, I had no experience to go on, and I felt totally out of my depth and inadequate to the task. Like all helping professionals, I had a strong desire to make things better for this family. We were doing our best, but although on the surface our practical suggestions were helpful, I knew that, underneath, nothing could really work.

One day, the parents requested an appointment without the children, and when we met with them alone, it was no surprise that what they wanted to discuss was whether they should tell Bobby that he would eventually die.

'We've told him the name of his illness,' they said. 'And obviously he knows that his muscles are getting weaker, but we haven't said anything about the future.'

Once again, I felt panicked and completely unequal to the task. They were asking us for advice? What did *I* know? I was little more than half their age, with no children of my own and a very limited experience of death. But of course, I had my professional training and reading behind me, so I gulped and tried to think of something to say that would reflect both this and a bit of how I really felt.

'I can't imagine how difficult this must be for you,' I said. 'I don't have children of my own, but I can see it's an overwhelming task. You don't want to frighten Bobby, but you don't want to keep secrets from him either, particularly knowing that he might find out the truth from somebody else if you don't tell him. I don't know. I honestly don't think there's a right or wrong answer. Perhaps that's what we need to spend some time exploring together: different ways of managing the situation, until we get to something you feel reasonably comfortable with.'

I think this did lead to some productive discussion, especially when thinking about how children of different ages understand the concept of death (because, of course, the question of what to tell Sarah was a very live issue as well). But I never felt comfortable, and I was always aware of the strong undercurrents dragging at our superficial chit-chat.

After several weeks, we decided mutually that we had got as far as we could for now, and met for our last session. The children had made us a 'Thank You' card, and the parents voiced their appreciation of our efforts.

Bobby's mum singled out my contribution for particular mention: 'I know this hasn't been easy for you because you haven't got your own children yet. But I want you to know how much I've appreciated your sensitivity.'

I found this very poignant. Bobby's parents didn't really want to deny what was happening in their family, but they were constrained in what they could say in front of the children. Bobby's mum must have picked up something of my discomfort about this, and rather than dismissing or ignoring my feelings, she made a point of acknowledging their authenticity.

I turn my attention back to poor Nigel. He, too, is busy denying what is really happening to him, pretending that everything is alright. And I am feeling intense discomfort all over again in the face of impending death. But more than this, I realise that my contact with Bobby and his family has many parallels with my experience of dating in general: there is the same uneasy sense of floundering, of feeling inadequate to the task, of not really knowing how to manage these dates with the deep sense of loss always in the background; there is the elephant (Paul) in the room on every date; there is the awareness that what other people expect of me feels profoundly uncomfortable; and there are the opposing forces of moving forwards and grieving, forces that wage a battle within me, much as they must have done with Bobby's parents. The dating knocks my confidence, just as my experience with Bobby's family had done, and I know that I don't want to do it again.

I reflect also on what Bobby's mother said about my sensitivity, and I realise that Jocelyn is not sensitive in this way. She wants me to be positive and move on, rather than dwelling on the painful undercurrents that are always there with the dates. She doesn't pick up on *these* feelings, so will we ever make any real progress? Perhaps the reason why I hardly remember a thing she says is because it doesn't resonate with me emotionally. I wonder again about packing it in with her too, and before long something happens to hasten my decision.

*

Just as Nigel and I are saying goodbye, Jocelyn announces that she's moving her practice to her home. This is nearer where I live, and will be more convenient, so I'm unprepared for the disruption that the change to my weekly routine actually brings.

Her new consulting room is in the basement of her tiny Victorian terraced house. Parking is no longer free, and the room is no longer bright and airy. It's so small that there's only just enough room for our two chairs, with a small table in between us. On it are the tissues, and a vase of flowers: not the elaborate bouquets of the previous room, but a few stems of uniform species and colour. I notice with distaste that these are sometimes lilies, which I detest for their cloying perfume, staining pollen and association with funerals. In order to get to the basement, we have to walk down a flight of stairs past a jumble of her paraphernalia, inexpertly concealed behind a heavy velvet curtain. There's something about this which feels as disorganised as her hair. I hate the new room. I feel uncomfortable there, claustrophobic.

One day in summer, a wasp flies in through the open window and buzzes fretfully against the windowpane. I've been terrified of wasps since I was three and was stung in the middle of my hand while picking an apple; I can't concentrate at all on what Jocelyn's saying. I'm even more mesmerised by the captive wasp than by her shoes. And suddenly I recognise, forcefully, what has been at the back of my mind for ages: how trapped I feel, how this is all wrong, not the answer, and how much I need to escape. I tell her I want to stop coming to see her, and soon. She's surprised. She advises that I should wind the sessions down gradually over at least three months. But I know I won't do that. I'm not properly engaged with her, but I will come a few more times so as not to appear rude. And, as there is a new message in my box, I will go on one last date. After that, I will definitely pack in the dating, too.

Chris sounds South African, and I have always liked the accent, provided it isn't too strongly Afrikaans. I ring him from the car (by now I have hands-free), and he doesn't beat about the bush but suggests meeting for a drink the next evening at yet another pub. This pub (his choice) is unlike the others in that it sits on a main road, surrounded by tarmac, and is ugly. Inside it is cavernous and noisy, the cheap décor illuminated by the perpetual blinking of the fruit machines. Chris is tall, fair and quite good-looking, but his arrogance is apparent from the outset, as he literally looks me up and down and then buys himself a drink. We sit down at a draughty table close to the door and, without preamble, he launches into the story of his previous dates. Mostly, he informs me, there is just one drink and then he's off. A woman is doing well if he stays for a second drink, but recently there was one he really liked and they ended up having dinner. It appears that I am to be put through some kind of test, and so I take a deep breath, turn on as much charm as is possible under the circumstances, and give him an annotated version of my recent life. He seems mildly interested, particularly in the fact that I live in a big house and have a job, and suggests another drink. Round one to me, then!

When he returns from the bar, he homes in on my domestic circumstances in more detail. I haven't mentioned children up to this point, and he's clearly disconcerted to hear that I have a son living with me. But it doesn't deter him from pressing on with what I gradually realise is his real agenda; he wants to arrange to come and stay for a weekend at my house. I'm appalled; I've only just met him, and the more time I spend with him, the more narcissistic and obnoxious I think he is. I don't want to antagonise him and so I list, calmly and rationally, the reasons why it would not be a good idea. These include the facts that Simon and I have tried to carve out a stable life for ourselves since suffering a massive shock, and that his GCSEs are just around the corner. Chris is completely unmoved – cross, in fact, as he snaps: 'So what's the problem? Isn't your son used to having house guests?'

That peculiarly South African euphemism makes me snap, too, and I stand up and tell him that I'm going home. We say a terse goodbye in the car park and, as I watch the tail lights of his Audi convertible screech off into the distance, I think, *Right, that's it. I am never going to do this again,* and I cry all the way home.

Over the next couple of weeks, I resolve to take back some control over my life. I delete all traces of myself from the internet and surrender my message box. At the same time, I know I must finally wind up my visits to Jocelyn's cramped basement, with its overbearing smell of lilies, and stop giving money to both her and her annoying car park every week. After all, with no more dates, there will be no more brief encounters with which to arouse her interest, and what will I talk about? By the end of the month, I've stopped seeing her and I'm standing on my own two feet, encased in their unobtrusive black ankle boots.

*

For a while, everything is OK. I'm busy with work and Simon's GCSE revision. We make a giant revision time-table on a roll of wallpaper lining paper, and we go to WHSmith to buy him index cards in assorted colours on which to make his revision notes. Over the next few weeks I learn a lot about different religions, the arguments for and against euthanasia, *Of Mice and Men*, how to work out the volume of solids, respiration in plants, the periodic table, and much more.

One evening we're practising for his French oral the next day, and the topic is the family.

I ask him, *'Qui est dans ta famille?'*

'J'ai une mère,' he says.

'Oui, et comment est ta mère?'

'Elle est assez vieille, mais elle est gentille.' (Well, that's alright, then!)

'Et tu as des frères ou des soeurs?'

'Oui, j'ai une soeur. Elle a vingt-deux ans. Et j'ai un frère. Il a vingt ans.'

'Et ton père?'

'Mon père est mort.'[1]

I'm gobsmacked, although I do try not to show it. For, after all, his father is very much alive; it's his stepfather who is dead. We haven't talked about it much, and we have probably each been trying to shield the other from further pain, but in that moment, in a foreign language, I get some inkling of just how devastating Paul's death has been for Simon, too.

*

As the summer unfolds, I put the house on the market. It's too big and expensive to run, and Simon and I agree that it would be better to move into the city, where he will start sixth form college in September. He gets an A for French, one of a full house of As and A*s, and I'm incredibly proud of him. I go as a parent-helper with the band he plays in on a concert trip to Croatia, where I get to grips with driving

---

1 'Who is in your family?' 'I have a mother.' 'Yes, and what is your mother like?' 'She's quite old, but she's nice.' 'And do you have brothers or sisters?' 'Yes, I have one sister. She's twenty-two. And one brother. He's twenty.' 'And your father?' 'My father is dead.'

in the mountains of the Istrian peninsula in the dark (*Paul, you would be proud of me*), and soaring high into the sky on a parachute attached to a speedboat. Nobody could say I wasn't trying. But soon after we return to England, there's an incident which leaves me terrified of being in the house alone at night.

Our house is old, detached and surrounded by tall pine trees. I'm fast asleep one night when I feel someone shaking me. Simon is standing by the bed in his boxers, quaking with fear. 'Mum, there's someone in the kitchen. I heard crunching on the gravel and Jess is going berserk.'

The dog is, indeed, barking furiously. My heart starts racing and the first thought that flashes through my mind is *what would Paul do?* I know he would go downstairs and investigate, and so I tell Simon that this is what we must do. My mobile phone is by the bed and I pick it up and dial 99, reasoning that if there really is a burglar downstairs, I will only have to manage one more '9' to summon the police. Simon disappears briefly into his bedroom, and comes back armed with a metal pole. I'm trying to work out where he found it when I realise that it's the bar he uses for working out – he has simply removed the weights from the ends.

The dog has suddenly and abruptly stopped barking, and my immediate thought is that whoever is down there must have killed her. We tiptoe down the stairs, me in my nightdress, clutching my mobile, and Simon in his boxers, armed with his pole. When we get to the kitchen door, all is quiet. Simon takes control of the situation. He raises his pole above his head and whispers, 'Mum, I'll count to three. On three, you open the door and I'll hit them.'

There is no time to remonstrate or even to think about the consequences, as he's already counting.

'One ... two ... three!'

I throw the door open and see ... nothing. Well, nothing, that is, except the kitchen as it normally looks at night, with the dishes from last night's supper piled by the sink and the dog asleep on her old sofa. We creep hesitantly round the room, checking the windows and the back door, still half expecting someone to leap out from the shadows, but there is nobody there. When we're quite sure of this, we go and check the windows in all the other downstairs rooms, to no avail. We go back upstairs, but Simon is still rattled, quite certain that he heard something, including (he now tells me) people talking beneath his window in deep, growly voices. Whether this is simply the effect on his dreams of listening to a lot of heavy metal, we will never know, but he asks if he can sleep in my room. He drags his mattress in and puts it beside my bed.

Even though there was nobody there, this incident spooks me, and as the evenings draw in, I feel more and more anxious about being in the house after dark. The house isn't selling, and when Simon starts college, I reluctantly take it off the market. The prospect of another long, dark winter on my own is looming, and I feel myself sinking back into depression. I still get up, feed the animals, go to work, do the shopping and cook the meals, but it all feels mechanical, detached from reality. I don't answer the phone when it rings, and I make excuses to avoid any form of socialising, apart from seeing my sisters and the closest of friends.

I think a lot about what I was doing with all that dating, which now seems preposterous; in spite of Mari's advice, I'm ashamed to think that I could ever have dreamed of 'advertising' myself in such a way. I think about Jocelyn too, and why I agreed to see her in the first place, and whether my meetings with her were helpful or meaningful. And then it suddenly dawns on me that there's a connection between the two: Jocelyn was my replacement for the loss of Jennifer, to whom I had become attached. And I knew that Jennifer wanted me to find somebody else, so I dutifully did as she asked. The 'dates' were my attempt to replace Paul. Although I sensed that he had given me permission to find a replacement, I still found all the 'dates' wanting when they weren't – and never could be – him.

I hadn't really been aware of making such direct comparisons at the time, but now I see that Pedro was too skinny where Paul was chunky, and his voice was whiny where Paul's was deep; that bumblebee jumpers felt wrong compared to Paul's dark blue heavy-knit sailing jerseys; that Mark's inability to drive or use a computer seemed wimpish compared to Paul's confident driving and self-taught ability to rebuild any computer from scratch. The dates were 'all wrong' because they weren't Paul, just as Jocelyn was 'all wrong' because she wasn't Jennifer. They allowed me a temporary escape from my grief, just as Jocelyn gave me a temporary respite from Jennifer's abandonment. But there was no way I would ever have allowed myself to get attached to her after Jennifer had let me down so badly. Jocelyn was little more than a useful sounding board in the background as I acted out my experiments with the men. I scarcely remembered a thing that she said to me – just as none of the men said anything of substance.

*

Although these insights help to make some sense of what I've been doing, they also leave me feeling bereft.

Confronted with an endless stream of domestic problems, and the realisation that Paul has gone for good and that dates are no substitute, grief resurges with a vengeance. As Stephen Grosz writes: 'For the person who dies there is an end, but this is not so for the person who grieves. The person who mourns goes on living and for as long as he lives, there is always the possibility of feeling grief ... grief can ebb and then, without warning, resurge ... grief can surprise and disorder us – even years after our loss.'

A dark dread seeps into me, pulls me down, and holds me there. The feathers, as always, provide some relief, but they cannot penetrate deeply enough. Paul feels too far away, and in the furthest corners of my mind, and in our isolated house, I still feel desolate. I've been distracting myself with Jocelyn and the dates, but they have brought only a brief reprieve. As I wonder again what to do, I find myself thinking about another patient, even though the case had nothing to do with bereavement – at least, not initially.

I was in my office in the Child Development Centre one day, when one of my paediatrician colleagues knocked on my door.

'I'm really sorry to disturb you,' she said, 'but I wonder if you could possibly come and have a look at this boy? He's laying waste to my room, and I honestly don't know what to do.'

This was most unusual. She was a highly experienced doctor who had worked for many years with children who had learning disabilities and challenging behaviour. I grabbed a balloon and a pot of bubble liquid and followed her. When we got into her room, Max was, indeed, busy destroying it. Sheets of paper, crayons, puzzle pieces and paper towels were strewn everywhere, and he was now trying to tug the telephone wire out of its socket. His mother, and an older woman, whom I later discovered to be his grandmother, were admonishing him and trying to tempt him away from the phone with sweets and Hula Hoops, but to no avail. I took in the scene of destruction and blew some air into the balloon. Then I held it above my head and let it go. It made a rude farting noise as it flew around the room, but it stopped Max in his tracks. He didn't like it – he put his hands over his ears – but it distracted him from the telephone wire for long enough for me to blow a stream of bubbles into the air. That did the trick. He ran over, popped a bubble with his finger and jumped up and down on the spot for more. After that, it was relatively easy to get eye contact with him, calm him down, persuade him to sit down at the child's table and even do one or two simple puzzles, using the bubbles as a reward each time he cooperated.

For me, that afternoon marked the beginning of a long association with Max and his family. Max was three at the time. He had autism and a learning disability, and his behaviour was consistently difficult to manage. His mother, Claudia, who was in her early forties, was a single parent. She was as resigned and pragmatic about that fact as she was about everything to do with Max's upbringing. 'He took one look at the bump and I never saw him again,' was all she ever said about Max's father. She lived with her own mother, Gloria, who came with her to most of our sessions with Max, and together we worked hard on bringing his behaviour under control. Then one day, Claudia turned up on her own, looking upset and tearful. She told me that Gloria had been diagnosed with breast cancer, and that it had already spread. I didn't ever see Gloria again; she went downhill rapidly and died within a few weeks of diagnosis.

Claudia was devastated. Losing Gloria amounted to losing a mother and a partner all at once, so closely involved had she been in their everyday lives and managing Max.

For several weeks, Claudia came to see me on her own, when Max was at nursery. We never actually discussed this – it just happened, and because it seemed to be what she wanted and needed at the time, it was fine by me. Eventually, Claudia felt better, Max went to school, and our sessions together ended. I did keep in touch, because Max became amenable enough to participate in a course that we ran on child development once a year, and Claudia was always delighted to bring him. Years later, over a cup of coffee at one of these courses, while we were waiting for Max, Claudia told me how much she had valued the sessions we had had alone together.

'It meant a great deal to me to have someone who would just listen,' she said. 'I remember how terribly upset I was, but you never minded me crying. Max didn't like it at all if I cried – it frightened him. I needed someone to dump all those feelings on to.'

I think about Claudia's words as my own despairing feelings resurface. I still feel that I need a meaningful relationship with a therapist if I'm to have any hope of getting properly better. My training and career have shown me again and again that therapy is what helps people who are distressed, and I'm drawn to it as the key to processing the trauma that has happened to me. My relationship with Jocelyn wasn't meaningful; my relationship with Jennifer was, but she let me down. Even so, I decide that I'm prepared to give it one more try, so I make some enquiries and off I go again.

*

The recommended therapist this time is called Margaret. She lives about ten miles away and she sounds friendly on the phone. Her house turns out to be 1960s vintage, surrounded by a rather unkempt garden. I've been instructed to ring the bell on the side door, and when she opens it, I'm confronted with another woman of similar age to me, wearing glasses, with her hair scraped back in a low bun. She shows me into a large room which is sparsely furnished, the predominant colour being a Farrow & Ball type of beige. The couch is there, with folded car rugs on the end of it, and there are two Victorian armchairs, one of which she indicates for me to sit in. There are one or two oil paintings of flowers and trees on the walls, a small bookcase containing works by Freud and other psychoanalysts, and some rather lovely plain pottery bowls. Margaret sits down opposite me. Between us is the inevitable low table with a box of tissues, but no flowers this time. She is composed and seems concerned as she invites me to tell my story. I find that I can talk easily about Paul's death, about my depression and about my families – both the one I have now and my family of origin. She doesn't betray a preference for any topic, and appears to have a genuine interest in anything I have to say. I like her. I feel that we've 'clicked', and it is with relief that I agree to come and see her on a weekly basis. Perhaps this time it really will help.

From that moment on, I begin to feel a bit better. As I'm talking to Margaret, I realise I'm not focusing on the trauma of Paul's death all the time, and I begin to make connections between losing him and other things that have happened in my life, some of them recent and some of them a long time ago.

A few weeks after I've started seeing her, I'm in the hairdresser's. This is my opportunity every six weeks to get free access to the women's magazines that I would never allow myself to buy, and I devour their contents. I can normally manage to get through *Hello!* or *OK!* in the time needed for the colour to 'take' on my hair. On this particular occasion, I'm struck by an article somebody has written on the subject of 'Drains versus Radiators'. The author claims that one's friends can be allocated to either one category or the other. 'Drains' are the people who suck you dry, who use you as a sounding board, or else pontificate endlessly about themselves and their achievements. 'Radiators' on the other hand, leave you feeling warm because they care about you and listen to you. I begin, automatically, to assign my friends, and discover to my surprise that there are quite a few Drains amongst them. In fact, I realise that I often find myself in situations where I feel exploited by 'friends' who will use an evening out to talk exclusively about themselves, with scarcely a passing concern for me. I mention this to Margaret and she's interested.

– Can you say more?

– People always tell me I'm a good listener. I suppose that's why I chose to work in the helping professions.

– But you say you feel exploited?

– Mmm. Not by my patients, because it's my job to listen to them. But by some of my friends, when I spend hours listening to them, but they're not interested in me. I do feel exploited, and I find it draining, but I don't ever say anything.

– Do you know why?

– I suppose I've never been any good at saying what I really want. When I was a child, I was always good, always responsible, always looking after my younger sisters.

– Can you say more?

– Well, one of my earliest memories is of my new baby sister being brought home from hospital. I was told by my mother to sit down on the low chair in the nursery and hold her and give her a bottle. I would have been two and a half, and there was already another sister between me and the new baby. I did as I was told, and from then on, I was always an obedient goody-goody, constantly trying to please my mother.

– Which meant not noticing your own needs?

– Exactly. I learned very quickly that one of the easiest ways to get noticed by my parents and singled out for praise was to be clever. I remember being taught to read in kindergarten – the flash cards and the *Janet and John* books. I found it very easy and I was a fluent reader in no time at all. My teacher was delighted, and so was Mum, and after that I always wanted to be top of the class. And I went on doing it for years and years. When I got my PhD, you can see Mum's radiant face in the photos taken standing outside the Royal Albert Hall – me in my red gown, four months pregnant with my daughter. Mum was much more excited about the PhD than she'd been when I told her that I was going to be a mother myself.

– So, your academic achievements were more important to your mother than your emotional life. I wonder how that made you feel?

– I don't know really. I was always anxious about not being good enough. But I just remember feeling gloomy and empty a lot of the time.

Margaret makes a link between what I've just been talking about and what I came in with.

– I wonder whether 'gloomy and empty' is how you feel when you sense you've been exploited?

– Yes, I'd say it's the same as the drained feeling.

– Perhaps you're attracted to Drains because you're so used to pleasing other people, doing the right thing, not thinking about yourself?

– Yes, that's probably true. I hate conflict, or offending people. It's been much worse since Paul died. He was the ultimate Radiator. He was always warm and comforting, and he always listened to me, *really* listened. He didn't care how much I ranted about work or my mother or anything – he always tried to understand and he always supported me.

– So, Paul was particularly good at understanding and meeting your needs, unlike your mother and some of your friends?

– Mmm. My mother always found me wanting, no matter how hard I tried to please her. And some of my friends just seem to want me to be a sounding board. With Paul, I could be myself. He liked me just as I was; I didn't have to try to please him. That's why I can't bear it without him.

Margaret asks me about my father, whether he was supportive.

– Not exactly. He didn't criticise, but he didn't take much notice, either. He was a kind of remote presence during my childhood. He was there in the background, up in his study working, or out in his shed mending something or building something, but he never really got involved in the dramas of family life.

– Can you say more?

– He was brought up in an isolated part of New Zealand during the Depression, and after the war he worked his passage to Europe by washing a million dishes on a cargo ship. I think he's very driven by his background of poverty and hard work. I never, ever remember him getting in a tradesman to fix anything around the house. Dad did it all himself, including every bit of painting and decorating. We lived in a big, draughty Edwardian house, so as soon as he'd finished all the rooms, it was time to start all over again. But he was also brilliant at making things for us three girls: he made us a tree house at the top of the poplar tree, where we used to have picnics and play our favourite game of runaway children; he put up a horizontal iron bar in the garden so we could do somersaults or hang upside down on it; he made all kinds of 'jumps' around the lawn when we wanted to play horses; he made cages for our guinea pigs and a huge structure enclosed in netting, full of tree branches and wooden walkways for Timmy, our pet squirrel; and best of all, he made us a trolley from planks of wood and old aeroplane wheels – we used to trail it behind our bikes and hurtle down hills on it.

– So, in that way, he was involved.

– Well, yes. I think he showed his love for us in very practical ways. There was one time – we would have been teenagers – when Annie decided she wanted to paint her bedroom black, like the inside of Biba. We could tell that Dad was reluctant, but he did it, including the ceiling and window frames. When it was done, we spent hours lying on the floor, listening to Pink Floyd at full volume.

– So, he was generous with his time and his practical skills?

– Yes, but he had a puritanical attitude to life, which could be tough. To this day, he never overindulges in food or drink, and he can still get into the suit he wore for his wedding in 1949. We never had central heating, and on schooldays in winter we would have a one-bar electric fire to get dressed by, with ice on the inside of the windows. We had ancient family cars that were constantly breaking down. I remember once driving down to Devon in the middle of a freezing cold winter with a paraffin stove flaring away in the back of our Bedford Dormobile as it had no heating – thinking back, that was incredibly dangerous. We went on camping holidays in north Wales or the Isle of Wight in tents that had no groundsheets and leaked at the top and bottom; we got a tiny black-and-white TV years after most of our school friends already had colour ones; we never had new bikes – Dad would always manage to find an old one and do it up. I still remember the bitter disappointment on my tenth birthday, when my birthday 'surprise' was an orange bike that dad had recycled from the rubbish dump. I'd been hoping and praying for a brand-new Raleigh – a blue one like the one my best friend had. We very occasionally went to a restaurant for a meal on a birthday or some other special occasion and I would automatically choose the cheapest dish on the menu … and I still do.

Margaret doesn't comment.

I sit quietly for a while and think about all this before speaking again.

– I suppose Dad didn't look after our material needs – he frowned on them, really. And Mum wasn't too hot on emotional needs. I think Paul rescued me on both counts. He was supportive emotionally and he didn't mind spending money and having nice things and going away to nice places.

Margaret considers this, then issues a challenge.

– You seem to be pretty good at picking up when your needs aren't being met, as with the friends you've talked about who exploit you. So perhaps you could begin to think more about how your needs *can* be met now?

Hmm. That might be tricky. I register what she says, but in the meantime, life moves on – and presents further challenges.

*

I've been trying to sell the house again, but the market is bad. Then one day, quite out of the blue, the estate agent rings to say that he thinks he's found a buyer.

Next morning, the Tomlinsons arrive in their shiny black Range Rover. Mr Tomlinson is abrupt and business-like, and doesn't want to engage in conversation about anything except the house. His wife is much friendlier to me. She tells me about their three children, and how she thinks this would make a lovely family home. I can tell that she really likes the house. He seems irritated by her keenness, and tries to shut her up. I'm soon to find out why. As the sale progresses, I discover that he is misogynistic and tight; he will only deal with me via the (male) estate agent, and his main objective appears to be to get as much of a reduction as he possibly can on the sale price for every single thing he can find wrong with the house (and, it being an Edwardian house with its original roof, he has plenty to argue over).

I rant about him to Margaret.

– He's a complete bastard. He's trying to do me out of every penny he possibly can. He thinks that just because I'm a woman on my own, he can walk all over me.

Margaret's response is calm and measured as always.

– So, you think he's out to exploit you?

– Yes, of course he is.

– So, what have you said to him?

– Nothing. I don't want to upset him in case he pulls out of buying the house.

– But you are angry with him?

– Yes, of course I am!

Margaret doesn't respond. She sits quietly and waits, eyebrows raised slightly in my direction. (*What is it about psychotherapists' eyebrows? Jennifer used to do it too – that quizzical look, inviting you to say more without actually asking…*) And then it dawns on me that we're going over old ground, and here I am again, reacting in the usual way, behaving well, not wanting to rock the boat. Now I'm annoyed with myself.

– OK, OK, I get it. I'm about to lie down and get trampled on, like I always do. I'm trying to please him … I know, I know … just like I always tried to please my mother.

Following this exchange, I do try to think hard about what my needs are, and I access a strong determination not to be wound down by Mr Tomlinson. I engage a painter and decorator to repaint every room in the house in either magnolia or gardenia (these being the much cheaper versions of Farrow & Ball's beige) and tell Mr Tomlinson that, unless he sticks to his offer of the asking price, I'm going to take the house off the market and rent it out instead. To my amazement this works, and once he has forked out the money for a full survey, I'm pretty sure that he's committed: I've stood my ground and the house really is going to be sold. This means, though, that I'm going to have to find somewhere else to live, and also pack up almost twenty years' worth of family history, much of which will have to be got rid of.

CHAPTER SEVEN

Attachment and Separation

Loss can apply to many aspects of our lives, not only the death of a loved one. Grief may occur after the loss of a romantic relationship, a pet, a home, a child leaving home, retirement, even a loss of trust.

JOHN W. JAMES AND RUSSELL FRIEDMAN,
The Grief Recovery Handbook

Finding another house is easy. Emily and I go and look at three in one afternoon, and we both agree that one of them is perfect; much smaller, but light and spacious, and five minutes' walk from all the facilities of the city centre, including the swimming pool, which is just around the corner. And it's in a Victorian terrace surrounded by other houses, so I imagine I'll feel much safer at night. I make an offer and it's accepted.

Packing up the old house consumes all my spare time for months. The huge, cobwebby attic and leaky stables are mostly full of rubbish, but they do contain a couple of items that capture my attention. There's a framed certificate proclaiming me to be the winner of *The Children's*

Newspaper National Handwriting Competition 1960, and, as if bearing witness to this accolade, a letter to my parents written at around the same time, in pencil, on pre-ruled lines, in immaculate writing:

Dear Mummy and Daddy,

I am having a lovely time in Dymchurch. Tessa and I have been swimming in the sea every day. I wore my new bathing suit. I hope you are both well.
With love from

Vanessa xxx

I'm struck by the formality of this letter, by the absence of any communication about how I really felt, because I do remember being particularly homesick on that holiday. I didn't know the family I went with very well (their daughter was an only child and they wanted company for her) and the father took great delight in walking me and Tessa round the beach and making us stamp on jellyfish with our flippers. I found this both frightening, in case the jellyfish stung us, and disgusting, because the squashed jelly spewed out everywhere.

I tell Margaret about this, and she encourages me to say more on my thoughts about the letter.

– It kind of sums up how I was as a child. The writing is perfect, and I'm telling my parents what they want to hear: that I'm having a nice time. But I'm not really. I'm just keeping the bad feelings to myself.

– Can you say more about the bad feelings?

– Anxiety, mainly. I was terribly anxious as a child. I tried hard to be perfect most of the time, but I was constantly worried that I wouldn't be good enough, or that something bad was going to happen.

– Do you have any thoughts about where the anxiety came from?

– My mother was incredibly anxious. She worried about everything. If Dad was late home from work, she thought something awful must have happened to him; if my sisters or I had a problem, she turned it into a catastrophe. She always said it started after she lost her first baby, my brother Patrick, because she couldn't trust the world after that. I don't know if that's true, because obviously I didn't know her before she had me.

– Did she ever talk to you about your brother's death?

– Mmm. A bit, although Dad never mentioned him. He was a full-term, normal baby, but during labour, the cord got stuck round his neck. If she'd been in a proper hospital, she could have had a Caesarean and he probably would have survived, but she was in a nursing home and the cord strangled him. I think she felt terribly guilty – she was a doctor, after all. She always made me and my sisters promise that we'd have our babies in hospital.

– And how long after your brother's death were you born?

– Just over a year, so I suppose I was the replacement baby. I always had this strong sense that I had to make up for something, that I had to really excel and make them proud of me.

– So, you were trying to replace your brother, to live up to their expectations of him?

– I didn't think that at the time. I've only really thought

it since I grew up. I think Dad would have loved to have a son, and probably Mum, too – in the end they never got one. I just had this really strong sense that I had to work hard to please them. And I think Mum was probably overprotective of me and my sisters, too, because Patrick had died … at least, she always seemed to be worried about all of us, especially if we were away from home.

– It sounds as though you were very sensitive to your mother's feelings and needs when you were a child. And perhaps you sensed that she wouldn't tolerate strong emotions from you?

– Yes, definitely. I remember one time when I was in hospital, I'm not sure how long for, maybe a couple of weeks. I had something wrong with my leg and it was pulled up in one of those traction things, to stretch it. I was only about three, and in those days, children were left in hospital on their own and their parents could only see them at visiting times. I remember Mum leaving after a visit, and me screaming and screaming as I watched her walk down the corridor. She came back and told me to be quiet, and stop making such a fuss.

To my surprise, tears well up as I recall this scene.

Margaret says: I'm struck by the sense of despair, desolation perhaps, of the little girl being abandoned by her mother.

I'm amazed at how much material can be generated by such a sparse letter. Clearly my horror of abandonment of any kind goes back a long way. No wonder Bryony and I felt so abandoned when Mum and Dad relocated to the most inaccessible corner of Devon. Is this why I feel so abandoned by Paul?

*

After what seems like months of spending every spare moment sorting, chucking and packing up the contents of the house, I've done all that I can. There are still some large items of furniture left which won't fit into the new house, and so I ask the Tomlinsons if they'd like to buy them at a knock-down price. They say they are happy to have them, but not prepared to pay me a penny. So, four days before moving, I'm left with a gas range cooker, two full-size trampolines, a pine dining table with ten chairs, a dishwasher and a huge American fridge-freezer. Thinking about what *I* want for once, I'm determined that the Tomlinsons aren't going to have them for nothing, so my sons and I dismantle the trampolines, and I sell one to a neighbour for £10, and drive the other down to Devon and deposit it with my father. I find a second-hand furniture man who is happy to take the pine table and chairs, and my son Will puts the stove on eBay. This results in a man with a van driving down from Essex early the next morning and handing over £1,000 in twenty-pound notes. I have to wake up every teenager who happens to have slept in the house the previous night to come and help lift the stove into his van. They are understandably sleepy and disgruntled, but I am filled with the joy of success. The fridge-freezer and dishwasher can stay. The freezer regularly malfunctions and encases the frozen peas and ice cream in blocks of ice, and the dishwasher floods the kitchen about once a week, so the Tomlinsons are welcome to them – their triumphant smiles will be wiped off their faces soon enough.

When I get into the car and negotiate the front drive for the last time, my feelings are mixed. The house and garden are full of memories, some wonderful, some dreadful, and it's sad to think that I'll never again see the inside of the place that has been my home for the past nineteen years. I'm aware, too, that Simon's A levels are not far off. It's beginning to dawn on me that he will soon be leaving home to go to university, and I'll be left on my own. The prospect of yet another loss, and the fear of being totally by myself this time, send me into a tailspin. I start to cry in my sessions with Margaret, and tell her over and over again how unbearable it will be to carry on living with another central pillar of my identity removed:

– I know I haven't been a wife for a long time now. I can cope with that. But I can't cope with not being a mother. I've been a mother for nearly twenty-five years. It's by far the most important thing I've ever done. How am I going to find any purpose in life without it?

… Since Paul died, the children have needed me to sort them out in lots of ways. It's kept me going. How will I survive when they don't need me any more? … Simon has been my only housemate and companion for the past four years since his brother and sister left home. How am I going to bear it on my own when he goes?

Margaret listens patiently to all of this, but when she responds, she's incredulous.

– Why do you think that you will stop being a mother just because the children aren't living at home? Why do you assume that 'out of sight' is 'out of mind' for them? Are they 'out of mind' for you when you're not with them? Aren't they still your children? … Surely you continue to be a mother to your children no matter where they are and not just when you're physically looking after them? Isn't successful parenting the kind of parenting that enables children to feel confident about separating and making their own way in the world?

I ponder these questions in my car, in the supermarket, on my walks with Jess. The memory of a young patient and her highly anxious mother comes into my mind. Janet was a tiny scrap of a girl, with thick brown hair cut into a severe bob. She had a high forehead and prominent eyes, the result of a rare syndrome with an unpronounceable name. Her short stature arose from the same condition, and although she was over two, she had no speech and she was only just beginning to take her first tentative steps. She had been referred to our clinic because of sleep problems, and she was brought along by her mother, Muriel. Muriel was in her late forties, and she told me that Janet had been a 'mistake', conceived well after her older three children had grown up and left home. Her husband, John, had been furious about the pregnancy and provided Muriel with minimal support. His work as a long-distance lorry driver kept him away from home for extended periods. Muriel seemed downtrodden and exhausted as she recounted how Janet was difficult to settle, and woke repeatedly during the night.

'She cries when I put her in her cot. I have to stay with her until she falls asleep, but if she hears me leave the room, she screams and I have to start all over again. Most nights, I have to crawl out so she doesn't see me leaving.' She went on to describe the remainder of the night: 'She wakes up at least every couple of hours and screams. I try to settle her down but it doesn't usually work. If John's at home, he goes mad at the noise, so I have to sleep in the spare bedroom and I take Janet in with me. If John's away, I try to leave her to go to sleep, but sometimes the screaming gets too much so I bring her into bed with me.'

Throughout this consultation, Janet sat on her mother's lap, clutching the toy rabbit she had brought with her and rubbing one of its ears rhythmically along the side of her nose.

On the face of it, this seemed like a classic example of the kind of sleep problem we often saw: an absence of an appropriate bedtime routine, and a tendency for the sleep-deprived parents to eventually give in to their child's demands, thereby unintentionally strengthening the likelihood that the child would wake again in the future. Providing parents with some education about developing good sleeping habits, setting up a proper bedtime routine and agreeing strategies for responding to night-time waking was often all that was needed to solve the problem, and usually fairly quickly. So, I sent Muriel away with sleep diaries to complete, and followed all the usual steps in setting up a sleep programme – but to no avail. As the weeks went by, Muriel reported an increase in Janet's night-time waking, and she herself looked more dishevelled and exhausted than ever. Janet continued to sit on her mother's lap throughout our sessions together, quietly stroking her rabbit. It was on the day when I decided to challenge this and get to know Janet a bit better that I began to get an inkling of what was really going on. I had brought in a selection of toys that were suitable for Janet's age and developmental level, but she refused to get down from Muriel's lap to investigate them.

'Can you have a go?' I asked Muriel. 'Just take her over to the table and see if she'd like to play with anything.'

But as Muriel tried to get up, Janet clung to her and screamed, and the only way we could get her to stop was by ignoring her again, sitting back down and carrying on with our conversation.

At the end of the session, I said to Muriel: 'I'd like to try something different next time. Could you bring in some of her favourite toys from home and put them on the table or the floor and play with her? No sitting down and talking to me at all – just playing with Janet.'

Muriel seemed anxious at the prospect of this change, but she agreed, and very slowly, bit by bit, over the ensuing weeks, we began to make some headway. At first, Janet was more receptive to playing with her own toys, but as time went on, she allowed me to join in with her and Muriel and to introduce some toys of my own. Then we invited one of the nursery nurses from our special nursery along, and eventually Janet was able to go off with the nurse to the nursery and play with the other children, provided she could take her rabbit.

This gave Muriel and me an opportunity to talk on our own, and she began to open up about how difficult things had been at home since Janet's birth.

'John's been in a foul mood with me ever since Janet was born. He didn't want another child at all, and especially not one with problems.'

'So how has that affected your relationship with him?'

'We don't have a relationship. He works away from home for days at a time, and when he is home, he sits in front of the TV with a beer and ignores me and Janet.'

'And how does that make you feel?'

'Upset, angry … but most of all, tired out, because I have to do everything for Janet, and the house, and the family. I feel like a single parent most of the time and I'm too old to be doing all this.'

She often cried when talking about her situation, but when asked how she felt about Janet and her disability, she was fiercely protective.

'I feel so sorry for her, poor little mite. She doesn't understand so much of what goes on around her. And she's all I've got. I love her to bits.'

This admission turned out to be the key to solving what was really a separation rather than a sleep problem. As Muriel and I talked, we came to understand how much Janet depended on her mother for support in an often incomprehensible world, and how much Muriel needed Janet in the absence of a supportive partner, as well as her intense feelings of protectiveness towards her because of her developmental difficulties. With this new awareness of what the real issues were, it was possible to make progress with the sleep programme, while at the same time building up Janet's independence in her daytime activities. As long as she had her rabbit with her, she was able to separate from her mother during the day, and eventually at night.

So, it seems that the issues surrounding separation between parents and children can be keenly felt on both sides. I remember my own separation from home when I was seventeen, and I tell Margaret about it.

– Mum and Dad encouraged us to be independent, outwardly at least, but I think the real message was something different.

– Can you say more?

– The absolutely best time with Mum was when I was a teenager. She really blossomed in our early teenage years. She definitely enjoyed our company far more than she had when we were young children. Just as many of my friends were starting to experience friction with their parents, Mum became our best friend. She often used to say how lucky we were to have each other, as she was an only child and had always longed to have sisters.

– So, you and your sisters provided the siblings she didn't have?

– Yes, it felt like that. She loved coming with us to buy clothes, and our first bras, and we had a lot of fun. But it didn't last, because I began to be aware that I wanted to lead a life of my own. I started to do things in secret. It began with compulsive eating: I would buy Skippy bars on my way home from school and eat them while I was doing my homework, before supper. I put on weight, which everybody told me was 'puppy fat', but I hated it. Then I discovered smoking. I could satisfy my need to have something in my mouth without the calories, and by the time I was fourteen, I was buying ten Embassy regularly on my way home from school and hiding them in my blazer pocket.

– So, you were, in fact, satisfying your own needs?

– Yes. And not long after, I met a boy, the brother of one of my school friends and fell madly in love. By the time I was fifteen, I was sleeping with him. It was difficult to organise because we were both still living at home, and it involved long walks by the river or in the woods, and a lot of tiptoeing around in the middle of the night in both our parents' houses.

– You were an adolescent girl. You were beginning to make a life of your own.

– Yes, and I would never have told my parents the details of what was really going on in my life outside school and O and A levels. My sisters soon began to get into drinking and smoking and boys too, and the more this went on, the more I noticed Mum beginning to get irritated and snappy. She didn't like my sisters' boyfriends; she thought they were unsuitable. She liked mine, because he was a public-school boy with a passion for English literature.

It was when he and I eventually broke up that she was cross. It was he who left me for someone more beautiful, richer and apparently better equipped to further his career aspirations than I was. I was devastated: the loss of him felt catastrophic. But Mum showed little sympathy and I felt I was to blame for letting her down. I sensed that I'd failed her. She didn't approve of my choice of A levels or career, either. She was one of the relatively few women of her generation who had studied medicine and she wanted me to follow in her footsteps, so I let her down there too.

– She didn't support you when things were difficult, when you had difficult choices to make.

– No, and it went on and got worse. Over the years, my sisters and I got married and had children of our own. Mum didn't much like my sisters' husbands, and often criticised them. She did like mine, who was like my dad in many ways: a psychologist, a quietly spoken man from the colonies who had had a similarly impoverished childhood. But when I divorced him and married Paul, she absolutely hated *him*, and never changed her mind, even on her deathbed. Do you know she didn't even come to see me when Paul died? Dad came. Mum said, over the phone, 'I didn't think you'd want somebody who didn't like your husband in your house.'

My eyes fill with tears as I think how unkind she was about Paul, how it didn't matter to her that I cared about him and that he made me happy. Her disapproval trumped everything.

– So, there's a strong sense of you feeling crushed by your mother?

– Yes, I felt that whatever I did was wrong. And it wasn't any better when I had children. In fact, her attitude to all her grandchildren was extraordinary. She appeared not to like them, or at least not to have any interest in getting to know them properly. She dutifully sent them birthday and Christmas cards, but she would often say: 'I don't know what's the matter with me, all my friends adore their grandchildren and I just don't,' as if that somehow excused her. She criticised us all the time as parents, for paying too much attention to the children so that it was 'impossible to have an adult conversation'. She was the first to jump on any of her grandchildren at the slightest sign of bad behaviour, and as the years went by, this situation got worse and worse, and we would often end up rowing about it. She and Dad would come and stay for a weekend, and to begin with she would be fine, eager to see us all. But of course, the children would make demands, the phone would ring, the food would need to be cooked. Dad would find something to fix or chop and Mum would become more and more sullen; sometimes she would sit in the middle of the chaotic kitchen with her face in a book; sometimes she would criticise openly and vociferously, and sometimes she would withdraw completely and sulk in silence. She scarcely bothered to hide her anger and resentment.

– You didn't feel supported as you tried to build your own life, to have your own home and family.

– No. Looking back, I think that, at the same time as all three of us were trying to separate and build our own lives, Mum was losing the sisterly relationships she really wanted, and she became increasingly envious of our relationships with our own husbands and children. She was an only child, and her father doted on her, so she must have found it difficult not to be the centre of attention, particularly as she got older and we all got busier with families and work. And of course, she no longer had the adulation of her patients after she retired, which was probably why giving up work was so hard for her.

– You are saying that separation was difficult for you, that although it seemed as though you were encouraged, you didn't actually feel supported in the choices you made, in having your own family.

– No, I didn't. Mum made it really hard. She seemed so angry, but in actual fact I think she badly wanted to cling on to us

I sit quietly and think for a moment.

– I don't know how you set someone free and feel OK about it.

I think back to how this conversation started, with my worries about my youngest son going off to university, and my memories of Muriel, who found it so difficult to separate from Janet, her own youngest child. I see now why it's a difficult area for me too, but unpicking some of it helps me to feel a bit more comfortable about Simon leaving. As Margaret says, 'Sometimes baby birds need a push from the nest.' She is making links between the difficulties and anxieties that I'm facing now and things that happened earlier in my life. My mother found it hard to separate from us; I find it hard to contemplate my last child going; separation from Paul, my greatest supporter, seems intolerable. No wonder I need a sensory thread to cling to him, just as Janet needed her rabbit when she was away from her mother. All of this makes a lot of sense, but is it really going to help me to feel better? I don't mind talking to Margaret, but I worry that I never have the sense of really wanting to see her that I had with Jennifer.

*

As my regular sessions with Margaret mark the passing of the weeks, I continue to see feathers in all manner of places. I pick them up constantly, and they often fall from my pockets when I'm searching for a tissue. I scarcely mention them to Margaret: I feel superstitious about it, as if placing them in front of her for analysis might remove some of the magic. Today however, I notice a small white feather on the tarmac as I walk up her driveway. I pick it up and put it in the pocket of my jeans. I'm still fingering it as I ring her doorbell. As always, she says nothing as I cross the room and sit down in my usual chair, but since the feather is at the forefront of my mind, I tell her about it.

– I found a white feather on your drive.

I take it out of my pocket and show her.

– I still find feathers a lot. And I still think they're linked with Paul in some way.

Margaret knows that it was my birthday yesterday, and that since Paul died, I have found any kind of anniversary difficult. She makes a link between this and the feather:

– You experience Paul's loss very keenly at this anniversary time. And perhaps the feather represents a way of keeping Paul in your mind, of keeping him close on a special day.

She doesn't dwell on the subject, but instead goes on to wonder how my birthday went. I hear what she says, but it doesn't resonate with me. In fact, it makes me annoyed. I feel that I have risked placing something before her that is very important to me, and that she hasn't understood, has even been dismissive. It feels unsatisfactory, and I decide that from now on, I'll keep the feathers to myself, as something special and private between me and Paul that I'm reluctant to open up to scrutiny. I know what the mean to me, and if they bring me comfort, why risk losing it?

*

As Margaret knows, my future feels precarious without Paul – and without my mother, my familiar old house and the reassurance of having my children around me. One anchor after another has been torn away, and now yet another one is causing me a great deal of stress. My work has always been there, keeping me grounded, offering me all kinds of challenges to grapple with, giving me a reason to get up in the morning, especially since Paul died. But over the years it has changed and I'm acutely aware that working in today's NHS has lost the allure it once had. I don't want to continue in this climate. We can no longer do preventative work to help our patients before things get out of hand. Managers who have no clinical training hold the purse strings: they tell us that there are now limits on the number of times we can see a patient, and that it costs too much to replace experienced staff when they leave. Support workers are used in place of clinical psychologists, as, according to these same untrained managers, 'anyone can do therapy'. So when an opportunity to take advantage of a resignation scheme comes up, I grab it. I have little time to stop and ponder the consequences, as part of the deal is that I have to leave by the end of the month and not work out the usual three months' notice. My staff are shocked, and I'm touched to find that some of them cry as I invite them one by one into my office to tell them about my impending departure.

I feel dreadful. I talk to Margaret about it.

– I feel so guilty. I know I won't be replaced in the

current financial climate and my staff won't have anyone to protect them any more.

– Whose needs are you concerned about?

– Theirs, of course.

Margaret says nothing.

– Oh, right, I get it … Not thinking about my own needs again.

– You said it. We've often talked about how good you are at looking after other people's needs. So, what *are* your needs? What do *you* want?

– I want to leave. I hate what's become of the NHS. But I also hate letting people down. I want to leave, but I think I *should* stay.

– Can you think of other times when you've done what 'should' do rather than what you want or need for yourself?

Of course I can think of other times: it's the story of my life. I hear what Margaret is saying, but I still feel guilty.

My immediate team arranges a tea party. They decorate one of our treatment rooms with balloons and flowers and set out the tea on a table adorned with a red-and-white-check tablecloth. It is charming, intimate, like having tea in a French café. Next day, three of the accountants from the finance department turn up with a cake that one of them has made, iced with pink roses. I'm moved to tears: these are the poor girls, young enough to be my daughters, who have helped me, month in, month out, to fathom the intricacies and anomalies of my budget. It has required great patience on their part, but I've grown fond of them for their lack of pretension and unfailing good humour. They tell me I'm their favourite manager. My boss, on the other hand, can't hide the glint of excitement in her eyes as she realises how much money she will save from my salary. She dutifully bakes and ices cakes, and makes a perfunctory speech about my service, which only betrays her ignorance of what it is that we actually do. After work that day I cry, and think that I would give anything to find Paul at home, cheerful and supportive, pouring me out a glass of wine and insisting on taking me out to dinner. But mindful of how I *should* behave, I send my now ex-boss a thank you note and a present; Bryony is currently making cake stands from vintage plates she collects from junk shops, and since my ex-boss likes baking, I decide that one of these will be perfect. I box it up, wrap it in pretty paper and deliver it to management HQ. She never acknowledges it. I'm hurt, but it vindicates my assessment of her, and makes finally leaving much easier.

*

Over the next few months, I have to adapt to ending my full-time career and living in a new place, both of which I had always thought I would do with Paul. Margaret is encouraging whenever I try out new things – watercolour painting, for example, and joining a choir – although I need her there to coax me to keep at it, and to remind me that I can't be perfect at everything at the first attempt. This is a new discovery: that I can enjoy doing something without being top of the class at it. I still can't help comparing my paintings or my voice to those of the women next to me, but over time I find that I can enjoy the activities sometimes just because they are enjoyable, and it begins to matter less if I find myself wanting.

One thing I know I must face is buying another car; the one Paul bought me is getting old and is too long to park easily in the city street where I now live. Paul knew a lot about cars; for years, he managed the fleet for the company he worked for, and he would often come home with a new Saab or BMW or Jag to try out. I'm scared of having to do this on my own. I moan about it to Margaret.

– How can I buy a car? I've never bought a car before. Paul always did it.

– Paul knew a lot about cars?

– Yes, he did. We used to go through loads of car magazines and visit car showrooms whenever it was time for him to change his company car, and whenever my car needed replacing.

– So, you learned quite a lot yourself?

– Yes, I got quite interested. I can tell pretty much every car on the road from its badge …

Margaret is raising her eyebrows in my direction again. I take her message on board and I resolve to do some research and get on with it. I think about my needs now that I'm no longer travelling to work and don't have to transport children and drum kits. I buy motoring magazines, and I search on the internet until I've decided what I want. I go to a local car salesroom armed with the results of my research and a good deal of confidence. What I have not reckoned with is the attitude of the car salesman to an unaccompanied woman. Des wears a cheap suit and a gold identity bracelet, but he's polite and welcoming, shakes my hand firmly and offers me a cup of polystyrene coffee. I tell him what I'm looking for, and he immediately offers me another car: the same make, but a less powerful model. I reiterate that I know which model I want, and arrange a test drive for the following Saturday. When I turn up for this, he insists on accompanying me, and the car he drives round to the front of the showroom is the less powerful model. I remind him that this isn't what I asked for, but he tells me he's sure that once I've driven it, I'll find that it is powerful enough, and spouts a load of technical jargon to support his claim. We belt up and he sits on the edge of his seat like a frightened rabbit. I drive off and he directs me around the local streets, where the maximum speed limit is thirty miles per hour. It's like having a driving lesson all over again: take the next turning on the right; go straight on at the traffic lights; mind the pedestrian/cyclist. I've been driving for over forty years and I've never had an accident or a single point on my licence. I find the situation ridiculous, and so I tell Des that I want to go on the motorway. He seems horrified, but I am adamant: how else am I going to test the power of the car?

Reluctantly, he allows me to drive from one junction to the next, clinging all the time to his seat and glancing anxiously in the wing mirrors. Delivered safely back to the showroom, he's both relieved and triumphant: 'You see, I told you it would be powerful enough.' He's not pleased when I respond that I would now like to drive the other, more powerful model. He doesn't think they have one in stock, but when I stand my ground he stomps off with bad grace and eventually manages to find what I want; this particular car belongs to one of the salesmen and isn't for sale, but I can have a drive in it if I must. After the second drive, I'm more resolved than ever to buy what I came in for in the first place. He's disappointed, but says he will look around and get in touch if he can find one. As I leave the showroom, I notice that there are several of the less powerful cars lined up for sale, so these are obviously what he wants to get rid of.

After this irritating encounter, I've got no further with buying a car. I resort to the internet and spend hours searching across the south of England. Eventually, I find what I'm looking for in a showroom about fifty miles away. I phone up, heart beating fast, and inquire whether the car is still for sale. It is, and I can test-drive it next morning. When I arrive at the showroom, the salesman is on his own. His colleague is sick, which means he can't come out with me for the test drive because he needs to answer the phones. I can barely conceal my delight, but he is nervous, not sure whether he can let me take the car out by myself. I point out that I have already driven fifty miles to get here, and finally, after making me sign insurance documents and hand over £20, he lets me go. I ask him the way to the motorway and he tells me that it's too far and I mustn't go there; there is a main road about a mile away that will suffice. As I drive off, alone, I think: *Sod you. I will find the motorway and I will give this car a proper test drive*. There's no way I'm going to part with thousands of pounds on the basis of a drive along a congested A-road at forty-five miles per hour. I love the car. When I return to the showroom an hour later, my announcement that I want to buy it diverts any questions about where exactly I have been all this time.

A week later, my almost new car is in my possession, and as I recount the tale of its purchase to Margaret, I feel proud that I held out for what I really wanted. There is another problem, though, which I hardly dare broach with her; indeed, I don't say anything for weeks, until the situation becomes critical. My old car had an indicator which displayed the tyre pressures. After Paul died, I carried a foot pump around with me so that I could pump up the tyres if the pressure became too low.

My new car doesn't have a tyre-pressure indicator and I don't know how to use the air machines in garages. Paul always inflated my tyres for me, my ex-husband before him, boyfriends before that and before them, my dad. I read articles in the newspaper about the number of accidents caused by wrongly inflated tyres, and I know I must face it, but the problem seems insurmountable. Eventually I dare to tell Margaret.

– You'll think this is really stupid, but I don't know how to put air in the tyres. Paul always did it. Why isn't he here to help me?

I start to cry. Margaret is never ruffled by any display of emotion from me. She is always calm.

– Tell me some more about the things that Paul did for you.

Where to start? There is a long list, but I settle for the things that are most relevant to what we're talking about.

– He was brilliant at DIY. He could fix anything that got broken, and he did everything for the cars: cleaning them, putting water in the windscreen washers, putting air in the tyres.

– So, you felt safe with him?

I consider this and realise that, yes, this is the point I keep coming back to when I'm thinking about Paul. I remember Mari telling me how safe she felt with him on one occasion when we were out on his boat and the weather deteriorated. I always felt safe with him, too, and not only because he knew how to operate a particular machine in a garage forecourt.

– Yes, I felt safe. I felt that nothing awful could happen so long as he was there.

The memory of something I told Jennifer pops into

my mind: *No wonder I reached out a finger or toe to him for security in the night.*

– But you have said that Paul encouraged you to do new things; that he thought you were capable?

– Yes, he believed in me. He used to tell me that I could do anything.

I think to myself that this is the important thing to hang on to. Venturing out to explore the world still fells tentative and scary, but Paul sowed the seeds of confidence, and Margaret is watering them. If I let her in on the things that frighten me, she can help me to believe in myself. I'm ready for her next question.

– Was Paul the only person in the world who knew how to inflate car tyres?

Of course he wasn't. I feel so much better now that this stupid problem is out in the open, and I begin to explore possible practical solutions.

The next time I'm at the supermarket, I take the car to the adjoining garage where I have seen two air machines. It seems important that there are two, so that if I take ages, I won't be keeping anyone waiting. I park next to one of the machines and read the instructions, but when I open my petrol flap to find the right level of inflation for my car tyres, I'm faced with a problem: the machine is displaying PSI and the numbers on my car's petrol flap refer to bars. There's nothing for it: I'm going to have to swallow my pride and ask somebody. I approach a middle-aged man covered in tattoos who is vacuuming his van at the valet station. He stops and comes over at once to help me. He's not sure himself how to convert PSI to bars, but we work it out together. He then talks me through the whole process of reading the pressure and inflating each tyre, and stays with me until the job is completed. He couldn't be nicer. He is neither patronising nor sarcastic, and we chat about the price of petrol and the council's plans for the local leisure centre while the air hisses into the tyres and I replace each of the tiny black valve covers. I thank him profusely, though he will never have any idea of how amazingly, eternally grateful I really am.

*

I've been enjoying my watercolour class, so I decide to go away on a weekend painting course. It is held in what was once a stately home with extensive grounds, near the sea. It's midsummer, very hot. At the end of the first day, I go for a long evening walk, out of the grounds with their man-icured gardens and on to the downs, rolling away towards the English Channel. I talk to Paul all the time, telling him what I've been doing and asking him, as ever, where he is. I look sporadically for feathers, but each time I think I see one, I find that I'm deceived; there are many sheep grazing these green hills, and the white blobs I can see everywhere are little clumps of their wool. I'm nearing the end of my walk, the great house in sight at the bottom of the slope in front of me, when a mass of white feathers is suddenly there on the grass, right in my path, right before my eyes. I smile. I say to Paul, 'Oh so you were here then, after all.'

I think to myself again that there must be a reason why I see these feathers now, but not when my mother or close friends died; why some people see robins and barn owls and others don't. I return to the notion that there must be something about the *strength* of the attachment to the dead person that influences whether or not these sensory experiences occur. From talking to Margaret, I've understood a lot more about the strength of my attachment to Paul, how much I depended on him to keep me secure and meet my emotional needs, particularly when a sense of security and emotional responsiveness had been lacking in my childhood. Paul always stood up for me, he helped me to believe in myself, he loved me and showed it. No wonder I still need a sensory thread to cling to, something to give me comfort as I negotiate the rocky path to separation. I think too about Julian Barnes' passionate writing about the strength and quality of his attachment to his wife – no wonder he dreamed about her after she died. The strength of my little sister's attachment to her son goes without saying – no wonder there were dreams, robins, wood smoke. The people in my survey who reported feathers, trees falling, magpies and so on, all had feelings of intense loss when their loved ones died. There is no way to bear the severing of a strong attachment, perhaps particularly when it is untimely, so the sensory thread becomes the way. It is the lifeline to the dead. Where the attachment is less strong, and perhaps when the death is long anticipated, no sensory thread is necessary. So, my father anticipated my mother's death and was able to process it adequately without recourse to feathers or barn owls or dreams; my attachments to my mother and brother-in-law were not of the same order as my attachment to Paul, and I just didn't need a sensory thread to cling on to.

*

Things have been going pretty well for quite a while. I've managed the not inconsiderable life events of retiring and moving to a new house, and much of the time I feel that I'm adapting quite well to my new and different life. I will never stop missing and wanting Paul, and I can never go back to being the person I was before he died, but I'm learning to live without him. Margaret's involvement has been useful: she has supported me in overcoming my self-doubt and my fears, and in helping me to make sense of my loss in the context of my particular family history. I haven't felt suicidal or even particularly depressed for ages now, so I decide that I can stop seeing Margaret; after all, I won't be standing properly on my own two feet if I'm still coming to talk to her every week. I think I'm ready to make the break and I tell her so. What's more, I've arranged a holiday in September, when air fares are cheaper, just after she has taken her month-long summer break, so I'll have six or seven weeks to get used to not seeing her.

I tell Margaret all of this and I'm surprised by her reaction. She doesn't agree or disagree with me, but points out that the ending of therapy will be another big loss. This time I have a chance to face it, to do it properly, to work through my feelings about it rather than being faced with another catastrophe. I need to be careful not to avoid it – by being away, or by cancelling sessions – or to trivialise it. What she says sounds sensible, but I don't really *feel* that it will be such a big loss and I don't change my plans to fly out to Crete to stay with my old friend who has a house there. This will be the only time I've been on a plane by myself; another first.

CHAPTER EIGHT

Ups and Downs

*The power of working in the here-and-now is what
distinguishes psychodynamic psychotherapy from
friendship and from other, more superficial forms
of therapy and counselling, which tend to focus on
the there-and-now (i.e. outside life) rather than the
relationship between therapist and client.*

IRVIN D. YALOM,
Staring at the Sun: Overcoming the Dread of Death

Over the summer, something unexpected happens. I'm in
John Lewis one day looking for a new kettle, when I bump
into a man whom I've known for years but haven't seen
for a long time. I spot him striding towards the tills with a
toaster under one arm. His name is Charles and we were at
university together. He was a medical student and he was
going out with one of my friends. I've seen him occasionally
over the years at weddings and university reunions, but I
have no idea what he's doing here – as far as I know, he lives
in Northumberland. We chat for ages and I find out that he
has just got a consultant post in the nearby hospital where I
worked for eighteen years. He's divorced, living in hospital
accommodation and doesn't know many people in the area.

He asks if I'd like to go out for a drink one evening and I readily agree: there's lots to catch up on and he has always been good fun. We go to a tiny pub in the country and sit at an outside table for hours, talking and laughing until it begins to get cold. He suggests dinner, but the pub doesn't have any food. He apologises, says that he feels bad about asking someone out on a date and then not being able to get anything to eat. I register the use of the word 'date', but make no comment. We drive to another pub where we can get food, and then he drops me at home. I examine my reactions. I like him a lot and I can see that he's quite attractive, but I don't really regard him 'like that'; he seems more like a brother than a potential boyfriend.

I go off to Crete and he texts me several times. My girlfriend is extremely curious and wants to know all about him and what I think his intentions are. I honestly don't know. When I get back to England, Charles and I go to the theatre, and then the cinema, and then he goes off on holiday for two weeks. The night before he leaves, he asks if I want to go with him. I can't, but he texts me virtually every day. I'm confused. I haven't done proper 'dating' – if that is what this is – for many years. He hasn't really said anything that leads me to believe that he's interested in me as a potential girlfriend. On his way back from holiday, he texts and invites me to the cinema again, to a performance that starts a couple of hours after he gets off the plane. He seems keen to see me, and I find myself going out and buying new skinny jeans and a leather jacket. After the cinema, we have coffee and then he drives me back to where my car is parked. This time, there is no mistaking his intentions. He kisses me ardently and asks if I want to come back to his hospital accommodation. I don't – I want to think about what is happening – but I feel exhilarated in a way I haven't for years as I drive home along the motorway.

I make a small attempt to tell Margaret, but I don't say much. I feel superstitious; if I make this out to be something big, then it will turn out to be nothing. There's also something about how 'straight' she is that makes me think she might disapprove, or be hard to talk to about a potential relationship.

My exhilaration quickly turns to confusion and anxiety as a pattern begins to emerge. Every pleasant evening with Charles is followed by him backing off. Sometimes I don't hear from him for days (he says he's working hard), and he disappears for weekends and sometimes whole weeks with no explanation. But the next time I see him, he's his usual extroverted self and behaves as if nothing has happened. However, I do begin to notice that, although he makes all the right noises when I tell him about Paul's death and my life as a widow, he doesn't really seem interested. He talks incessantly about himself: his work, his children, his friends and his many glittering achievements; in fact, he has many of the features of a Drain. I often feel that he's putting on a show (for my benefit or his?), selecting just the right CD to play in the car, leaving just the right newspaper on the back seat, arriving fashionably – but not rudely – late. Then one day, he tells me that he needs a partner to accompany him to a posh work do, and asks if I'll go with him. I say yes. I'm scared, but also excited at the prospect of meeting some of his colleagues, and pleased that he wants to take our friendship into a social setting. I buy some strappy sandals with heels and put on a smart black dress and a brave face. I needn't have worried. His colleagues are lovely, I have no difficulty at all joining in with the conversation and I feel that the evening goes very well. Afterwards, we drive back to his accommodation and he invites me in for coffee. This, inevitably, is when the seduction takes place. I haven't spent the night with a man for almost seven years, and ironically, it's the night that the clocks go back. Early next morning, as he drives to work and I catch a train home, I feel unexpectedly happy; perhaps, after all, it may be possible to have another relationship, to love and be loved in return.

I should have trusted my initial instincts. After this, Charles backs off big time and is suddenly working all hours of the day and night. I'm hurt and mystified and ask if we can meet for dinner to talk about what's going on. He texts (yes, *texts*) to say that he's enjoying our friendship, but feels that I want much, much more. I'm furious – absolutely mad with him. How dare he put the blame on me and take advantage of my situation? I feel outraged, humiliated, exasperated.

I try to calm myself down and think back to other relationships I have had in the past: after all, I have been a psychologist for over thirty years and I do know that old patterns tend to repeat themselves. I have enough insight left to realise that I've fallen straight into the old trap, dating back to my teens and twenties, of being attracted to precisely the wrong kind of man: the kind who is attentive, successful, good-looking, who will work hard to reel me in, but be completely insensitive to whatever I might want from the relationship. (Indeed, I discover later that Charles had a girlfriend all along, who lived several hundred miles away, but he somehow never got around to mentioning her.) In trying to meet my own needs, something that Margaret is always banging on about, I have managed to do the complete opposite and sabotage them. I thought I needed a man like Charles, but in fact he was most definitely not the sort of man I really needed.

A good friend, who also happens to be a psychotherapist, makes this crystal clear over supper in Prezzo's: 'What he did is nothing to do with you. He's a narcissist. He doesn't see *you*; he doesn't know you. He only sees himself. He groomed you, sensing your vulnerability.'

She's right. I read in an article somewhere that, on the one and only occasion when Freud met Virginia Woolf, he presented her with a narcissus flower. I would dearly love to present Charles with one now, although I suspect that the symbolism would be lost on him. Come to think of it, it would be an appropriate present for my first serious boyfriend too; with his literary background, he might actually understand the message, even if he wouldn't appreciate it.

(Years later, I would reflect a lot more on the toxic combination of Charles's narcissism and my vulnerability. Of course the widowed are emotionally vulnerable, being starved of the affection and support of a loving relationship, and hence more likely to be susceptible to misjudgements about the attentions of unsuitable men. One striking and tragic example of where this can lead is the murder of the widowed author Helen Bailey by a manipulative predator who exploited her vulnerability to his own advantage.)

Walking up to Margaret's side door for my next session, I feel nervous. She greets me with her usual nod and goes to sit in her chair. As usual she says nothing, but waits for me to speak first, and today I find this intimidating. I try to talk to her about Charles, but I find it very difficult. It's humiliating to be rejected, and I don't feel comfortable about presenting myself in such a bad light, as someone who could make such a massive and stupid error of judgement. But whenever I do try to broach the subject, she links it with my decision to end therapy.

– It takes bravery and self-confidence to explore the possibilities of a new relationship without becoming hung up or needy or desperate. I'm wondering whether you're actually feeling desperate about coming to the end of therapy, whether you thought you could ride off into the sunset with a new man to talk to and not need a therapist any more?

This strikes me as being rubbish and I tell her so.

– It's nothing to do with ending therapy. I thought I'd found somebody to have a relationship with and now I feel humiliated.

She's like a dog with a bone.

– You've done a lot of work on building up your confidence and belief in yourself. You didn't need a partner before. I think you're bringing this here because you feel desperate about ending with me.

This just makes me angry. I feel she's not listening to me – I want to talk about what has happened with Charles and she wants to talk about my decision to end therapy. For weeks, I grow more and more silent and sit sullenly in my armchair, avoiding eye contact and refusing to say a word. All of my thoughts are negative. I hate her. She's useless. She doesn't understand me. She doesn't want to listen to what I care about. I want her to say something to make me feel better and she doesn't say it. I'm furious with her. She drives a rubbish green car; green, for God's sake? She wears frumpy shoes. How could I possibly talk about sex, anyway, to somebody who wears frumpy shoes? This goes on and on and I fantasise often, and seriously, about either walking out or not turning up at all.

– I'm fed up with coming here. I'm not getting anywhere any more and I haven't for ages. I'm sick of talking about Paul and my mother all the time because they're both dead and it's depressing.

She considers this.

– I think there's something important here about your relationship with women. It's very difficult for you to allow a woman to give you something that's good. If you rubbish therapy and rubbish me you can leave without any sense of loss, without taking anything good from the relationship.

I'm quick to contradict her.

– Of course I'm not rubbishing therapy. Why do you think I've been coming all this time? I just don't think it's working any more.

What she says next stuns me.

– I don't see much evidence of you having a real interest in psychotherapy, of thinking about what we talk about between sessions, of *you* making an effort to work. I feel denigrated by the way you tell me that it's all my fault, that I have nothing to offer.

I'm stung by this criticism. Afterwards, I *do* think about the session and I realise that I have been expecting her to 'rescue' me, to say some magic words that will suddenly make everything better. I see at once the parallel with my relationship with Mum: I felt criticised by her, for not doing the right thing, for not being a nice person, and I felt angry, resentful and sulky in return.

Next session I pluck up the courage to say: I thought you were very critical of me last time, when you said that there was little evidence of me working between sessions, and that you felt denigrated by me. I thought you were really nasty.

My heart is pounding at my daring to be so rude. I'm expecting her to be furious, or at the very least to get back at me. Instead she is silent for a while, and then she speaks.

– You have survived your mother in me.

*

Afterwards, I think that this seems important: a turning point. I've kept on coming when it has felt really difficult. My mother was only supportive when I was good, when she approved of what I did, but Margaret hasn't stopped being there for me despite my rude and uncommunicative behaviour. As the psychotherapist Valery Hazanov puts it, niceness and politeness are killers of intimacy, in psychotherapy and elsewhere. Even the most unpleasant emotions are part of psychotherapy: it should never be lukewarm. Margaret doesn't validate or praise me for my achievements as other people do, but accepts me, warts and all. It has taken a long time, but I'm beginning to trust her in a way that I never trusted Jocelyn, and this means being able to show her my less attractive qualities.

There's something else that I've noticed about Margaret. Instead of concentrating on what's going on in my life outside or even my childhood, she now keeps homing in on what is actually going on in the room between her and me. Whatever issue I bring up, she uses it to navigate us into the here and now of the therapy session. She used not to do this, and to begin with, it seems strange and uncomfortable and I want to resist it, as with the impasse we reached over ending therapy. But I can also see that it might yield results.

Soon afterwards, I have a dream that my four-month-old baby is critically ill. She needs open-heart surgery. A

woman surgeon comes who is going to perform the operation. The baby is white, hardly breathing. In another scene,
the baby is a little girl with long blonde hair, wanting to run
and play with the other girls, but unable to keep up. After
the operation, she is fine.

Margaret is very interested in this dream. I tell her that
I'm sure I am the little girl with long blonde hair. She asks
whether I have any more thoughts about it.

I find myself saying: I think it could be a metaphor for
therapy – the lifeline that I need, provided by a woman, to
come alive again.

I'm pleased; I feel that I 'get' something about the
process of therapy which I hadn't understood before. It
also occurs to me that Jocelyn worked very differently. Her
interest was in what was going on in my life outside, and
she never once commented on my relationship with her,
nor on the fact that my seeing her was precipitated by the
loss of Jennifer. There was nothing wrong with Jocelyn's
therapy: she was supportive, but it felt superficial, just like
the relationships with the internet men. The big difference
with Margaret is that I *am actually feeling*, rather than just
talking about feelings.

Then I have a dream about Paul. I dream that he's
holding me and my children prisoners in a dark house,
and he has a gun. Only I am allowed to open the front
door. A woman knocks and forces her way in, saying: 'Is
there something going on here that I should be concerned
about?' I try to reassure her that everything is OK, that
I'm just here with my family. She leaves, and part of me
hopes that she'll call the police. But another part of me is
terrified that Paul will now kill me for letting her in. I'm so
frightened that I wake myself up, and keep myself awake

by turning on the bedside light and distracting myself with a book.

Margaret asks me to say how I feel about Paul in the dream.

– I don't know. It scares me. I hardly ever dream about Paul, and this is the first negative dream that I've had about him.

– I wonder whether you do feel imprisoned by Paul? By his memory? By his death? Perhaps you want to break away, but you're not sure how?

– But why am I so terrified in the dream?

– Perhaps it's very frightening to think about letting go of him. But you might be able to find a way of escaping with the help of a woman?

I think back to the internet dates and how much they were influenced by my continuing attachment to Paul. No wonder the dating felt so disloyal to him.

Months later, Ariel Sharon dies. He went into a coma the month before Paul died, and had been in this coma for eight years. I've often thought about his family, keeping watch over him, wondering whether he would wake up. Margaret likens their vigil, over now, to my own silent vigil for Paul. Keeping close to his death is a way of staying close to him, but I'm denying myself the chance to be alive, to live my own life.

My birthday falls in the same month as the anniversary of Paul's death. A friend brings me a bunch of snowdrops picked from her garden. Of course she doesn't know it, but snowdrops always remind me of the harrowing scene at the funeral parlour, when I was unable to put the bunch from our garden into Paul's frozen hand. Margaret is struck by this connection.

—A gift that you couldn't give because of stiffness and coldness, which made you feel unwanted, unloved. This is a very strong metaphor in your life, it touches something very deep.

I know. I see it now. It's so sad.

*

There's something wrong with Jess. Her walking is becoming slower and slower, and a couple of times recently she's lain down in the middle of the field, or the road, or wherever we happen to be, and I've had to pull her back up again. Today I take her for a walk down the hill, and on the way back, she lies down on the pavement and simply won't get up. Every time I help her into a standing position, she just flops down again. There's nothing for it: I'll have to carry her home. She's a big dog, and people stare. One kind lady driving past stops and winds down her window and asks if she can help, but by then I'm nearly home. Jess perks up when we get inside and I decide not to ring the vet because I'm worried about what he might say. Next day I take her for a very short walk to the end of our road, but she can hardly put one paw in front of the other. When we get back inside the house, she flops down on the doormat, and this time she can't get up. I ring the vet and he tells me to bring her in. He knows her well, and he says that if she can't walk inside, he will come out to the car park and carry her.

When I park at the surgery, I open the boot, where Jess is lying, and sit on the edge to keep her company while we wait for the vet. As I'm sitting there, an extraordinary thing happens. There's a lamp post on a traffic island in the middle of the road immediately outside the vets, and a car drives straight into it. There's an enormous crash, followed by the sound of shattering glass, which brings all the vets and nurses running out to see what has happened. (Is it a warning? Like the 7/7 bombs?) The vet carries Jess into his consulting room and listens to her heart.

He looks at me. 'I think it's time,' he says. 'We could embark on a long and expensive programme of trying to keep her going for a bit longer, but she's old, she's had a long life.'

I know he's right, but how can I be the one to make the decision to condemn her to death?

'You're not. *Nobody* could have looked after this dog better than you have. You're doing the kindest thing you can to let her go now, before she suffers any more pain.'

I tell him that I've never done this before, that all of the many cats in my life had died natural deaths, or were hit by cars. He explains that he'll give her a sedative to make her sleepy and then give her the lethal injection. A nurse comes in to assist him, and that is exactly what happens. It looks as though Jess is sleeping on the table in front of me, just like Paul in the ambulance. The vet listens to her heart again and says: 'She's gone.' I burst into tears and start to kiss her fur without even thinking about what I'm doing. The vet is tactful and says he'll leave me with her for a while. I hug her and kiss her more, far more than I hugged or kissed Paul after he died, but this time there are no paramedics watching. After a while, the vet comes back and asks if I'd like one of the nurses to drive me home. I say I'll be fine, and he shows me out through the back door to the car park. (Isn't that interesting? I hadn't noticed that vets' surgeries have back doors before. It's just like at the funeral directors', with their heavy net curtains shielding the 'viewing room' from any members of the public who might walk past, and the back road where the hearses come and go, and the hospital mortuary: unseen, unlabelled. People try to make death invisible, even when they're dealing with it on a daily basis.)

Amazingly, I'm fine. I'm comforted by the thought that Jess is with Paul and that he will look after her now. As I walk to the car, I'm thinking back to the moment when the vet injected Jess, and I wonder whether Paul has found her yet. Just as I have this thought, a tiny white feather floats down in front of me.

I give Jess's bed and the leftover dog food to my dad, and when her ashes are returned a couple of weeks later, I scatter them on the pond in the New Forest where Paul's were scattered eight years earlier. I notice that the water lily which I put in 'Paul's end' of the pond last year has taken root and is flowering. I'm very pleased about this.

I find myself saying to Margaret: 'It occurs to me that out of death, it's possible to find new growth.'

*

I suddenly decide to stick all the photos from the past eight years into albums. I haven't been able to face this since Paul died, but now I find that I can and I enjoy it, sharing many of the memories with my daughter. The piles of albums and photos are on the kitchen table for weeks.

Margaret likens this to a new phase in psychotherapy: I'm beginning to be able to organise some of the 'mess' of the past, to think more positively about the memories, to feel more alive. I go out for lunch one day with an ex-colleague who has become a friend since we both retired. We're sitting in the café of a garden centre and we're talking about the area where she lives. It turns out that she used to know Jennifer; in fact, their children shared lifts to school. I mention that Jennifer used to be my therapist, and that I know she moved back to her home country. My friend is undeterred by this revelation; indeed, the piece of gossip she's about to reveal will be even more fascinating with both of us knowing the person concerned.

'Yes, she went back home – created quite a scandal in the village.'

'Really?'

'Mmm, she went off to live with a man she met on the internet. She was dating him for a while, going backwards and forwards' – *Don't I know it!* – 'and then she packed up and left altogether.'

What? She abandoned me for an internet date? How COULD she? But of course I don't say this. There was no dying relative, then, but escape in pursuit of a man, presumably a prince and not a frog. While she was warning me off internet dating, she was actually doing it herself! I'm so glad I didn't know this at the time, because it would have left me feeling even more devastated to think that she could leave me for such a trivial reason. It also makes me realise how preoccupied I was with death: naturally, I assumed she had a dying relative; I thought about nothing but death, twenty-four-seven. The fact that I actually knew nothing about her real life simply exposed my own fantasies and concerns. I do feel deeply annoyed, though: it doesn't seem like a very ethical way to behave towards a patient who has felt suicidal when faced with abandonment and loss.

That night, I dream that my psychotherapist friend (the one who exposed Charles as a narcissist) has something seriously wrong with her. She has to have a tracheostomy (an operation performed through the front of the neck to open a blocked trachea, the tube that carries air from the throat to the lungs), and I'm trying to talk to her about it, but there are other people in the room who seem oblivious or insensitive to the fact that anything is the matter.

Margaret asks me what I'm feeling in the dream, and I reply at once that it is acute anxiety. She and I have been talking again about whether I'm going to continue with therapy, and she links this discussion with the feeling in the dream.

– The decision to carry on with therapy is risky, difficult. Therapy, like a tracheostomy, is a lifeline for the mind. It seems you are worried that something might happen to me. After all, you have lost many people, including a previous therapist.

Therapy *is* difficult. No psychotherapist is ever going to produce the magic words that will make everything clear, make everything better. It is I who must make an effort to engage, bring material, think between sessions, make a commitment, do the work, and change. The work is hard, but as I grapple with it, I notice that I'm learning from the process itself. There is no obvious 'goal' as there would be in a clinical psychology treatment programme; rather, engaging with Margaret, week after week, in that rather strange time and space that demarcates the psychotherapy hour, is what seems to bring about change. The process still feels unnatural, and I have many moments of doubt, when I wonder whether the passage of time alone would have resulted in similar changes, but for now I keep on going. It's a predictable slot in the week that keeps me grounded.

*

As summer arrives again, Emily reminds me that next weekend we're going to do the Great North Swim. This seemed like a good idea six months ago in the depths of winter, when we were looking at pictures of Cumbria on her laptop in the comfort of our cosy kitchen, so she signed us both up and paid the entrance fee. The prospect now seems daunting. We've elected to swim a mile in Lake Windermere, in open water, wearing wetsuits, along with 30,000 other people, to raise money for charity. Naturally, I take my anxieties to Margaret (will I be too old/too slow/ unable to keep up? Will I get cramp? etc., etc.) but there is no going back, and anyway, Emily is keen.

We travel up to the Lake District by train and a charming Polish taxi driver takes us to the B & B we've booked. Our hostess greets us with the news that a man in his fifties died doing the swim earlier that day. He was airlifted to hospital, but despite their best efforts, the paramedics were unable to save him.

Our swim is to take place the next day. I find it hard to sleep following the news about the dead man, who was undoubtedly somebody's husband, and even harder to touch the full English breakfast of local produce that is put in front of us the following morning. We walk the three miles to Windermere and emerge from the peace of the fells into the frenetic razzamatazz of the lakeside; traffic jams everywhere, crowds of people in various states of undress, bunting, loudhailers blaring, fast food at every turn. It certainly isn't going to be the peaceful open-water swim that we'd both anticipated, but we're committed now and so we elbow our way to the giant marquees which serve as changing tents. Have you ever tried to squeeze your body into a wetsuit in a boiling hot tent surrounded by hundreds of other sweaty women who are similarly occupied? It's not easy. A website that I had looked at earlier (having never worn a wetsuit before) said that your arms and legs will go in better if you put a carrier bag over them first. I've come equipped with two bags from the Co-op and one from Waitrose. For this particular purpose, the Co-op bags prove to be more reliable, as the Waitrose one splits almost at once.

It's a great relief to get out into the fresh air again, but a pity that we didn't think to hire any of the rubber shoes that other, more seasoned, open-water swimmers are wearing, because it's painful negotiating the stony path to the starting area in bare feet. We're placed in a 'holding pen' with the other 298 swimmers in our 'wave', all wearing identical bright yellow swimming caps. After doing a few warm-up exercises to some very loud disco music, the klaxon blares and we're off. Emily is a good swimmer and can go much faster than me, but she knows that I'm anxious, and she promises to stay with me for as long as I want. In the event, I quickly discover that it is, after all, possible to swim in the constraining wetsuit, and I tell her to go ahead; I'll be fine.

I start to swim my usual breast stroke, which involves putting my face in the water, but it's a murky brown colour and I don't like it at all. I swim with my head above the water instead, but this hurts my neck and I quickly get out of breath. I start to panic. I haven't even reached the first giant plastic buoy yet, and I calculate that there must be at least twenty of them marking out the one-mile course. There are safety canoes with marshals in them all along the route, and I'm just about to swim over to one when I stop myself. *This is ridiculous*, I tell myself. *It's only sixty-four lengths of the swimming pool. You know you can do that. You do it every week.* So why am I exhausted after only a couple of hundred yards? *You have to swim your normal stroke. Forget about the dirty water and pretend you're in the swimming pool.* This is positive self-talk. I was always encouraging my patients to use it, and now I have a chance to put it to the test. To my huge relief, it works. I get into the rhythm of my normal stroke, closing my eyes periodically when the murk gets too much, and before too long, I reach the halfway mark at the end of the lake.

The second half of the course presents further challenges. I can see that I'm near the back of the yellow-cap wave, and soon we are overtaken by bright pink caps swimming fast front crawl. These people are from the pink wave, which set off half an hour after we did. It's very discouraging. I decide to stick close to a small group of middle-aged yellow caps who are swimming at about the same pace as me. They are being encouraged by a young lady in green goggles, who is swimming on her back with her head out of the water and chatting to them. I don't know if she's a marshal or just another swimmer, but I find her presence reassuring.

As we near the finish line, I start to get cramp in one leg; it hurts like hell, but I'm determined to keep going. I swim on my back, on my front, on my back again, trying to relax, and eventually, mercifully, I cross the line and haul myself out of the water. I'm exhausted and exhilarated in equal measure. Emily has been waiting for twenty minutes, but she's delighted (and relieved) that I've made it. We collect our medals and a goody bag each, and munch our way through a whole packet of cereal bars, washed down with mugs of hot chocolate.

When I give Margaret my account of the swim the

following week, it proves to be a fertile source of material for us to work on. There is my horror at the middle-aged man's death and the obvious connection with Paul's death after swimming. I tell Margaret that just before the start, my heart was thumping so hard that I didn't know if I would be able to swim at all. She considers the relevance of the palpitating heart.

– In Paul's case, it was heart disease. In your case, it is fear. I wonder whether you have concerns about your own mortality?

She's right about that: from the outset, I was secretly worried about the wisdom of undertaking a swim like this at my age.

Then there is the murky brown water of the lake. Psychiatrist and psychotherapist Irvin Yalom writes that: 'Diving into deep water not uncommonly symbolises the act of diving into the depths of one's unconscious,' and Margaret, too, makes much of this analogy.

– I wonder whether you want to explore further into the murky depths in therapy, or just go on 'coping'? … I wonder whether you are frightened of what you might uncover if you look under the surface? Perhaps it is easier to skim the surface than to look underneath, where you can't see where you're going?

All of this makes sense in the context of our discussions about whether – or when – to end therapy. We have also been talking about whether Emily, now in her late twenties, should move out. She's come back to live with me for the time being, as she has a job near home. Margaret links this with my account of the swim.

– You want to let your daughter go. It seems you don't want to hold her back. But you are also worried about whether you will manage OK without her.

Then she asks: When your daughter goes, is there anyone else who can guide you? Can I?

For some reason, I think immediately of the girl with the green goggles and tell Margaret again how reassuring I found her presence towards the end of the swim. Then I realise that I have answered her question. I smile. She smiles back.

– Even down to the goggles, she says.

(Margaret wears glasses!)

A few weeks later, and I've broken my ankle. My left leg is in plaster up to the knee and I have to walk with crutches. The break happened when I was alone, many miles away, and I had to drive myself to the hospital and later, when my leg had been plastered, hire an automatic car so that I could get home. I felt desperately lonely, and the night before going to the fracture clinic, I found myself missing Mum and sobbing in a way that I hadn't done at all in the more than seven years since she died. I tell Margaret this when I see her two days later. I cry throughout the session. Margaret thinks it's significant that I miss Mum when I'm ill.

– When you are a patient and your mother is the doctor, you have something to offer each other.

It doesn't escape my notice that I am Margaret's patient, too, and indeed, she makes this link. I then tell her that the main reason I hired the car was so that I would be able to drive to see her today; that it was important for me to get here.

She says: I think this is a real turning point. At last you are thinking about your own needs.

*

Back in the real world of running a home and managing children and animals, the neighbour's cat is wreaking havoc in our house. He is Jasper, a scrawny tabby, and he's been wandering in for several days now. Generally, he stands in the kitchen looking bewildered and yowling, until I give him some milk. The neighbour says, with a shrug of his shoulders, that Jasper is dementing. I can hardly complain, since our own Fatcat, a huge ball of white fur with a meow inside it, visits their house regularly, whenever he fancies a second dinner. I tolerate Jasper for several days, and even begin to grow fond of him, until I notice that dark patches are appearing on the mat inside the front door. Then one morning, I pick up the wetsuit that I wore for the Great North Swim from my bedroom floor, and find that it's soaked in a stinking yellow liquid that runs off on to my hands and the carpet. I scream, hurl the wetsuit into the bath, and text Em.

'Jasper's weed all over my wetsuit!'

She's at work, and busy. 'Shut him out, then.'

'He can get in through the cat flap.'

'Block the cat flap.'

'Then Fatty can't get in.'

'Get a magnetic cat flap.'

I can sense her exasperation. But she's right, it's a sensible solution, so I drive (still with my leg in plaster) to Pets at Home, and select a cat flap that will only open to a cat wearing the correct magnet on its collar. I'm determined to fit it myself: I have Paul's old toolbox in the airing cupboard, along with his drill, and there are instructions inside the box. I talk to Paul.

'I'm sure I can do it; you'll help me, won't you?'

The first problem is getting the old cat flap off. I manage

to get three of the long screws out fairly easily, but the fourth screw's head is 'blown'. I simply can't get the hand-held screwdriver to grip on to it. I read the instructions for the drill, and realise that it doubles up as an electric screwdriver. Surely this will be able to exert more force than my hand? I try it, but it doesn't work: it won't grip, either. Then I notice that there's a small nut holding the screw in place on the other side of the door: if I can get this off, I think I will be able to loosen the screw manually. The drill has a fitting for loosening nuts, so I try this, but it doesn't work; perhaps I've chosen the wrong-sized piece to fit in the drill – but how on earth are you supposed to know which piece is the right size? By this point, it's starting to rain, I'm crouching on the wet ground outside the back door with my leg in plaster, and I'm stumped. I begin to panic, but swallow my pride and go and knock on my neighbour's door. There's no reply. I go across the road and knock on the door of another neighbour, who has been building his own conservatory, so must have good DIY skills. He's out, too. I think of a third neighbour who fixed his own roof after a spell of heavy rain, but then remember that he and his family have gone on holiday. There's nothing for it: I'll have to try again. I think about the positive self-talk that helped during the swim and say to myself: *Come on, it can't be that difficult to undo a screw. There must be a tool somewhere in the toolbox that will do it.* I appeal to Paul: 'I know you'd be able to do it; please help me now.' I search through the toolbox again, and in a compartment that I hadn't looked in before, I find a tiny spanner. I try this on the nut and it works. The nut loosens, I undo the screw, and the old cat flap is off.

I'm excited, now, as I take the shiny new cat flap out of its box. But my pleasure is erased when I find that it's too big for the hole in the door. I refer to the instructions, which tell me that I need a jigsaw. Luckily a picture of this is provided, and I know that I don't have one – in fact, I dimly recall throwing one away when I was clearing out the sheds in the old house. I go back to Paul's toolbox and find a small handsaw with a jagged blade. I think that this will probably do the job of shaving off the edge of the existing hole, and I find to my relief that it does. The hole I end up with has one edge with a rough, splintered surface, and it's not centred properly in the door panel, but the cat flap fits. The last thing I have to do is secure the flap to the door with the screws provided. The instructions tell me to mark in pencil the place where the holes are to be drilled. I break the lead in three different pencils before I conclude that any pencil is going to be too fat to fit through the holes in the cat flap. Then a picture of Paul using the drill itself to mark a position on a wall flashes into my mind. I try this, and the problem is solved. Finally, at last, I'm ready to drill the four holes in the back door. I work out, by trial and error, that masonry drill bits won't work in wood, and that there's a difference between hammer action (which I don't want) and drill action (which I do), and the holes are drilled. The cat flap is replaced, the screws are fitted and the job is done.

This whole enterprise has taken well over three hours. You might think that I'd be exhilarated at the end of it, proud of myself, but all I can do is cry. 'Why weren't you there to help me, Paul?'

There's something about using his tools that brings me very close to him again. I remember how tidy and organised he was: all his drill bits are lined up in the right order, and the spanners, hammers and screwdrivers are neatly arranged in different compartments of his toolbox. It has made this job easier for me, but remembering how he was makes me miss him so, so much. I think again of Stephen Grosz's contention that, for as long as the person who mourns goes on living, there is always the possibility of grief. For him, the notion of closure – of having finished with grief – is delusive. Living grief just cannot be permanently deadened.

But neither, it seems, can the sensory threads of comfort. The day after the cat flap nightmare, I decide to reward myself by buying a new barbecue. Although it's the end of the season, the weather is still very warm, and a friend has told me that you can get them at knock-down prices. So, I go to Homebase, find a bargain barbecue, and two delightful young men who agree to assemble and deliver it. The fact that my leg is still in plaster has undoubtedly helped in these negotiations, as the store doesn't usually deliver or assemble. As I hobble back to the car, I'm thinking about Paul: the last barbecue I bought was with him, more than ten years ago, and I tell him that he would like the new one, and it's a pity that he's not going to be around to try it out with me. As I approach the car boot to open it and deposit my crutches, I see that there is a tiny white feather clinging to the rear windscreen wiper. The knowledge that Paul hasn't *really* put it there doesn't diminish the sense of connection and comfort that it brings.

I don't tell Margaret about the cat flap because we are on a summer break of five weeks. I do remember telling her, not long before the break, about my son Will's PhD crisis. He has funding for three years, which is a rarity in these days of financial constraints, but he's not enjoying it: he feels very unsupported by his supervisor, and he's not sure that he wants to carry on. Margaret linked this with my concerns about continuing with therapy: would it be worthwhile? Would I get what I want out of it? Would I feel adequately supported? I think now about what I've gained so far, whether I've made progress. I came to therapy in the first place because I was so panicky and depressed following Paul's death. Psychoanalyst Alice Miller claims that: 'The true opposite of depression is neither gaiety nor absence of pain, but vitality – the freedom to experience spontaneous feelings.' I do believe that I have made some headway with this; I have learned that loss and separation have always been difficult for me, long before the catastrophic loss of Paul. I think about the strong sense of anxiety, gloom and desolation that pervaded so much of my childhood, and of the misery surrounding the losses that preceded Paul's death: my first serious boyfriend leaving me; the ending of other relationships, even if it was I who instigated the break-up. Paul's dying was the ultimate abandonment, followed swiftly by Mum dying and Jennifer leaving. Talking to Margaret has helped me to see this, and her support has helped me to take tentative steps forwards, and to pay more attention to my own needs. I may not be jumping for joy, but I do feel more alive. So why do I still have reservations? Even after all this time, I find the ritual of the 'fifty-minute hour' rigid and unnatural, and Margaret's silence at the beginning of each session disconcerting. I hardly ever look forward to my sessions with her. I know I can learn from her, but I feel very little attachment to her as a human being.

*

Returning from the summer break, I'm very annoyed with Margaret. To begin with, she has taken holiday in September rather than her usual August; and during the holiday, I sent her a cheque, but she mislaid it and sent me an apologetic note asking for a replacement. I hand the second cheque to her grudgingly as I enter her consulting room.

– Thank you. I'm sorry about mislaying the previous one.

– Yes, I was annoyed about that. In fact, I was pretty hurt. (I hear my voice breaking.)

– Oh? (Her eyebrows are raised.)

– Yes, I wondered what it meant. Why did you lose it? Is it because you're fed up with me? You'd like to get rid of me?

– You seem to be taking it very personally.

– Yes, well, why wouldn't I? After the last session, I sent you a long text, which I knew you wouldn't reply to, explaining why I thought you had shifted the goalposts about the break. You know I always go away for the first two weeks in August.

– So you're upset about the mismatch, about the fact that your break and mine didn't coincide?

– Yes. I'm sure you've *never* gone away in September before.

– Which is why I give plenty of notice.

– Yes, but that doesn't make any difference – I'd already booked the ferry.

– In *May*?

– Yes. The earlier you do it, the cheaper it is.

– You don't think I'm entitled to a break?

– It's not that. It's that you seemed to be suggesting that I was being difficult about coming in August, that *I* was lacking commitment, that it was my fault, when actually it

was you who changed the dates. That's why I think you're
fed up with me and you want to get rid of me.

– You seem to be taking it very personally, when it might
not have been just your cheque that was lost.

– Yes, but you're not going to tell me if there were others, are you?

– No. But the point is that *you* take it *personally*. You
jump straight to the conclusion that I'm fed up with you,
that I don't like you.

– Yes, I know, *blah blah blah*. We've been here before.
I think you're being nasty and critical of me, just like my
mother was. I *know* that, but I don't know where to go next
with it.

Margaret is thoughtful for a while, and then she says:
Self-knowledge? Self-awareness?

By halfway through the session, I feel better. I can lash
out at Margaret and she doesn't rise to the bait, but uses
what I say to try to understand something about how I
habitually react. And I'm aware, too, that she is responsive
to my needs: by putting out a stool for my broken ankle,
and by changing the day or time of our therapy session
to accommodate changes in my weekly timetable, for
instance. She provides me with safety and emotional care.
This is a different kind of mothering. I notice these things,
and I appreciate them, but the seeds of doubt won't go
away, either. I remember a time a few weeks ago when she
mistakenly referred to Paul as 'Alan'. I was horrified at the
time, but she glossed over it, apologising for having got in
a muddle. But then, a few sessions later, she repeated the
same mistake. Is she *really* listening to me? I once read an
interesting study which looked at how suicidal patients
communicate emotional pain, and whether professionals

are successful at receiving their communications. It found that patients feel depersonalised when professionals forget their personal details. By contrast, when their personal information is remembered, it's hugely impactful in patients feeling 'heard'. This resonates strongly with my own feelings about Margaret's forgetfulness. On another occasion, shortly before the break, Margaret finished my session fifteen minutes early, again by mistake. She phoned me on my way home to apologise, and said we could talk about it next time, but the topic was never raised again. So, does she *really* want to see me? I know I should raise these things with her, but I shy away from confrontation. It's difficult.

*

Time marches on, and the next anniversary of Paul's death coincides with my session with Margaret. I have been off antidepressants for over a year, and although there have been ups and downs, I've been getting on with my life and involving myself with lots of projects and people. On this day though, I can't stop crying.

I say to Margaret: I'm fed up with living a half-life.

Margaret says: You like half of it, but not the other half, of being bereaved, being a widow.

– Yes, I hate it. Paul promised he would never leave me.

– He knew you were vulnerable, but he made you a promise he couldn't keep. I think this taps right into your terror of being abandoned, a very early fear, something that goes right back to when you were a young child.

So here we are again, back with this theme that keeps on coming up.

CHAPTER NINE

Impasse

Academic and practitioner conferences are like fashion shows: therapy models are presented by emphasising the benefits, without mentioning their limitations.

MIRANDA WOLPERT AND
TONY ROUSMANIERE,
Talking Failure in Therapy and Beyond

There is more abandonment to come. For months, Dad has been slowing down, physically and mentally. Em and I decide to go down to Devon for the weekend of Mothering Sunday. Dad is now ninety-one. He's a bit slow on his feet and forgetful, but he's eating well and still walking every day – in fact, he insists on taking us for a walk and, instead of sticking to the lanes and footpaths, he launches out across the fields and through the woods, hacking away with his scythe at any vegetation that hinders our progress. Back at his home, we work our way through piles of general knowledge crosswords, bequeathed to him daily by one of his neighbours, and littered across the kitchen table. Mum would be horrified if she knew that we simply push this pile to the end of the table to make room for the plates at meal-times. But it is to Mum that my thoughts turn on Sunday, and I find that I'm thinking of her fondly, and missing her. I gather an armful of daffodils from the back garden and take them to her grave in the churchyard next to the house.

Over the next few weeks, my sister Annie reports a slow, downhill course. I notice that Dad never phones me any more, and that when I phone him, he's often breathless from getting himself out into the hallway, and can't think of anything to tell me about his daily life. I feel that the father I know is slowly receding, and yet he still has the tenacity to carry on with living independently, going for walks and voicing strong opinions about politics and current affairs. Then my sister reports a sudden deterioration – Dad has stopped taking any medication, is eating very little and can only walk as far as the church next door. A rare visit to his GP suggests that he may have intestinal cancer, but he refuses to have any further tests or treatment. When I next go down to see him, I'm shocked by the change in his appearance – he's asleep in his chair when I arrive, and he's thin and sallow – but he perks up a lot when he sees me and we spend the weekend doing more crosswords and watching TV, though he sleeps through everything except *Dad's Army*. The crossword activity, too, is becoming unproductive, as by now Dad has significant retrieval problems. I can see that an answer is often on the tip of his tongue, and I find myself holding back and willing it to come to him, but it seldom does. Then, suddenly he will exclaim 'Borodino!' or 'Oxymoron!' in response to a clue that came up half an hour ago. I can tell that this is exceedingly frustrating for him, and it feels to me as though he himself is gradually slipping out of reach, just like the elusive crossword solutions.

Margaret's attitude, when I tell her about Dad, is one of concern and kindness. She says she is very sorry, and asks me how I'm feeling. I say I'm distracted. I thought I'd lost my towel the last time I went for a swim, and sent my friend Jane down to lost property to look for it, only to realise as the swing door banged behind her that it was wrapped around me. I also tell Margaret that I'm scared of sleeping in Dad's house alone with him, in case he dies in the night. But that is an awful thought.

Margaret says: I'm glad you had it, because it's a selfish thought. You're thinking about your own needs.

Emily has always been very fond of her grandad, and she's determined to see him before she goes away for the summer, so the next time I see Dad, it is with her. It's Father's Day, and we take him cards. Mine is the sentimental sort of card that I would never normally buy, expressing gratitude for help and support over the years and pride at being my father's daughter. These are things which seem impossible to say to a man who never talks about feelings, and yet I want to express them, so I let the card do it for me. Em's is a sparkly card with a Snoopy-like character on the front proclaiming: 'Everybody thinks they've got the best grandad in the world…' and inside '…but I'm the only one who's right!' Dad is amused by this, and he seems touched by both the cards. He says, perhaps jokingly, perhaps not, 'I think I might cry,' and asks us to put the cards on the dressing table at the end of his bed where he can see them.

The rest of the weekend is difficult. Dad isn't getting dressed any more, and he's hardly eating. Em is distressed, and Dad is angry and cantankerous. I toast him half a muffin for breakfast and cut it into four tiny pieces, but he eats only one. Annie and I help him to sit himself up in bed, and he shouts and swears at us. Dad has never liked being fussed over, but the sight of the person he was slipping further and further away is hard to witness. He manages to shuffle into the conservatory in his pyjamas to join us for lunch and is violently sick. He insists on going outside into the garden, but has to give up after four or five paces. His constant refrain is: 'This is awful, awful.' We hear this on and off during the night, through the thin wall separating his bedroom from ours. When we drive off at the end of the weekend, Em is sobbing; she knows she will never see him again.

I describe this weekend to Margaret in a matter-of-fact way, and again she tells me how sorry she is. I tell her that Emily is upset, and accuses me of having no feelings, because she has been crying and I haven't.

Margaret asks: I wonder where your feelings are?

– I don't know. I think Paul's death inoculated me against ever feeling anything again, it was so awful.

– I sometimes feel close to tears when you talk about your father. Emotions don't keep appointments. They come unbidden.

Much later, I will reflect on how right she was about this.

After a few days, Annie texts to say she has had a dreadful night with no sleep and Dad in a state of constant agitation. I get straight into the car. When I arrive in Devon late that night, Dad is propped up in bed, hiccuping uncontrollably, but very pleased to see me. I settle myself on the bed beside him with a bottle of beer and take his hand. He doesn't let go, and every now and again he squeezes my fingers, very gently. I don't think I've ever held Dad's hand before, and it feels magical, like a spell I don't want to be broken. Of course, it is broken, but only after more than an hour, when the phone rings. It's the out-of-hours nurses, saying that they've managed to get hold of the medication we need for Dad's hiccups, and asking if we can come and collect it from Bideford, almost an hour's drive away. And so I set off in the car again, along eerie, unlit roads in the deep countryside, and I get lost and have to ask a police officer for directions, but eventually I end up in an Asda car park in an out-of-town shopping centre, where an NHS car has been waiting for me for some time. When I get back with the drugs, Dad is asleep, so my sister and I make tea and eat half a packet of chocolate brownies; we both feel an overwhelming need for something comforting and sweet. By 4.30 a.m., Dad is awake again, shouting, swearing and hiccupping. We manage to conceal the new medication in a spoonful of yogurt, which he takes, but it makes no difference. Throughout the day, he alternates between periods of sleep, when we rush around doing washing and shopping and making phone calls, and wakeful agitation, when we do our best to make him comfortable. It reminds me of listening out for the baby alarm when the children were tiny.

The next day, a lovely young carer comes from the hospice and washes Dad, and shows us how to turn him, clean him and change the sheets on his bed. A cowardly part of me longs to shy away from the sight of my father naked, and the gross indignity of witnessing a giant nappy being put on him, but the capable part knows that it has to be done, and wants to do it for him. Later on, the community nurses come and set up a syringe driver so that Dad can have a continuous supply of drugs to keep him comfortable and control his agitation. Annie and I also know this means that he won't be conscious for much longer, so now is the time to say our goodbyes. We sit either side of him on the bed, and hold his hands, and stroke his poor, worn-out forehead, and cry and cry as we tell him that he can go now, that we will look after each other, that he doesn't need to fight any more. Then we each spend some time alone with him, and after I've said what a great Dad he's been, I tell him how grateful I was that he came after Paul died, and that he never judged me. He is beyond speaking now, but he squeezes my hand, and makes a small noise, and I feel sure that he has understood. The nurses have told us that hearing is the last sense to go.

After that, all is much more peaceful. Bryony arrives, neighbours come and go, Dad remains asleep almost constantly, and periodically we turn him, wash him, change his pad and moisten his lips with water, all the time talking to him, stroking him and kissing his forehead. The next day his breathing is bubbly and we know that he has pneumonia. Bryony and I make another dash to Bideford Hospital, and the same Asda in Atlantic Village, to get more morphine and drugs to dry up the secretions from his chest. Then we go out for a long walk with the dog while we're waiting for the nurses to arrive and top up the syringe driver. They never come. When we get in from the walk, we find Annie sitting on the bed cradling Dad in her arms, tears streaming down her face. It's 6.31 p.m. and Dad, my Daddy, died at 6.30. It was very peaceful – he just gradually stopped breathing.

We make Dad as comfortable as we can, and tie his mouth shut with Annie's pink lacy scarf. Although it looks incongruous, we discover by trial and error that it works better than ribbon or string. We light some candles by his bed and then open a bottle of wine and drink to him. We ring the hospice, and they promise that the out-of-hours nurses will come as soon as they can to verify Dad's death;

we can't call the undertakers until this has been done. We eat some supper and sit through a DVD of *Far from the Madding Crowd*, but none of us can concentrate with Dad lying dead in the next room. Eventually, very late, the nurses ring. They're some distance away and would prefer to wait until the morning to come. Annie is talking to them, and agreeing to this, but I find myself screaming hysterically at her.

'No! Tell them they've got to come tonight.'

Annie is embarrassed. She puts her hand over the receiver. 'Why?' she hisses. 'They're miles away. It'll take them hours to get here.'

'I don't care. It's their job.'

She hands me the phone. She's furious. 'You tell them, then.'

The irritated nurse on the other end reiterates that they are at least two hours' drive away, but I refuse to back down.

'I'm sorry, but we'd like you to come tonight. It will delay everything if we wait till the morning.'

I know that by tomorrow, Dad's body will have deteriorated, and we may then have to wait several more hours for the undertakers. The nurses do, grudgingly, agree to come, but Annie is angry. She accuses me of being unreasonable by making them drive so far in the middle of the night.

'I don't fucking care,' I say. 'They're on night duty, for God's sake. They're meant to be working.'

When they eventually arrive at 1.30 a.m., they are disgruntled and we are shattered. We all go into Dad's bedroom, and already his face is waxy and drained of blood; I find it frightening. After the nurses leave, I still feel hysterical. I can't get rid of the vision of Paul as he looked several days after he died, and I don't want to see

Dad like that. In fact, I don't want to see his body again.

Next morning, the undertakers come at breakfast time and take Dad away. We all hide in Annie's bedroom until they've gone.

In the days that follow, I find that I'm not devoid of emotion. I feel very tearful, as if a big void has opened up in my life. When I tell Margaret about Dad's death, she is struck by the importance of the fact that he communicated something about his feelings for me by holding my hand, and by the fact that I was able, in the end, to communicate how much I appreciated him. I also tell her that he has made me his executor in his will.

– So, you had a special place, a special importance for him.

– I don't know about that. But I do feel different from how I felt when Mum died. I feel as though a big hole has opened up.

– That is because your father was able to hold you in mind, and care for you, in a way that your mother didn't.

She is concerned that I will miss my next session because of Dad's funeral, and offers me an alternative time. She is showing caring now.

The alternative session is on what would have been Paul's birthday. It's also the tenth anniversary of the London bombings. I tell Margaret that I want to go to the New Forest, to the place where Paul's ashes are, but I'm preoccupied with choosing readings for Dad's funeral. One of them is called 'Overwhelmed.' She picks up on this at once.

– So, you are feeling overwhelmed with feelings.

I tell her that I am, but also that it's difficult to find readings that bear no reference to life after death, which Dad didn't believe in.

Margaret says: I think this links with the feathers you've been noticing since Paul died. I think you want there to be life after death.

I'm quick to contradict her.

– But I've thought for ages that the feathers are a construction of my own mind. I don't think I really believe in life after death.

– I think you got very close to believing. As a child you would want, long to stay close to your parents. I think it's important to keep that child in mind, now that your parents are gone.

Then she makes a link with the ending of therapy.

– You are talking about this – about death, the end, hanging on to somebody – because you know that therapy will end. Now is not quite the right time to finish, but therapy will not go on forever.

I do know this. The question is whether I will be able to manage when bad things happen again in life, as they inevitably will.

I haven't seen any robins or barn owls or rainbows since Dad died, but early on the morning of his funeral, when Bryony and I have just woken from an uneasy sleep in our ancient childhood beds, she tells me that during the night, she smelled perfume and tobacco smoke. Later in the day, when we're having lunch in Dad's garden after his funeral, both my sisters catch a whiff of tobacco smoke at the same moment. Dad smoked a pipe many years ago, and they believe that this confirms he is with us. I experience nothing, although I have whispered to Dad, unbeliever though he was, to let me know, if he can, that he's OK. That night, when I'm back home alone and fast asleep, all the smoke alarms in the house suddenly go off. The noise is deafening, and I leap out of bed and rush down to the kitchen in search of the fire. But there is nothing; the air is calm and fresh. Moments later, the alarms stop. Back in bed, wrestling with what is now a fitful sleep, I catch a sudden whiff of perfume, too brief to identify, but without question there.

'You see,' Bryony says when I ring her next morning, 'Mum and Dad are looking out for all three of us.'

As I get back into the routine of daily life, I notice that there is a tiny white feather that clings stubbornly to the front doormat. I leave it there, because it makes me think that Paul knows where I am every time I enter or leave the house; I need the reassurance that it brings. I have a framed photograph of Paul in my bedroom, taken by a friend and fellow sailing enthusiast. It shows Paul at the end of his boat with his back turned to the camera, contemplating the sea. Since Dad died, I have put a lovely photo of him in the same frame, next to Paul. I tell Margaret that I like to see these two men who meant so much to me the moment I wake, and I comment on the fact that Paul is turned away, while Dad is facing the camera.

– Yes, she says. You are able to face your father's death.

*

But am I? Sometimes in your professional life, you get it wrong. I don't mean the kind of wrong that happens a lot in the early days, when you're inexperienced and unsure, as I was with Kerry, but the wrong that can happen when you set out on a well-worn path, only to find that there is a complete mismatch between where you thought you were going and the agenda of the person sitting in front of you. This happened with Connor, an eleven-year-old boy who had come for an autism assessment. I was working, as usual, with my speech therapist colleague. We had seen hundreds of children together over the years, and we had a whole range of tricks up our sleeves (sometimes literally – it was a good place to hide balloons) to gain the cooperation of children who were unenthusiastic about the assessment tasks we needed to complete. Connor was one such unenthusiastic participant to begin with. He had brought his Game Boy into the room with him, and he was determined to play on it rather than look at any of the toys in our test box. The big craze at that time was Pokémon; fortunately both my colleague and I had a good working knowledge of the characters, gained from our own sons. Connor seemed both surprised and impressed by this, and we were soon immersed in conversation about the merits of Pikachu versus Venomoth. After that, we managed to persuade him to agree to a two-minute access to his Game Boy as a reward for completing each assessment task. We wrote out a list of all the tasks we needed to get through so that he could tick each one off as it was completed, and it worked like a dream; Connor cooperated fully with the assessment, and at the end we concluded that he wasn't on the autistic spectrum. He did have some of the features commonly shown by ASD children – his eye contact was variable; he was not amenable to adult direction, at least initially; he had a circumscribed interest in Pokémon (more than our sons did?) – but these were not sufficient to merit an ASD diagnosis. Indeed, Connor was a sociable boy once engaged, well able to take turns in a conversation and enjoy the reciprocity. We were sure that his parents would be pleased with this outcome when we joined the rest of our team to feed back our findings to them.

We met in the consulting room where we had carried out the assessment. It was sparsely furnished, with chairs, a low table and a mirror running the full length of one wall. This doubled up as a one-way screen, through which Connor's parents had watched part of our assessment earlier on. I was sitting next to Connor's father as the child psychiatrist in the team gave an overview of our findings. As she was speaking, I watched with horror as the colour rose from his neck to the tips of his ears and then the top of his head. He was incandescent with rage. He slammed his fist down on the table in front of us and laid into each member of the team in turn, egged on by his wife. They were both deaf to our praise of Connor for his cooperation with the assessment, blind to the examples of his work that we had brought to show them, and dismissive of our predictions of an optimistic future for him. They had wanted an autism diagnosis, and we had denied them it. The conversation then took a more sinister turn, as Connor's father turned to the female members of the team and said: 'I know where you park your cars, and I'm going to get you.' With that, he and his wife marched from the room, slamming the door behind them.

As you might imagine, there were many discussions within the team and beyond following this episode. What had upset the parents so much about their failure to get an autism diagnosis? Did they think they would miss out on financial benefits? Would having a diagnosis absolve them of any responsibility for Connor's behaviour, which was challenging at times? Could we have handled the situation differently? Better? Incident forms were completed, personal alarms were issued, but on reflection, the important point for me was the mismatch between our view of the situation and that of Connor's parents. We weren't sensitive to where they were coming from, and we had made the mistaken assumption that our enthusiasm about a positive assessment outcome would be shared by all the families who came to see us, including Connor's.

As it turns out, Margaret is wrong about me being able to face Dad's death. Dad dies in the summer, and his death coincides with the usual long break from therapy. Margaret doesn't seem unduly concerned. I know I have a phone number for her somewhere, but she doesn't encourage me to get in touch if I need to in the way that Jennifer did when Mum died. By the time Margaret returns in September, I've been feeling low for weeks, and Em has gone. The dark dread has returned and won't go away. I tell Margaret how hopeless I feel.

She says: It may be easier to feel hopeless than to live through this current period of grief and see what emerges.

– Like what?

– We don't know yet.

I find this profoundly unhelpful. I feel she is not 'hearing' my despair. Paul died out of the blue. And not long after that, Mum died. And then my brother-in-law. And then Jess. And along the way, Jennifer left and I was rejected by Charles. People die – of course they do. And people move away, and people get rejected – it happens to most of us. But that is quite a lot of loss and abandonment in a short space of time. And now my lovely dad is dead, too, and my daughter has moved out. What I really, really need, more than anything, is someone to hug me. Instead, there is the prospect of another long weekend on my own.

Friday night. Paul and I never cooked on Fridays. To celebrate the end of the working week, we went out for dinner, and if we were too tired, we phoned for a takeaway to eat in front of the TV. It was an unchanging ritual, whether or not the children were with us. Now Friday night looms empty, mocking, devoid of comfort or company. The empty house. When I was at the centre of a big, bustling family, I used to long for a day alone in the house, and relish such days when they did, occasionally, happen. Now that the house is always empty, I approach it with foreboding and enter it with an anxious dread. The silence is menacing; the loneliness sucks every drop of optimism from me and leaves me inert with misery. How did it come to this? Why isn't anyone here to welcome me with a smile and a hug? When I was a busy wife and mother, it never crossed my mind that I would end up like this, alone and unwanted. And yet that fact is reinforced again and again, after every excursion, every visit to the shops, every walk up the road to post a letter. Each time I get home and open the front door, the silence slams me in the face.

I spend the weekend in the clutches of the nameless dread, looking at suicide websites. I quickly discover that taking an overdose is an unreliable method, unless you also put a plastic bag over your head. Jumping in front of a train is much more effective. I don't think I would have the guts to do that. I recall a patient I used to see when I was working in one of the huge psychiatric hospitals that once existed around the fringes of London. I was in my second year of training, and the patient was a young racing driver in his early thirties. His career had not lived up to its initial promise, and he was depressed. I was seeing him for what was loosely termed 'supportive counselling', and I was supervised by a pleasant psychologist who had a very laid-back attitude to work and was always complimentary about my handling of the cases I brought to supervision.

One Monday, I turned up for work, only to be ushered into a side ward by my supervisor and the superintendent of the hospital. My patient had attempted to hang himself in a hospital toilet over the weekend, but had been found and cut down just in time by one of the nurses. Nobody blamed me, although there was some discussion over whether he had been a suitable case for a trainee. I, of course, felt awful, but I was simply told that I wouldn't be seeing him any more, and that was the end of it. Thinking about that episode now, I don't think that I would have the guts to hang myself either, but I do begin to formulate a plan based on the large amounts of medication I have stashed away upstairs. I feel strongly that I need to do the abandoning before I'm abandoned yet again myself.

I cry from beginning to end of my next session with Margaret, and tell her that I want to die. I tell her that the house is properly empty now, that I've spoken to nobody at all for four days and that I find this extreme loneliness unbearable. Margaret says I should contact my GP and go and get some antidepressants. I know I won't do this. The last thing I can manage when I feel like this is to phone anyone at all, and certainly not the hostile receptionist who guards the phones at the GP's surgery. We go round and round this topic for what seems like ages, until eventually Margaret says she will ring the GP on my behalf then. I don't sense that this is offered willingly; rather that she's exasperated at my refusal to cooperate.

The GP takes my suicidal thoughts seriously, and the next day I'm visited at home by a psychiatrist from the adult mental health crisis team. He's a charming young man, tall and dark with a gentle manner. He accepts a cup of coffee and chats for a long time about my life, my work and everything that has happened over the past few years. He is warm, caring and positive. He tells me I'm depressed, and prescribes medication, but he also says that there are good reasons as to why I should be feeling so low now, and he's sure that in years to come, I will look back on this as a 'blip'. He says that he'll come back and see me again, and in the meantime, he'll send his team of nurses round to give me some support. He asks how I would feel about having some Cognitive Behavioural Therapy (CBT). I tell him I've been seeing a psychodynamic psychotherapist. He seems only vaguely interested in this, and says we can return to the question of therapy at his next visit. His visits are on Thursdays, which would usually be my therapy day with Margaret.

The team of nurses are brilliant. One of them visits every day, sometimes late in the evening, but I never get the sense that I'm being 'fitted in' to a busy schedule. They stay as long as I want. The one called Jim has been assigned specifically to me, so he visits most, except on his days off. He's middle-aged, casually dressed and has a moustache and what I judge to be quite long hair for a health professional. He reminds me of the hippies I used to hang out with at university. I like him. He's warm and friendly, and he always accepts my offer of tea. He notices things – my books, my vinyl record collection, the photos of the children on the mantelpiece – and asks me about them.

So, I don't mind when he also asks, as he invariably does: So, have you been looking at any more websites?

To begin with, I feel agitated and restless, and I don't talk much. But as the days pass and the antidepressants kick in, I begin to relax, and we talk about our children, the state of the NHS, and much else besides. I look forward to his visits, but I'm already aware that they can't continue in the long term, and this begins to make me anxious.

– I know you can't keep on coming forever. But I'm worried about what will happen when you stop. What if I get suicidal again?

– You're right. This is a crisis service, so we can't carry on in the long term. But we won't stop until you feel OK about it, and we'll wind down gradually. And now that you're on our books, as it were, you can access us again very quickly.

This makes all the difference. The fact that the door will be left ajar. This team has shown nothing but kindness and concern. They have given me time and space, and contained the anxiety and agitation I've been feeling. The psychiatrist visits again, and suggests that I talk to the psychologist on the team about having some CBT. He tells me, as I already know, that a combination of medication and CBT has a good, evidence-based track record in treating depression. But seeing a psychologist? One of my own profession? That would be weird.

As it happens, she's brisk and efficient, and it's much like any other professional consultation. She asks me what my goals would be if I were to have some CBT, and I find, somewhat to my surprise, that I can articulate them quite clearly.

– I want to build resilience. My reaction to Dad dying has really scared me, and I want some strategies to help me manage better when bad things happen and I feel myself going down. And I want to find a way forwards with my life, to find something meaningful to do without sabotaging myself with negative thoughts about being no good, not good enough, not likeable.

Her advice is that CBT would be appropriate, and protective. I say I will think about it, but first I know I must talk to Margaret.

*

I feel reluctant and upset as I walk through Margaret's bedraggled garden to the side door. I feel that since Dad died, she hasn't been looking after her garden or me. As I sit in my usual chair, I stare at the worn Persian rug on the floor. My eyes lock on to its monotonous pattern of dark reds and blacks: anything rather than look at her. I tell her how the episode with the crisis team has really frightened me, and how concerned I am that psychotherapy hasn't prevented me from becoming suicidal. I tell her that CBT has been suggested, and I wonder, out loud, whether I should try it. She seems annoyed.

– You have a choice about whether to continue with psychotherapy, but you have to be committed; you have to be interested in the question of why out of sight is out of mind – (meaning, presumably, my reaction to her summer break) – why you can't draw on the resources of family and friends when you need them, why you 'forget' your own needs.

– But I am interested. Otherwise why would I keep coming?

– Maybe you want me to sort it all out for you, but this isn't how psychotherapy works.

– But if I haven't made progress in all these years, why should I make progress now?

– That's assuming you haven't made progress.

(But she doesn't actually say that I have.)

– But why would I come if I'm not committed?

– Maybe the whole thing is a big rivalry – you want to prove me wrong by showing that psychotherapy doesn't work.

She hasn't said this before, and it makes me feel annoyed. There is clearly rivalry between us; I suddenly recall a remark she made several weeks ago, about me needing to acknowledge that someone in my profession could be helped by someone in hers. So, the rivalry is not all coming from me.

At the next session, I'm furious. She has charged me for the two sessions I missed because of seeing the psychiatrist.

She says: That's the agreement. I charge for cancellations.

I think this is unreasonable, given the circumstances and the state I was in at the time.

I say: I don't want to come any more.

I sit in hostile silence for a long time, until eventually she asks what I'm thinking.

– It isn't working. It didn't prevent me from being suicidal. The crisis team are kind – you're not. You didn't give me your email address when you were away after my dad died, and you charged me for sessions I missed when I was suicidal.

– You didn't *ask* for my email address. You didn't say you weren't OK. Having a seven-week break around the time your father died was always going to be a problem.

– I was responsible for three of those weeks because I had to be in Devon; Dad was *dying*. You were responsible for the other four, and you didn't give me your contact details.

– You have my telephone number.

– I don't like talking on the phone.

— I didn't know that. Contrary to popular belief, I'm not a mind-reader.

— You're not caring.

— You won't acknowledge any empathy.

— I see no evidence of it.

— I did contact your GP when you were feeling low.

—Of *course* you did! I was suicidal! You would have been totally negligent if you hadn't. That doesn't mean at all that there was any empathy or caring for me.

— The question is whether we can learn from this together.

— I don't know what 'learn from it' means. I can't see any point in flogging a dead horse.

— It's sad that that's how you see yourself, that your needs aren't worth thinking about.

— I know that. We've been over it again and again and we never get anywhere.

Her answer is that I should increase the number of times a week that I come, and that I should lie on her couch. This makes me mad, given that I'm a widow currently supporting two children through master's degrees. Can't she see how vulnerable I am? That I need kindness?

The next time I see her I tell her: I don't think you like me. You think I'm a bad person. I feel that, since Dad died, you've been detached and critical, whereas what I've needed is warmth and reassurance.

— I don't recognise myself in your description. I don't recognise you either. Your strengths are very apparent.

— People tell me that, but I don't see it. I'm disillusioned with coming to see you to focus on the negative and have a hard time. It makes me feel worse about myself. I want to build resilience.

– I can see that, but there is still important work to be done.

– But I can't bear any more of this negativity – it will literally kill me.

*

By the next session, I've been to Devon again and have been sorting through Mum and Dad's papers with my sisters. I find a shocking letter from Mum to Dad, dated New Year's Eve, when I would have been seventeen. In it, she acknowledges her often critical and undermining behaviour towards him, with a quote from the Bible: 'For the good that I would, I do not, but the evil that I would not, that I do' (Romans 7:19). She also acknowledges what he has said about her behaviour, that it 'diminishes' him, and that he has almost reached the limits of his tolerance. She apologises, and promises to do better in the New Year – a new start. Of course, this never happened; she remained overtly critical of Dad right up to the time of her death, yet he never spoke to any of his daughters about it. This was surprising, given that he witnessed similar behaviour being directed by Mum towards me and Bryony whenever we visited them in Devon. There would be a 'honeymoon' period for the first day, followed by attacks and harsh criticism (of our clothes, our behaviour, our children), followed by apologies and recriminations after we'd left, and promises (never kept) that all would be better next time. I tell Margaret how damaging it has been to be on the receiving end of this behaviour, how it has destroyed my self-esteem and that of my sisters, how it has made me so sensitive to criticism.

– How could she do that to her children? I could never do that to mine.

– But you were prepared to kill yourself, and that would have the same damaging effect on your children.

– But I don't understand her behaviour. What on earth was she doing?

– She had strong emotions that she couldn't control, so she was raving, all over the place. Being suicidal is also about strong emotions, equally destructive, but turned in on the self.

We found another, earlier letter from Mum to Dad, written when I was three and my sisters were eighteen months and four months old. Dad had gone away skiing with a friend, leaving Mum to look after us, and we were all ill. She sounded at the end of her tether, admonishing him for leaving her, and warning him that he certainly wouldn't be doing it again. I had a high temperature and a boil, and she describes me lying for a whole day completely still and not speaking, worried that the boil would hurt if I moved.

Margaret's comment: You're still doing that. Suffering in silence.

– Why would I do that?

– Perhaps because of there not being a sense of a mother there who is concerned, to whom you could turn?

And it's true. I used to feel that Margaret was concerned, but I don't any more.

We've also been talking about my decision to try six sessions of CBT after Christmas. We've agreed that I'll stop seeing her while this is happening, and then have a review session.

She says: I worry about who will 'keep you in mind' when CBT is finished.

Unfortunately, I no longer feel that she can do this in

a way that is helpful. I would like her to be the concerned mother, but I no longer feel that she is.

*

So, what happened? I found Margaret supportive for a long time, but as time went on, I had a sense that we were drifting further and further apart.

Irvin Yalom wrote a fascinating book about a twice-told therapy, *Every Day Gets A Little Closer*, in which he and his patient each wrote their own accounts of every session. After several months, they compared what they had written, and eventually the two accounts were published together. Frequently, the accounts of patient and therapist were so different that it was hard to believe that the two had been in the same room together. Yalom writes: 'Even our views of what was helpful varied. My elegant interpretations? She never even heard them! Instead she remembered, and treasured, casual, personal, supportive comments I had made.'

No doubt Margaret's account of what happened with me after my father's illness and death would be very different to my own. I can only speculate, because I have no access to her records. I did ask, but she refused to tell me whether she had even kept any, let alone allow me to see them. But from what she actually said in our sessions together, it seems that she was noticing lack of commitment; failure to engage properly; unexpressed anger at loss or abandonment turned in on myself; lack of trust; difficulties with intimacy; and maybe much else besides. From my point of view, none of this mattered, and it wasn't helpful to express it, because what I wanted was support and kindness and warmth in the face of so much loss and despair. I did say this, often, but I felt that she didn't hear me. I tried to tell her how awful I was feeling and she came back at me with pronouncements about ending therapy, or the need to focus on what could be learned. There was nothing wrong with this per se, but it was mistimed and misplaced. She seemed wedded to the theory underlying her therapeutic practice, whereas I just needed someone to respond to me on a human level, to acknowledge my despair and distress and make me feel safe. As Stephen Grosz puts it: 'The most important thing is that the patient should feel that what she came to say, needed to say, has been said, listened to and thought about.'

Scott Peck was a psychiatrist and psychotherapist. In the 1970s he wrote the bestselling book *The Road Less Travelled*, in which he describes how the difficulties and suffering of human beings, if properly confronted and faced, can result in spiritual growth and a higher level of self-understanding. He describes a particularly intransigent female patient, with whom he struggled three times a week for well over a year with no signs of improvement. She wouldn't talk about the things he wanted her to talk about, and often she wouldn't talk at all. At the same time, she began a period of extreme promiscuity in her life outside therapy.

One day she asked Dr Peck: 'Do you think I'm a bit of a shit?'

Dr Peck's training suggested that he should respond by turning the question back towards his patient, by saying, for example: 'I wonder why you ask that?' or 'What's important is not what I think of you, but what you think of yourself.' But his gut feeling was that his patient deserved an honest answer. So, he described how, despite the struggle and lack of progress, she had continued to come and see him, come rain or shine, and concluded that: 'I do not think I would feel that someone who works as hard on herself as you do is a bit of a shit. So, the answer is no, I do not think you are a bit of a shit. In fact, I admire you a great deal.'

This was the turning point in the patient's therapy and in her life outside – the end of the struggle. Dr Peck reflects: 'My going out on a limb by revealing my genuine positive feelings for her – something I felt I was really not supposed to do – apparently was of great therapeutic benefit.' He provides other examples, criticises the tradition of the aloof and detached analyst (which, incidentally, was promoted by Freud's followers rather than Freud himself), and concludes that: 'In order to be healed through psychotherapy, the patient must receive from the psychotherapist at least a portion of the genuine love of which the patient was deprived (from parents or parent figures).' If a psychotherapist cannot genuinely love a patient, genuine healing will not occur, no matter how well trained the psychotherapist may be.

Yalom makes a similar point: 'The therapist's venture is not to engage the patient in a joint archaeological dig … a therapist helps a patient not by sifting through the past but by being lovingly present with that person; by being trustworthy, interested; and by believing that their joint activity will ultimately be redemptive and healing.'

That was the kind of therapist I so desperately needed at that point in time. Margaret hardly ever said anything positive about me, or acknowledged my persistence in attending week after week – year after year, in fact. This hadn't mattered so much when things were going reasonably well, but it did matter now. There's a whole body of research that shows how important 'therapist variables' are in influencing outcomes of therapy, much more so than differences in theory or technique. Margaret and I were no longer 'clicking' in a way that felt helpful. The kind of mismatch that occurred between us can result in things going badly wrong.

Most descriptions of therapy are written from the psychotherapist's point of view, but there are a few accounts by patients, which the psychoanalyst Robert Morley believes are just as valid and often just as illuminating for understanding the process of therapy.

What emerges clearly from these accounts, as Yalom discovered with his twice-told therapy, is how different the reports of patients and therapists are. There often appear to be 'discordant agendas' regarding what each believes will be helpful in their treatment. This can lead to the patient feeling misunderstood by the therapist, ultimately resulting in therapeutic difficulty and failure. Sometimes discordant agendas arise because the therapist is more interested in the theory underpinning their work than the emotional realities of the patient. Freud himself claimed he was more interested in theory than in therapy and confessed that he often felt bored while working with patients. The most positive patient accounts were from those who benefitted from a warm, consistent and interested relationship with their therapist, suggesting again that this might be the essential therapeutic element in any type of psychotherapy.

Thinking back to our meeting with Connor's parents, it would have been helpful to check out where they were coming from, and what they had hoped to get out of their son's assessment, before launching into our findings, however positive these findings seemed to us. In other words, we should have found out what their agenda was before blundering in with what we thought they would be pleased to hear. Had we done this, we could have started by agreeing with them about all the autistic features we had in fact observed, and talked about Connor's difficult behaviours and how we could support them in managing these before going on to talk about his strengths. Had we pursued this agenda, which accorded much better with theirs, the meeting might have gone a lot better. It all comes down to listening, really listening, to the client.

CHAPTER TEN

Resolution

[Negative thoughts are often] well-known features of the landscape of depression. They are not reliable readouts on truth or reality.

MARK WILLIAMS ET AL.,
The Mindful Way through Depression

My problem in finding a CBT therapist is that many of them are clinical psychologists, and so I have connections with them through work in my local area. I turn reluctantly to the internet: I know there are all sorts of 'therapists' with all manner of qualifications out there, so I'm careful only to look at those who are properly accredited by the professional body that regulates CBT therapists. The first person I contact has glowing reviews on his website, and he comes across as friendly and professional on the phone, but he has no vacancies, and a waiting list. I feel disappointed: he must be good, but I can't see him. I go back to searching. There are plenty of therapists, all properly qualified, but beyond that I'm not really sure what it is I'm looking for. I phone a woman who looks about my age – perhaps I think I'll 'connect' better with someone who has reached a similar stage in life? She is friendly, and professional, too, but about to retire, so that's no good. I like the look of another woman who lives just outside my area (meaning my professional links won't be an issue). She has a round, open face, and is smiling broadly at the camera. Looking back, it seems extraordinary that I should base my choice on such flimsy criteria, but after my recent experience with Margaret, 'warmth' is clearly something that matters a lot to me. Sue has limited vacancies, but she's happy to see me for an initial consultation and take it from there. Phew – she sounds nice.

Sue's house is on a modern estate a few miles outside the city where I live. I set off far too early, and have to kill time sitting in a lay-by just outside her village. I'm nervous. There are several cars in the short driveway outside her house, but she has told me it's OK to park behind the blue Fiat, so that's what I do. I see her through the window before I've finished parking. She waves and comes straight out through the front door to greet me, and shakes my hand. I'm amazed by this, mentally comparing it with my initial encounters with Jennifer, Jocelyn and Margaret, all of whom greeted me with scarcely more than a nod before retreating into their consulting rooms. But I like it – it feels normal. She asks me about my journey, and that feels normal too.

Sue's consulting room is also different. It's a small room at the front of the house, overlooking an area of communal garden. There's no couch, but two modern armchairs and a low table between them with a carafe of water on it, and the usual tissues. Otherwise, it's an office, with a sizeable desk, built-in cupboards, a computer and a printer. The room is painted white, the furniture shades of grey: comfortable but functional. Sue herself is as open and friendly as her photograph promised. She's in early middle age, wearing glasses, her auburn hair cut in a short bob. She smiles a lot. She invites me to sit in one of the armchairs, and she sits in the other one. She begins by telling me something about herself: her qualifications, where she has worked and works now, and what I might expect from coming to see her. This in itself is a revelation: none of the others told me anything about themselves, nor did they go into any detail about the way in which they worked. Perhaps that was why I so often felt that I didn't know where we were, or where we were going. Then she asks me to explain why I've come to see her, and what the difficulties are that I'm facing at the moment. Of course, I tell her about Paul, but also about the recent depressive episode prompted by Dad dying and the last of the children leaving home. I explain how low and anxious this has left me feeling, and how terrified I am that the suicidal thoughts will return. She asks me a lot about my childhood and my relationships with my parents and my sisters, and I'm surprised by this – I had thought CBT focused only on the here and now, and that the past was irrelevant, but I was wrong about that.

Throughout the session, I feel that Sue is genuinely interested in what I have to say, and that she's listening, really listening, actively and intentionally. I have her full attention. She doesn't take any notes, but towards the end, she summarises what she thinks she has learned from what I've said, betraying the fact that she has indeed absorbed every detail of my story. I'm impressed. Her initial formulation goes something like this:

– You have some very negative beliefs about yourself. For example, you've said that you feel a failure, and that people don't like you. That's hardly surprising when you consider that your parents and your school had very high expectations of you, and your mother was often critical. From what you've said, your father was quite a remote figure in your childhood, and your mother was working, so perhaps you didn't get a lot of emotional support? You've also said that your mother was a very anxious person, and that both your mother and sister were depressed, so there might be a genetic predisposition towards depression and anxiety. When major life events occur, like your husband and then your father dying, they tend to activate these basic assumptions about yourself which were already there, and this can lead to a downward spiral of negative thinking, which further feeds into feelings of depression and anxiety.

Then she asks me what I think of this. *She asks me what I think!* I'm completely unprepared for this – no therapist has ever asked my opinion before! We are having a reciprocal conversation, and it feels very odd ... but in a good way. Sue goes on to explain what I might expect from therapy with her.

– The idea is that we work collaboratively. When you're depressed, your thinking tends to be negative and distorted, so we can work together to identify these negative thoughts and think about whether there really is evidence to support them – and whether there's evidence against them. The aim is to challenge the thoughts and to replace them with thinking that's more realistic and balanced. Your fundamental beliefs about yourself have been around for a long time and will be much harder to dislodge. Realistically, they're not going to be eliminated, but we can try to shift them a bit.

Again, she asks me what I think. I'm very attracted to the idea of working collaboratively; this should minimise the chances of there being any discordant agendas. And I like the fact that she's trying to give me a realistic view of what is – and isn't – achievable. I wonder how long she thinks the work will take?

– We shouldn't need more than ten, or at most twelve sessions. I think it would be helpful to build in a review after six sessions, so that we can both consider how it's going. And if you need or want more 'top-up' sessions in the future, you can come back at any time.

Only ten to twelve sessions, and the door left open? It seems too good to be true. There will be an end in sight, something to work towards, unlike the open-ended marathon of psychotherapy. I'm pleased when we manage to find a regular time that suits both of us, and as I drive away, my predominant feeling is of huge, blessed relief.

*

Sue and I meet weekly for an hour. Not a fifty-minute 'therapy hour', but a full sixty minutes. She gives me 'thought records' to fill in between sessions, in which I record any unhelpful thoughts that occur to me, and facts that support or challenge them. I find this vaguely helpful, but in the end, we make little use of them and focus instead on the material I take to each session. I find I have plenty to say. Sue remains open, interested and actively listening throughout, and I respond by talking openly and freely. She educates me about my unhelpful thinking styles, of which there are many, and together we work on more balanced ways of thinking, and build up strategies for managing situations or people I find difficult. An early example is a party I've been invited to by some friends who live in a big house in London. I don't want to go at all. Sue asks why not.

– I feel extremely anxious even thinking about it.

– What is it that you're anxious about?

– I don't know what to wear. I feel fat and old and unattractive.

– Anything else?

– Yes. What will I do if nobody talks to me? And what if there's dancing? What will I do then? I haven't got anyone to dance with … and I don't want anyone to dance with me out of pity.

– We've already talked about your core belief that you're not good enough, that you're unattractive physically and socially. If you walk into the party firmly believing that to be the case, it's quite likely to result in a self-fulfilling prophecy. So, let's think about it. What's the evidence that you're unattractive?

– Plenty. A man one of my friends introduced me to a few weeks ago as a potential date told her later that he was expecting me to be younger; there's the ghastly Charles who ran a mile as soon as he thought I was getting too interested in him; and there's the friend's brother I met last year. He was single, but he clearly wasn't interested in me, and then later I heard that he'd got engaged to someone twenty years younger than me.

– What do you think of all these men now?

– They're all wankers.

– I rest my case. So, let's think about any evidence that you are attractive?

Silence.

– Come on, I'm sure there is some.

– Well, I suppose people do sometimes tell me that I look nice, or that I look well. But they're probably just being polite.

– What else? Try to think of some examples.

– Well, on Saturday I had coffee with a guy who used to live in my road. I hadn't seen him for twenty-five years, and he told me I looked just the same. And I do a lot of swimming and walking, so I know I'm fitter and slimmer than quite a few women of my age. The children sometimes say that their friends think I'm cool, and fashionable.

Sue adds to this: Everyone else at the party will be middle-aged too. And if somebody isn't interested in talking to you, is it your fault or theirs? Are the other people at the party likely to be any 'better' than you? What's the worst that could happen?

We talk about this for a bit, and then reflect on the catalogue of unhelpful thinking styles that are colouring my view of the party and my attractiveness rating. There's 'selective abstraction', a sort of tunnel vision which involves dwelling on just one negative aspect of a situation and ignoring the rest, such as focusing on one example of someone saying I looked old compared to numerous others of people saying I looked good; 'mind-reading', which is jumping to conclusions because we assume we know what someone else is thinking, such as thinking that people are being polite if they say I look nice (they might actually think that I look nice), or would only ask me to dance out of pity (they might ask out of friendship, or even attraction). Often these conclusions are a reflection of how we think about ourselves (I'm unattractive; a pitiful widow), and because we think poorly about ourselves, we believe others must, too. Then there is 'catastrophising,' which is all the 'what if's that I imagine about the party situation, blowing it out of proportion until it seems beyond my control. And finally, there's the one I do more than any other: 'black and white thinking'. This style is typical of the student who doesn't get straight As and therefore thinks they're a failure, or the person who thinks: 'If I'm not the best at what I do, I'm worthless.' In this 'all-or-nothing' style of thinking, you see only one extreme; there are no shades of grey, no in-betweens, no middle ground. So, if someone is not talking or dancing or interacting with me constantly at the party, I must be a total waste of space.

Together, Sue and I work through my anxieties and try to come up with a more balanced perspective: I'm going to be more attractive to some people than others – everyone is; if conversation doesn't flow, it may be because we don't have much in common – and, at any rate, it's no more my fault than the other person's; and so on.

I go to the party and I survive it. I don't enjoy it much, but that has more to do with a horrendous journey there and back and deafeningly loud music than anxiety. Afterwards, Sue reflects that I can always choose whether or not to do things.

– It's important to distinguish between *can't* (because of anxiety or unduly negative thinking, which does need to be challenged) and *choosing not to*.

Another unhelpful thinking style, and again one that I am very prone to, is 'should-ing' and 'must-ing,' where you use 'should' or 'must' statements to put unreasonable demands on yourself. My mother was a past master at this, so it's not surprising that it comes so easily to me. Sue's revelation that I actually have a choice seems liberating, so I go away and start to exercise that choice in all kinds of ways: I don't *have* to meet the annoying woman from my choir for coffee because I think I should – I can say no politely and not feel guilty about it; I don't *have* to stay in all weekend in case one of the children decides to come home – I can choose to do something else and enjoy it.

This collaborative way of working with Sue has immediate pay-offs and helps me to manage all kinds of situations: I sail through an interview for voluntary work which has been keeping me awake with anxiety; I manage to take a balanced view of my daughter pulling out of a walk we'd planned together; I reflect on whether a friendship I'm finding unsatisfying really is important to me; I manage to see both good and bad things about my birthday when it didn't go perfectly, whereas before I would have judged it to be a complete disaster. Sue's unconditional interest and pleasure in any progress I make feels profoundly supportive. And we laugh! The material we talk about is often serious, but there's plenty of room for humour, too, and I really feel that she likes me. This makes all the difference. Once, long ago, I felt that Jennifer liked me, but she left. Now, Sue likes me and she has an open door. It's what I need.

*

After six weeks of seeing Sue, I'm due to have a review with Margaret. I'm dreading it. I've decided that I definitely don't want any more psychotherapy, and I'm scared of telling her this. But I do think I should see her face to face rather than just writing a letter, which would be the cowardly way out.

On the day, my heart is thumping as I drive up to her house. I notice that the green car isn't there, but the garden, unadorned and sodden with winter rain, looks as unkempt as ever. As I stand waiting outside her consulting room, I notice a tiny, bedraggled feather clinging to the empty hanging basket above the door. *Thanks Paul. You're here to hold my hand.* It's enough to slow my heartbeat fractionally. Margaret opens the door with her usual terse nod of greeting, and goes at once to sit silently in her chair. Now that I've become used to a different type of greeting, I find this intimidating, but I brace myself and come straight out with what I want to say.

– I've come to tell you that I've decided I don't want to continue with psychotherapy. I did find it supportive to begin with, but for ages I've found it very negative and I don't like coming any more.

I tell her a bit about CBT and the things I've found helpful about it.

– It's given me a way of moving forwards, whereas psychotherapy got me stuck in feeling very negative about myself.

Margaret's initial reaction is hostile:

– You seem to be denigrating psychotherapy and praising CBT. CBT can't *possibly* have achieved so much in six sessions. The groundwork had been done in all the work you've done in psychotherapy.

– I'm trying to be balanced about it.

A lesson learnt in CBT: avoid black and white thinking.

I continue: I did find psychotherapy supportive, but not recently, and especially not during the episode last year, when it didn't prevent me from almost killing myself.

Margaret is defensive.

– I hold my hands up! I did work supportively to begin with because you were so distressed when you first came to see me. I moved towards working in a more analytical way because that's what I do.

Yes, I think, *you refuse to be flexible.*

– I've said for ages that I don't think I'm being helped with this way of working. But I don't think you hear me.

– I've suggested that you come more frequently, and lie on the couch, but you don't want to do that. If you don't have the interest or motivation to explore in that way, then there is no point.

I don't say this at the time, but afterwards I reflect again about our discordant agendas: she doesn't 'hear' what it is that I want or need; or, if she does, she doesn't acknowledge it in a way that is helpful. Instead, she seems to be driven by her own theoretical background and training into what seems to me to be a fairly rigid way of working. Her solution to my misgivings is to offer me more of the same. I don't feel that we relate as human beings, and I certainly don't feel that she shows any of the genuine love towards me that Scott Peck believes to be so crucial for a successful therapeutic outcome. Indeed, I feel blamed for not being the kind of patient she wants me to be.

What I do tell her is more about my life and the new things I'm doing, like voluntary work and learning to play the piano again. I say that I'm feeling a lot better, and that people tell me that I look better. It will be the anniversary of Paul's death tomorrow, and the thought isn't freaking me out – I can think about it in a more balanced way.

To this, she responds: For what it's worth, I don't think that your psychotherapy has been a total waste of time. I think you have been able to reflect on many things in your life.

If this is praise, it feels as though it's delivered grudgingly, although I must be careful not to engage in mind-reading.

Then it is 'time': the moment when fifty minutes is up,

and no matter what is being talked about, you must stop. As I leave, Margaret stands stiffly in the middle of the room and says she appreciates me coming to say goodbye and wishes me well.

And that's it. After all these years, not even a hand-shake or a smile.

As I drive away, I do feel sad; after all, it has been a long time. But I also feel OK, and positive about moving forwards with my life. I think about what she said about psychotherapy laying the groundwork for CBT. There may well be a lot of truth in this, but it seems that CBT has quickly got to the heart of the matter and given me strate-gies for managing situations, taking risks and changing my behaviour, all of which are incredibly helpful, as there is an immediate pay-off. I'm not convinced that I would ever have got there with psychotherapy alone. Both approaches are probably trying to get to the same heart of the matter, but they have completely different methods, timescales and recipes for finding the way forwards. And there's no doubt that I find Sue easier to relate to than Margaret.

Valery Hazanov refers to the 'tiresome' and 'absurd' fight between the proponents of 'depth' therapies, like psychodynamic psychotherapy, and 'behavioural' thera-pies, like CBT. In his view, a patient has different layers of suffering which can be reached in many different ways, and sometimes simultaneously using different approaches. And he, like Scott Peck and Irvin Yalom, stresses the importance of the connection between the therapist and the patient: 'Conceptualisations, theories, interventions ... only matter if the patient remembers a *person*, something that *person* said or did for her that was real' (my italics). Perhaps, all those years ago, this is what had mattered to Kerry – not the rewards she earned, or even the weight she lost, but a connection with a *person* who cared about her.

*

I return to Sue for another four sessions of CBT. We carry on in much the same way, talking through difficult situations that arise and rebalancing my thinking about them, always acknowledging that the past exerts its influence, and that I have fundamental core beliefs about myself that won't shift easily. I continue to feel a lot better.

In the last session, Sue asks me why I think things have improved.

I reply: It still feels fragile, but I notice that I'm not operating on my usual default settings. In the past, if people asked me how I was, I'd say I was OK, but never mean it. Now I can say I feel OK and actually *mean* it, and it feels really weird.

– Can you think of actual examples of things that have changed?

– Yes. I've been living on my own for more than six months now and it's OK. In fact, in some ways I really like it, because I have complete freedom over what I choose to do. So, the thoughts I had before, that it would be dreadful, have been replaced by evidence that it's OK. I can please myself, so I've arranged to do lots of nice things over the summer.

– So, it turned out not to be the catastrophe you were expecting. That's very important. Is there anything else you can think of?

– Yes, when I had to have Fatty (the cat) put to sleep. I was dreading it because he'd been with me all the time since Paul died and I loved him. I surprised myself by realising that it might be better to have someone with me at the vets. So, I asked Jane – she's quite a new friend who lives just round the corner. Of course, it was terribly sad, but it made a big difference having someone with me, and afterwards we went home together and had a large glass of wine. My friendship with Jane is also a bit of a revelation. The fact that she seems to think I'm worth knowing challenges lots of my negative assumptions about myself. We do a lot of swimming and walking together and it's a reciprocal relationship which seems well balanced – I've got IT skills and she hasn't, and she's a much better cook than me. I took a risk getting to know her better, and it's paid dividends.

Sue agrees.

– I think you have become better at challenging negative thinking and taking some risks. The more you can do this, the more you'll build up a firm foundation against future knocks.

I recall what the participants in my survey wrote about the things that most helped them to cope following a bereavement. They were the support and kindness of family and friends, having a structure in their lives, and physical activity. Some people also wrote about finding inner strength or resilience. I can relate strongly to all of this, and I like to think that for me, therapy has provided a way of helping to access that inner strength.

Sue and I agree to meet again in six months to review how I've been getting on, but she reiterates that I can contact her to arrange top-up sessions at any time if there is a wobble. I find this extremely reassuring. She comes out to my car with me, shakes my hand, says she hopes I have a lovely summer and waves me off as I drive away. No stiff, withholding goodbyes from her.

*

One day in July, close to Paul's birthday, I'm watering the garden. There isn't much space, so I plant hanging baskets and tubs to give a good splash of colour in the summer months. I've put troughs brimming with pink and red geraniums on the front windowsills. Although drunken students occasionally knock them off on a Saturday night, I judge that, on the whole, it's worth keeping them there because they brighten up the road. As I emerge through the front door, taking care to leave it on the latch, I'm thinking about Paul and all the things that have happened since he died that he doesn't know about. It's not a depressing thought exactly, but rather one tinged with sadness that he's missed out on so much, coupled with a strong desire to talk to him and tell him about everything. I lift the watering can and notice that a white feather is lodged between the petals of the largest, pinkest flower. How could it have got there? The window has a wide overhang, so it couldn't possibly have fallen from a passing bird. But that's not important. I smile to myself. I think: *So, you do know where to find me, and maybe you do know that Mum and Dad died, and that all the children graduated, and that you have grandchildren. It comforts me to think so. And to know that I can still rely on you, now that Sue has gone.*

So far, I haven't needed any top-up sessions with Sue. It's almost a year since I last saw her, and I've been off medication for almost a year, too. Life certainly isn't always easy, or fun, but I'm coping OK. I seem to be able to manage situations with greater equanimity and far less of the emotional turmoil that characterised the early years following Paul's death. Two different encounters with shop assistants illustrate this.

A few years ago, I was in Debenhams around Christmas – always a difficult time of year for the bereaved. I had psyched myself up to buy perfume, as mine had run out. I hated the thought of having to do this. Paul always bought me perfume, and he was also instrumental in choosing it, usually in the duty-free shop of the P&O ferry to Cherbourg, where we would giggle, and waft the air with sprays of this and that until we found the scent that we both liked best. I selected a bottle of the perfume I was wearing when Paul died, and took it to the till. The sales assistant was a bird-like woman in her fifties, with a thick cake of make-up covering her face and eyebrows drawn on top of it with black pencil. As she rang up the price, I remarked on how expensive the perfume was.

'It is, isn't it?' she said. 'Can't you get your husband to buy it for you for Christmas?'

A perfectly innocent question, but to my embarrassment, I found tears spilling down my face as I explained that I was sure he would if he could, but unfortunately, he couldn't because he was dead. I could see her face reddening with embarrassment, even under the thick layer of foundation. She apologised profusely, and offered to give me a free makeover if I came back in the new year.

A few weeks ago, I was shopping in Boots for a new electric blanket. The old one still worked, but it took ages to warm up, and I was sure technology must have moved on. I found two blankets on a low shelf among the hot-water bottles. One had dual controls, and the other a single control, and although they looked identical in every other respect, there was quite a big difference in the price. I tracked down a sales assistant to ask about this.

'Well,' she said, 'the single control means there's only one place where you can switch it on and off and control the temperature. With the dual control, you can control your side of the bed, and your husband can control his. So, if you want to be nice and warm and he's too hot, it doesn't matter – he can turn his side off!'

I didn't flinch. I smiled, and said I'd have the dual control. Not, of course, to cater for the preferences of my husband, but because Annie and I sometimes share a bed if the house is full of people. Since her dog often ends up wedged between us, it's quite nice to be able to turn down the heat.

'I think that's a wise choice,' the assistant said. 'I bet your husband will be pleased.'

*

Not long after the electric blanket purchase, my old friend Mari invited me to stay with her and Toni in Barcelona during the Easter holidays. I hesitated. The last time I'd been there was with Paul and the children, and I wasn't sure if I could face going back alone. It would be a real test of whether I was able to cope better with life – but was I ready for it? As soon as I began to think about the trip in these terms, I was reminded of a patient who faced his own, very literal test.

Adrian was almost eighteen, one of our oldest patients, since all of the children eventually moved on to adult services. He came with his parents, Reg and Joyce, who were both in their sixties and very concerned about what would happen to Adrian as they got older and less able to care for him. Adrian was on the autistic spectrum, and he had a mild learning disability, but he was at a further education college gaining some qualifications, and there was a good chance that he would be able to work independently, so things were, in fact, looking fairly bright for his future. The problem his parents brought to our session was Adrian's inability to pass his driving test.

'Technically, he's a very good driver,' Reg told me. 'But he's failed his test three times now, and he just doesn't seem to realise what the other drivers on the road are doing.'

'That's right,' affirmed Joyce. 'And it's very scary being in the car with him, because he might come up to a round-about or a junction and carry straight on, without thinking that he should give way to other cars.'

One influential theory about the difficulties that people with autistic spectrum conditions have in everyday situations is that they lack 'theory of mind', or the ability to put themselves in somebody else's shoes, to see a situation from someone else's perspective, or to make a clear judgement about what someone else's intentions might be. It seemed likely that this was what lay at the root of Adrian's driving difficulties. I asked him if he liked driving.

'Yes, I do,' he said. 'I love cars. I'm a good driver.'

I'd noticed him eyeing a box of toy cars in the corner of the room.

'Yes, your dad told me you're very good,' I said. 'Do you have any problems with driving at all?'

'Well,' he said, 'sometimes people hoot at me.'

'And do you know why?'

Adrian looked a bit mystified. 'Not really,' he said. He kept looking over at the box of toy cars.

'Would you like to play with those cars?' I asked. This was a bit of a gamble, as he might have considered the suggestion very childish, but in fact he leapt at the chance.

'Yes please,' he said, his eyes lighting up, and he went straight over and started vrrrmmming the cars around the floor.

Further questioning of Reg and Joyce revealed that Adrian was desperately keen to have his own car, and that his parents also wanted him to have independent transport, partly because they thought it would lead to better job opportunities. We agreed that I would see Adrian for a few sessions to try to raise his awareness of other road users, and Adrian was happy to come along.

We met weekly. Adrian was a charming young man, whose dress made him look like someone from an older generation. He had a short, neat haircut and glasses, and he wore baggy brown trousers, creased down the front, and a series of Fair Isle jumpers and waistcoats, presumably knitted for him by Joyce. He was extremely polite, and always happy to engage with me, even if this meant kneeling on the floor for an hour and pushing toy cars around. I had decided that the key to treating him lay in his interest in the toy cars, but first I needed to pinpoint the precise nature of his driving difficulties. I bought a copy of the Highway Code and tested his knowledge of road signs. He displayed a phenomenal memory for this sort of information, giving the correct answer in every single case. It was in situations involving judgements about others' actions that his difficulties revealed themselves.

'So, what do you do when you come up to a roundabout, Adrian?'

'When turning left, approach in the left-hand lane. When turning right, approach in the right-hand lane. When going straight on, select the appropriate lane.' This sounded very much like a direct quote from the Highway Code.

'But what if there's somebody else who wants to go around the roundabout at the same time as you?'

'They approach in the left-hand lane if turning left, the right-hand lane if turning right ...'

'OK, let's try it with the cars,' I suggested. I gave him a toy car, took one myself, and used the apple I'd brought for lunch as an improvised roundabout.

'Pretend you're coming up to the roundabout, here, and you want to turn right.'

Adrian correctly selected the right-hand lane, but took no notice whatsoever of my own car coming in from the right, which he would have smashed into, had it been a real roundabout. He looked surprised, and again somewhat mystified.

'OK, Adrian, I think this is something we could work on,' I said. 'Would that be alright with you?'

'Yes,' he said. 'I want to pass my driving test.'

My own son, Will, had been passionate about playing with toy cars when he was little, and we had bought a number of cardboard 'roads', which we stuck on to a huge sheet of hardboard to make a complex road system, around which he would 'drive' his toy cars for hours at a time. I managed to transport this road system into work, and it formed the basis of my treatment sessions with Adrian. We used Duplo bricks to create an environment with which he was familiar: his 'house', his 'college', the 'bank', the 'station', and so on, and I would then give him the task of 'driving' from one location to another.

'So, Adrian, start off from home and drive to college. Which way are you going to go?'

He would describe a route, which I would then

intercept at various points with my own toy car. The aim was to build up his awareness of other road users, and to create a system of 'rules' which he could use to anticipate their intentions – a sort of concretisation of the 'give way' concept. We wrote these rules on cards and practised them over and over again. So, at a roundabout, for instance, as well as getting into the correct lane, Adrian learned to 'Wait. Look right. Go when there are no other cars coming around the roundabout towards you.'

We created rules for every junction and manoeuvre I could think of, and Adrian had no trouble at all memorising them. We then moved on to unpredictable hazards, using Playmobil people to act as wayward pedestrians and lolli-pop ladies. We practised these scenarios endlessly as well.

The next step was to generalise Adrian's learning into real-life situations, generalisation being something that autistic people often have difficulties with. But we had our set of rule cards, and Reg was happy to take Adrian out driving with the cards, reading out the relevant one every time he was faced with a situation involving awareness of other road users. The crunch came when we decided that Adrian was ready to take his test for the fourth time. I was so nervous that morning – far more agitated than when my own children took their driving tests. We had arranged to meet after the test so that I could say goodbye (if he passed), or decide next steps (if he failed). I knew the outcome as soon as the little family walked into my room, grinning from ear to ear.

'I passed my test,' Adrian announced, thrusting out his certificate for me to see. And, well, it's not often that you hug your patients, but on this occasion, I couldn't help myself.

*

Adrian was one of the successes of my working life, but will I manage a successful trip to Spain on my own, and cope with all the inevitable comparisons with the last time I was there? I decide to go with Jenny, a fellow child psychologist whom I've known for over thirty years. She and I had worked at the same hospital in east London, and we each have three children of similar ages. She's never been to Barcelona, and she is keen to go, so she seems like a good choice for a travelling companion. I haven't seen her for a few months, but we rebond quickly at Gatwick airport over our mutual fear of flying, and once on the plane, stiff drinks in hand, we talk non-stop for the duration of the two-hour flight. Much of the conversation is about our respective children, which gives me an opportunity to reflect that, despite all that has happened, and my own on-off depression, my children have shown remarkable resilience, and have all grown up into sociable, caring and productive adults.

After we arrive, we spend the first two days based in Toni's sister's flat in the centre of Barcelona, walking the streets of the city. I can't help making comparisons with 'before', and it is certainly different – and far more grown-up – on this occasion. We don't go to the zoo this time, and we do spend time inside the Sagrada Familia, which we'd only seen from the outside before, reasoning that a cathedral wouldn't appeal to young children. I love Gaudí's architecture of natural forms: the huge columns created from a medley of different stones that thrust up towards the roof like a forest of giant trees, the light suffusing the coloured glass windows – warm on one side, cool on the other, to reflect the diurnal rhythm. Even more impressive is Casa Batlló, with its twisting chimney pots, undulating curves of coloured tiles and wave-like window frames, which make the whole building resemble a living creature. I realise quite quickly that I am enjoying this city in a different way. And on this occasion, nobody steals our holiday money on the steps of Barcelona cathedral.

Moving on from Barcelona to Montserrat is much more difficult. I recall vividly from 'before' the children's exhilaration and my terror at the ride in a bright yellow cable car up to the monastery, perched on a sheer mountainside high above the clouds. This time, the cable car is still bright yellow, and my terror just as real, but there is no Paul to reassure me. At the top, my travelling companions make a perfunctory visit to the monastery, but they are really more interested in finding lunch. I badly want to queue up to file past the icon of the Black Virgin, because Paul and I had done that before, but the others aren't interested, so instead I have to settle for tourist paella and beer from a plastic cup. I miss Paul, and feel tearful and lost.

After Montserrat, we go to Mari and Toni's house in the deep countryside. They had bought a plot of land and designed and built the house themselves, and I haven't seen it until now. It is stunning: ultra-modern, ultra-light, with huge windows and tiled terraces looking out over mountains on every side. We stay there for several days, eating, drinking, walking and talking until late into the night. One particularly memorable walk takes us high into the mountains, following in Gaudí's footsteps, to see the pinkish-red rock formations that had inspired his architecture. You can pick out the curves and fissures of the Casa Batlló in the weird, pockmarked outcrops of rock, and I take pleasure in the thought that Gaudí himself walked here more than a hundred years earlier and translated what we are seeing now into those remarkable buildings.

We stop for coffee in a remote café next to a tiny church, which is famous, Mari informs us, 'as the place where you can pray to St Antonio for a husband'. She makes much of this, exhorting me and Jenny to go into the church. But in fact, as I sit at that worn table with its crocheted placemats, savouring a *café con leche*, I realise that I don't want to pray for a husband at all. I might decide to light a candle for Paul, but there is no need to pray for a different husband. Mari has found, in Toni, her own solution to the loss of Pepe, but that isn't the only way forwards. It strikes me, forcefully, that I've had a wonderful time in Spain without Paul, and that I've managed to derive pleasure from doing things differently. There have been moments when I've missed him dreadfully, but they have passed. My friends, my sisters, my children and the many wonderful places and experiences on offer in the world are capable of filling a good part of the void in my life and making it worth living. If coming back to Spain has been a test, I have passed it, and like my patient Adrian, I can smile gratefully. I am left with a sense of hope, the same sense of hope that sustained those parents in my group who were able to find a way forwards with their shattered lives.

On our last evening in Spain, Mari and Toni drive us to a tiny village high up in the mountains. It's a long drive, the route embracing a series of progressively tortuous hairpin bends as we climb towards our destination. But the view from the top is worth every anxious moment of our odyssey to get there. The village itself is ancient: houses of a uniform rough stone hugging the slopes; the landscape arid, yet interspersed with patches of abundant vegetation. There are clumps of purple irises surrounded by bright yellow valerian, all set on the crest of a mountain with breathtaking views in every direction. We go for a walk, and then to a bar inside a building which must have stood in the same place for centuries. Its cool, dark interior affords us a brief respite from the hot sunshine, but we soon emerge on to a terrace which hangs out over a void, the mountainside sloping away steeply beneath us. We can see for miles: as far as the sea on one side, and across mountain ranges of grey and pink rock, the road we had negotiated earlier no bigger than a length of string unravelling away from us. We sit down on rough wooden stools and take in the view.

'Paul would love this,' I say to Mari. 'I wish he was here with us. Do you think he is?'

'No,' she replies firmly. 'It's a nice thought, but life has to move on.'

Mari is, as ever, the realist, although I do pick up her implied message that I need to move on, too.

I let this go, but reflect to myself that, in fact, I am happy sitting here, *enlivened* by the thought that Paul might be here, too. The misery is gone. It feels almost as if I have internalised some essence of Paul, which is giving me the strength to face whatever challenges everyday life might throw at me. I wonder whether all those hours of therapy have helped me to build up this resilience? I can see that I've changed a lot since Paul died, but perhaps I would have done anyway. I'll never know how much of the change was due to therapy, family, friends, or just the passage of time: it isn't possible to do the controlled experiment.

The waiter arrives with a bottle of red wine and four glasses.

'I'm paying for this,' I say, and he hands me the bill on a small white saucer.

We drink the wine and spend a congenial hour chatting about our families, and holidays we have planned for the future. When it's time to go, I pick up the bill, and go inside to the counter to pay. My eyes take some time to adjust from the bright sunlight to the gloomy interior. At first, I think they are playing tricks on me, but as I lift the bill and hand it to the barman, I can just make out, lying underneath it on the saucer, a perfect white feather. I stare at it, mesmerised by the thought that Paul has been with us after all. A small smile edges along my lips as I look up to face the barman, who is chatting away to me in Catalan, quite unaware of the presence of the feather or the reason for my smile. I pay the bill, and as I leave the bar I lean over, pick up the feather from its saucer and put it in my pocket. I don't think the barman notices, and if he does, I don't care, because I have an overwhelming urge to take the feather back to England with me. Months later, I will come across it in the pocket of the jacket I was wearing that day. Its discovery will make me smile again, and will strengthen my belief that Paul will find me, wherever in the world I choose to go.

*

I didn't say anything to Mari about my encounter in the mountain bar, and I don't say anything when I find feathers in other places, but they are always there. I sometimes reflect on the changing nature of my feather experiences. I no longer cling to them in desperation as I did in the early days after Paul died; these days, they are more likely to make me smile, and I see them as a kind of affirmation that I'm doing OK. They are, and always will be, my link with Paul, but they are also, I now see clearly, the link that allows me to begin to separate from him: just as a young child's chosen comforter helps him or her to tolerate separation from a caregiver and gain independence, so the feathers help me to build resilience as time passes and Paul slips further away. I probably don't notice them as often as I did, but when I do see one, I nearly always pick it up and put it in my pocket and stroke it. Nobody knows, nobody sees me do it, but still it gives me comfort.

Enduring Loss

When one door of happiness closes, another opens, but often we look so long at the closed door that we do not see the other one that has been opened for us.

HELEN KELLER,
To Love this Life

A few weeks ago, I booked to go on a silent retreat. It was just a weekend, and I thought that it might do me good to step out of my busy life and have a bit of time for reflection. I had never done anything like this before, and I felt curious, but also anxious about what I might be letting myself in for. It turned out to be an opportunity to crystallise some of the important lessons that I'd learned on my journey through grief.

The retreat was held in a ramshackle old house, deep in the Surrey hills. We gathered in the sitting room, which had an enormous leaded bay window looking out over the extensive gardens and woodland beyond. The walls were heavy, wood-panelled and painted a rather sickly green. There was a large Persian rug on the floor, in the centre of which our teacher had placed an elaborate vase of fresh flowers: white lilies, chrysanthemums, phlox, mauve daisies. Twelve chairs were arranged in a neat circle around the flowers. The walls were lined with books on history, philosophy and religion, and there were many pictures, mainly photographs of countryside and seascapes, interspersed with Buddhist hangings and cut-outs of strange symbols and runes that I couldn't decipher.

Into this restful scene on Friday evening trooped our small group of retreaters, all women apart from one man accompanying his wife. We introduced ourselves briefly, listened to the teacher delivering some ground rules – and then it was silence until Sunday afternoon.

To begin with, this seemed alien and awkward. I felt way out of my comfort zone, not knowing how to behave when I passed a fellow retreater on the stairs or found myself alone in a room with somebody else. Eating our meals in silence was particularly challenging: if the salt and pepper were out of reach, they were unobtainable; I couldn't fathom how to work the toaster on the first morning, so I ended up having to eat bread and honey. But as time went on, something began to change, and what had felt strange and awkward at first began to feel liberating: it was a relief not to have to make decisions about food or activities, nor to socialise or make conversation at mealtimes. The food actually tasted better without the distraction of conversation. A small group of us went on a silent walk in the surrounding countryside, and the silence felt oddly companionable as we took in the changing light and the scenery with no talk to divert us.

At the end of the second evening, I decided to have a bath in the bathroom shared with the others in my corridor. It was a large room with a sash window, a dark lino floor, and strips of swirly patterned carpet beside the bath and under the sink. The central light was operated by a pull switch, and the flush by a pull chain. On the rusting metal tray across the bath lay a bar of yellowish soap. I recognised it by its shape and its smell before I turned it over to reveal the black and red Cussons Imperial Leather label. On the edge of the bath was a rectangular cleaning sponge, squashy on one side and scratchy on the other, and next to it a pack of Vim: that unmistakeable cylindrical container with a perforated metal top that would get rusty after weeks of sitting in a damp bathroom; the cardboard sides that would go mushy if they got wet; the grey, scratchy powder inside – a direct line to my childhood.

And it was at that moment that something fell into place, something that I knew already but now felt at a visceral level. Naturally I had been thinking about Paul during the hours of silence, but I suddenly saw with complete clarity that the story of my grief began *not* with his death, but with my earliest memory of abandonment by my mother in hospital at the age of three. This was *my* story, *my* reality, and the first important lesson of my journey through grief: *everybody who suffers major bereavement will have their own grief journey shaped by their own personal history.* Everybody's history is different. For me, loss, rejection and abandonment are all the same thing: Paul's death was a catastrophic loss, but it was also the ultimate rejection and abandonment. He promised he would never leave me, and then he did just that, in the most spectacular way. A few moments in an old-fashioned bathroom was enough to reinforce for me the importance of early influences, the direct line linking my ever-present grief with memories of things that happened long ago, something which those endless hours of therapy had helped me to see.

That lesson deepened my understanding of what was happening to me, but would understanding alone help me to manage future losses any better?

On the final morning of the retreat, we were given time to walk in the gardens. It was January, so there wasn't much out, but I soon noticed a clump of snowdrops beside the path. Now that the silence had tuned me in to savouring every taste, smell, sound and sight, I knelt down and investigated one tiny flower with great care: the perfectly formed white petals, the vivid green leaves and stem, and, buried deep inside, a tiny yellow stamen heart. I'd never noticed before that snowdrops have hearts. I thought back to the bunch of snowdrops that I had tried to force into Paul's frozen, unyielding hand, and it occurred to me that it could never have worked. Those snowdrops were cut off, dying, and just like Paul, they could never come alive again. But this beautiful snowdrop in the garden was alive, and so was I, and deep inside, a heart was beating. And that, I realised, was the second important lesson of my grief journey: that *I, and I alone, held the key to my future happiness*. I think that Margaret was trying to tell me this when she went on and on about paying attention to my own needs, but she never quite managed to find the words to resonate with me in a way that made me understand properly. Sue gave me the tools to build resilience, and I myself used – and still use – the feathers as a source of comfort. But most of all, my patients taught me that I alone could find a way forwards. Time and again, they helped me to reflect on what was happening to me, and to see it in a new light. Their struggles paralleled my struggles; their losses mirrored mine; their bravery helped me to find the inner strength I needed to move on.

On the last afternoon of the retreat, we had a sociable tea together, sharing our experiences of the weekend. As I drove home, I thought some more about my own experience, and it occurred to me that the weekend had evolved in much the same way as my journey through grief. That was my third important lesson: *the landscape of grief changes*. To begin with, it is a strange, hostile place, but it alters gradually as new experiences unfold and new learning takes place: what at first seems stifling may become liberating; as one door closes, others open; a silence that seemed oppressive may turn out to be enlightening. In the end, with luck, there is a sense of acceptance. Both the weekend and my longer struggle had taught me that I can always be there for myself: I will never leave or abandon myself, ever.

I got married
I got married to myself
I said yes
A yes that took years to arrive
Years of unspeakable suffering
Crying with the rain
Locking myself up in my room . . .

I felt good together with myself
Just like me
I felt good together with myself
And so
From one day to the next
I got married
And am together
And not even death can separate me.

Susana Thénon, 'Nuptial Song'

The Life That Never Was

After this long period of separation, they could no longer imagine the intimacy that they had shared nor how a being had lived beside them, on whom at any moment they could place their hands.

ALBERT CAMUS,
The Plague

It's ironic that I'm swimming up and down the pool alone this morning – and I mean completely alone. The pool (a different pool) is empty apart from me. I suppose there aren't that many people attracted to getting up this early on a Sunday morning. Sunday. That is significant. You died on a Sunday, and although it was many years ago, the anniversary seldom falls on the same day of the week. I'm willing time to turn back as I shift my goggled eyes under the water and search for your baggy swimming shorts. But all I see is the muffled glow of the underwater lights. I glance up at the clock and register that it is 7.45. Are you alive still or have you died? I don't know, and this troubles me. Even after all these years I can't locate the exact time;

I don't know precisely what happened. I still have a strong urge to pinpoint it, but I know I can't. The best I can come up with is 'sometime between 7.45 and 8.45' and this feels profoundly unsatisfactory.

On the way back I reach for your hand in the car, but there is nothing but empty air and the canvas straps of my swimming bag. Sunday Worship is on Radio 4 so I switch automatically to Spotify. I know I'm going to play music that will make me cry. Why? Because I want to feel close to you today. I have a playlist punctuated with songs from our youths that we would sing loudly, raucously together. If you were driving your car ahead of me, I would see you jigging up and down in your seat and flinging your arms about in time with the music. God knows what other drivers thought, but you certainly wouldn't have cared – you were full of the joys of life. Today I play Phil Collins – the song that brought us together, my way of letting you know that I was in love with you. It takes me right back to the evening when you put it on the CD player in my car and heard it for the first time. It's unbelievably sad to think of how we began and how we ended, but I've listened to this so many times over the years that tears don't fall anymore. Next Enya, and she has me sobbing instantly. You loved Enya, and I played her at the crematorium as your coffin rolled away. But you didn't know this song: I only heard it after you died. 'Is there a way I can find you? Is there a sign I should know? Is there a road I could follow... to bring you back home?' Her haunting voice is singing directly to you as I sing with her, tears streaming down my face. I'm begging you too, although I know it won't work. But I do know what the sign is: it's the feathers of course, those fragile signals which somehow bridge the divide, just a tiny bit.

Back home and it's nearly 9, so I know you're dead. I feel flat, but the cats are demanding food, and that snaps me out of my reverie. I light a candle and kiss your photo. The glass is hard and unyielding, quite the opposite of how a real kiss would feel. Later, I drive to see you in the New Forest. It's a beautiful day and the sun is shining as I walk to the pond that you share with Jessie and Fatcat. The water level is low, and a forest of bulrushes seems to have overtaken most of the waterlilies. I sit down on the bank at the far end, preoccupied with the many stressful issues in my daily life. I stare at the sun twinkling on the water and there, right there in front of me is a white feather clinging to the straw-like stem of a bulrush. It is tiny, fluffy, pristine and a marker of your presence. So you're here, I think, and yet you're not. Your love is long gone, but I often wonder how life would be if you had survived. Would we have walked in the Forest again together? Might we have had a picnic on the banks of this pond?

We had talked about moving to Dorset after the children had left home. Then, it seemed like a distant dream, but we did drive round the outskirts of Weymouth a couple of times and fantasise about houses we saw for sale. You wanted to be near the sea so that you could sail; I wanted to be near the sea so that I could walk. Then, we would have done these things together, and you would have insisted on a dog to come with us. You would have at least seven grandchildren by now: I've seen pictures of them on Facebook, although I've never been introduced to them. I have a grandchild too, and it saddens me to think that you will never meet her. It would have been exciting for us to have young children in our lives again. We would probably have continued going out on Friday nights after we retired, and you would certainly have continued to bring me a cup of tea in bed in the morning – that tradition never wavered, and to this day I miss it. Then, I couldn't have imagined anything more blissful than the prospect of these things continuing forever, but now I'm not so sure.

A future that never happened is devoid of details. It's blurry round the edges and monochrome, like an out-of-focus black-and-white photo. Then, it was clear and perfect – a brightly coloured print of an idyllic place by the sea and one big, happy family. But that was then, and this is now. I hated sailing, and I'm glad I don't have to suffer it anymore. You were never that keen on walking, and now I go for long walks on my own. I always preferred cats to dogs and now I have two. I've discovered a lot about my own company and the capacities I have to sort things out and make things happen. And I can make my own choices about who to socialise with. I still miss your company, of course I do, and most of all the hugs. I still keep your ring on my finger: it will always give me strength, but the baggage that came with you has melted away into the ether.

Back at home again, there's an e-card in my inbox from your cousin. She was adopted as a baby. She only discovered you a few years before you died, and yet you recognised something in each other that marked you out as kindred spirits. She always remembers the anniversary of your death when almost everybody else has forgotten by now. Swathes of lilies and tulips and primroses sprout from the screen of my laptop, followed by a quote from Victor Hugo: 'Even the darkest night will end and the sun will rise.' Cliched perhaps, but I appreciate her kindness, and

I do know, looking back from now to what was then, that a different life is possible. It may turn out to be as good as the one I thought I would have: perhaps even better.

March 2023

Notes and Sources

Preface

All of the stories about my patients are true, but I have changed their names and, in many cases, other identifying details in order to protect their confidentiality. The identities of my therapists have also been altered, but my dialogue with them is accurate, within the limitations imposed by my memory and my perception of the interactions that occurred between us.

Chapter 1: *Tsunami*

Mark Williams, John Teasdale, Zindel Segal and Jon Kabat-Zinn. *The Mindful Way Through Depression*. Guilford Press. 2007.

Chapter 2: *Aftermath*

John Bowlby. *Attachment and Loss, Volume 3: Loss*. Penguin. 1980.
C.S. Lewis. *A Grief Observed*. Faber and Faber. 1961.
Thomas Holmes and Richard Rahe. 'The Social Readjustment Rating Scale'. *Journal of Psychosomatic Research*, 11:2, 213–218. 1967.
– Commonly known as the Holmes & Rahe Stress Scale, this is a questionnaire developed for identifying major stressful life events.

Chapter 3: *Grenade Moments*

Cathy Rentzenbrink. *A Manual for Heartache*. Picador. 2017.
Stephen Grosz. *The Examined Life*. Chatto & Windus. 2013.
Wayne Fisher, Cathleen Piazza and Henry Roane. *Handbook of Applied Behavior Analysis*. Guilford Press. 2013.
Elisabeth Kübler-Ross and David Kessler. *On Grief and Grieving*. Simon & Schuster. 2005.
– This is an accessible guide to negotiating the five stages of loss, which are based on Kübler-Ross's original five stages of dying.

CHAPTER 4: *The Dating Dilemma*

John Bowlby. *Attachment and Loss, Volume 3: Loss*. Penguin. 1980.
Vanessa Moore and Helen McConachie. 'Communication between blind and severely visually impaired children and their parents'. *British Journal of Developmental Psychology*, 12:4, 491–502. 1994.
Vanessa Moore and Helen McConachie. '"Show me what you mean": helping young visually impaired children to communicate'. *Health Visitor*, 68, 105–107. 1995.
Roald Dahl. *The Twits*. Jonathan Cape, 1980.

CHAPTER 5: *Interlude: Sensory Threads*

King's College London, Doctorate in Clinical Psychology, *www. kcl.ac.uk*
Vanessa Moore. 'The relationship between children's drawings and preferences for alternative depictions of a familiar object'. *Journal of Experimental Child Psychology*, 42, 187–198. 1986.
Vanessa Moore. 'The influence of experience on children's drawings of a familiar and unfamiliar object'. *British Journal of Developmental Psychology*, 5, 221–229. 1987.
Sam Hayward. *Black to White*. New Generation Publishing. 2015.
Gloria Hunniford. *Next to You: Caron's Courage Remembered by her Mother*. Penguin Books. 2006.
Julian Barnes. *Nothing to be Frightened Of*. Vintage. 2008.
Julian Barnes. *Levels of Life*. Jonathan Cape. 2013.
Jonathan Cott. *Dinner with Lenny*. Oxford University Press. 2013.
Vanessa Moore. 'A Survey of Reactions to the Death of a Loved One'. Unpublished study, available from the author.
Eben Alexander. *Proof of Heaven*. Piatkus. 2012.
Stephen Grosz. *The Examined Life*. Chatto & Windus. 2013.
Sigmund Freud. *The Interpretation of Dreams*. Standard Edition 4–5. 1900.
Neville Symington. *The Analytic Experience*. Free Association Books. 1986.
Donald Winnicott. *The Child, the Family and the Outside World*. Penguin Books. 1964.
C.S. Lewis. *A Grief Observed*. Faber and Faber. 1961.

Chapter 6: *Moving on Again*

Anthony Roth and Peter Fonagy. *What Works for Whom? A Critical Review of Psychotherapy Research*. Guilford Press. 2006.

Stephen Grosz. *The Examined Life*. Chatto & Windus. 2013.

Chapter 7: *Attachment and Separation*

John James and Russell Friedman. *The Grief Recovery Handbook*. William Morrow Paperbacks. 2009.

Chapter 8: *Ups and Downs*

Irvin Yalom. *Staring at the Sun: Overcoming the Dread of Death*. Piatkus. 2011.

Helen Bailey. *When Bad Things Happen in Good Bikinis*. Blink. 2015.

– Helen Bailey wrote this memoir based on her blog, *Planet Grief*, some years after her husband's death by drowning. While I was reading it, Helen went missing. She writes in the memoir about the Gorgeous Grey-Haired Widower she met through an online grief forum and subsequently moved in with. He turned out to be the man who murdered her and her dog, and hid their bodies in the cesspit under his garage.

Valery Hazanov. *The Fear of Doing Nothing: Notes of a Young Therapist*. Sphinx. 2019.

Irvin Yalom. *Love's Executioner and Other Tales of Psychotherapy*. Penguin Books. 2013.

Alice Miller. *The Drama of the Gifted Child*. Basic Books. 1997.

Christine Dunkley et al. 'Hearing the suicidal patient's emotional pain'. *Crisis*, 39, 267–274. 2018.

Chapter 9: *Impasse*

Miranda Wolpert and Tony Rousmaniere. 'Talking failure in therapy and beyond'. *The Psychologist*, 30, 40–43. 2017.

Irvin Yalom and Ginny Elkin. *Every Day Gets a Little Closer: A Twice-Told Therapy*. Basic Books. 1974.

Stephen Grosz. *The Examined Life*. Chatto & Windus. 2013.

M. Scott Peck. *The Road Less Travelled*. Arrow Books. 2006 edition.

Irvin Yalom. *Love's Executioner and Other Tales of Psychotherapy*. Penguin Books. 2013.

Robert Morley. *The Analysand's Tale*. Karnac Books. 2007.

CHAPTER 10: *Resolution*

Mark Williams, John Teasdale, Zindel Segal and Jon Kabat-Zinn. *The Mindful Way Through Depression*. Guilford Press. 2007.
Valery Hazanov. *The Fear of Doing Nothing: Notes of a Young Therapist*. Sphinx. 2019.

EPILOGUE: *Enduring Loss*

Helen Keller. *To Love this Life: Quotations by Helen Keller*. AFB Press. 2000.
Susana Thénon. 'Nuptial Song'. *The Oxford Book of Latin American Poetry: A Bilingual Anthology*, edited by Cecilia Vicuña & Ernesto Livon-Grosman. Oxford University Press. 2009.

AFTERWORD: *The Life That Never Was*

Enya. 'If I Could Be Where You Are'. *Amarantine*. Warner Music UK, 2005.

MIND (*www.mind.org.uk*) is a mental health charity for England and Wales. Their website is a rich source of information about mental health problems, their treatment and how to access therapy.

SANE Australia (*www.sane.org*) is a national charity for Australians affected by mental illness which has fact sheets and guides on different types of therapy and how to access them. Beyond Blue (*www.beyondblue.org.au*) is a source of information on mental health problems and how to access help.

Mental Health America (*www.mhanational.org*) and the National Alliance on Mental Illness (*www.nami.org*) both have information on different types of mental health treatment and how to access them. The National Alliance on Mental Illness is the largest grassroots mental health organisation in the USA.

Acknowledgements

Grateful thanks are due to Helen Corner-Bryant and Cornerstones Literary Consultancy, who gave the first independent appraisal of my writing and made me believe that I could do it; to my agent Charlotte Robertson, who pulled me out of a desperate place with her positivity and enthusiasm for my work; to my publisher Joanna Copestick and her talented staff at Kyle Books: it isn't easy to manage the entire editorial process on Zoom, but despite the challenges of the pandemic Jo and her colleagues guided me every step of the way towards turning my manuscript into a book with unwavering calm and good humour.

I would like to thank the wonderful colleagues and ex-colleagues at University College London, the Institute of Psychiatry, the Donald Winnicott Centre, University Hospital Southampton NHS Foundation Trust and Solent NHS Trust, who guided my professional development as a psychologist and worked alongside me with many of the cases described in this book.

I am extremely grateful to all the people who agreed to be interviewed and surveyed about their views on death and its aftermath. I would like to extend particular thanks to Julian Barnes, for giving so generously of his time and reflections.

Thanks are also due to the four therapists described in the book. They bore the brunt of much of my grief and frustration, yet helped me, in their different ways, to inch my way forwards, and in doing so taught me much about the process of therapy. I am also deeply indebted to the patients with whom I had the privilege of working, and who helped me to move on in countless ways, without ever knowing that they had done so.

Many fantastic friends supported me, showed unwavering interest in my writing and kept me going through one of the darkest periods of my life – you know who you are and I am eternally grateful. Three people in particular encouraged me during the earliest stages of this project and helped to nudge it towards fruition: my old friend Debbie Taylor, who sowed the first seed of an idea when we both witnessed a white feather in her beautiful garden in Crete, and who has held my hand in many different ways ever since; Jenny Walters and Miranda Passey, whose insightful comments on the first draft helped so much to shape the book into what it eventually became, and whose presence and friendship over the years has been invaluable.

My wonderful friend Maria Terrazas Gonzalez (Mari) deserves a special mention, because she loved Paul, because she always understood, and because I owe the original title of this book, *One Thousand Days and One Cup of Tea*, to her. Thank you Mari, for always being available in spite of the thousand miles that separate us.

Finally, I could not have done this without the love and support of my family – my two sisters Bryony and Maryanne (Annie), who have been there throughout all of life's ups and downs and who can still make me laugh until I cry, my ex-husband Etienne who has given so generously of his friendship and his many thoughtful insights into the vagaries of the therapeutic process, and my daughter Emily, who has read and commented on every draft, and whose unstinting enthusiasm for the book kept me writing when I was at my lowest ebb – thank you Em, for your time, and for giving me the confidence to keep going.

My three amazing children have always been there for me, always supportive and always interested. They are a constant source of pride, joy and inspiration, and this book is dedicated to them.